SUBSISTENCE PATTERN OF THE KABUIS OF MANIPUR

An Ethnoarchaeological Study

Dr. Kh. Manglembi is currently working as Associate Professor, Department of Anthropology D.M. College of Science, D.M. University, Imphal. She obtained her Post Graduate in Anthropology from Guwahati University and Ph.D. Degree from Manipur University, for her work on Ethnoarchaeology. She completed one UGC Sponsored research project and guiding Ph.D. Scholars.

SUBSISTENCE PATTERN OF THE KABUIS OF MANIPUR

An Ethnoarchaeological Study

Dr. Kh. Manglembi Devi

Associate Professor

Department of Anthropology

D.M. College of Science, D.M. University, Imphal.

AKANSHA PUBLISHING HOUSE

4649-B/21, Ansari Road, Darya Ganj, New Delhi-110 002 (India)

AKANSHA PUBLISHING HOUSE
4649-B/21, Ansari Road,
Darya Ganj, New Delhi-110 002
Phones : 011-23263193, 09435116718
E-mail : ektabooks@yahoo.com
visit us : www.akanshapublishinghouse.com

Subsistence Pattern of the Kabuis of Manipur : An Ethnoarchaeological Study

First Published : 2021

ISBN 978-81-8370-593-6

PRINTED IN INDIA

Published by Akansha Publishing House, New Delhi - 110002.

CONTENTS

Foreword *ix*

Preface *xi*

Acknowledgements *xiii*

List of Tables *xv*

List of Figures *xvii*

List of Photo Plates *xix*

List of Maps *xxiii*

CHAPTER 1

Introduction 1-11

Theoretical Orientation

Aim and Object of the Study

Methodology

CHAPTER 2

Geographical Settting and the People 12-85

About Manipur : Location

Physiography

Hydrography

Climate

Flora and Fauna

The People

About the Villages Under Study

Location and Boundary
Settlement Pattern
The Kabuis : A Brief Ethnographic Profile
Origin and Migration
Family and Marriage
Clan Structure
Property and Inheritance
Dress and Ornaments
Festival
Religious Beliefs
Age Grading System and Grading of Social Status
Burial system

CHAPTER 3

Material Culture And Subsistence Pattern **86-195**

Gathering and Production of Food
Food Collection
Food Gathering
Hunting
Fishing
Food Production
Pastoralism
Horticulture
Agriculture
Food Habits
Household Implements

CHAPTER 4

Pre Historic Evidences **194-231**

Prehistoric Cultures of Manipur

Palaeolithic Culture
Hoabinhian Culture
Neolithic Culture
CHAPTER 5
Discussion and Conclusion **232-246**
Ethnographic Postulates about the Kabuis
Ethnographic Analogy
Conclusion
Bibliography **247-262**
Index **263-267**

Foreword

The book, which is a scholarly product of a dedicated and committed teacher, who has earned a reputation not only as a teacher but also as a researcher in her own field of specialization, is a worth reading book, for, in the first place, it is a regionally rooted archaeological ethnography, delineated precisely and elaborated succinctly in the light of the ethnographic parallelism, a theoretical understanding widely employed by the ethnoarchaeologists in the interpretation of archaeological remains of far off days; second, it explores the socio-cultural life of the Kabuis living for ages in three different eco-settings of Manipur with a view to giving the fullest account of their modes of adaptation to different habitats; third, it gives a brief but fascinating insight in to the prehistoric cultures of Manipur through the in-depth study of the prehistoric tools so far discovered from the different sites of Manipur; lastly , it makes an earnest attempt to reconstruct the prehistoric ideational culture which has been faded away in to the mystery of history by way of drawing an analogy between the material way of life of two different groups of people living in two different periods of time: one living in the ethnographic present and the other in the prehistoric past. Truly speaking, the authoress, drawing on an impressive array of carefully observed ethnographic facts of the Kabuis of Manipur, particularly the subsistence pattern of the people, reconstructs the livelihood pattern of the prehistoric forerunners who left behind only the stone tools, which they used in their economic pursuit, as the tangible evidence of their existence.

I found the book challenging and ultimately convincing. Not only does it make an important contribution to our understanding of the prehistoric culture of Manipur, but also it is a very welcome addition to the literature on ethnoarchaeology.

Prof. W. Nabakumar
Formerly, Dean,
School of Human and Environmental Sciences
Manipur University.

Preface

Past is the womb from which present is born. They are inseparable and inalienable. As the knowledge advances by steps not by leaps, actions of men which are the best reflection of his thoughts are also changing step by step. There is an unbroken link, in one form or the other, between the steps.

The book, based on the empirical study of five Kabui villages located at different geo-ecological settings, concerns itself with the study of the subsistence pattern of the Kabuis on the one hand and its relationship with the prehistoric cultures of Manipur in the light of the theoretical understanding of ethnographic parallelism, a domain of research of ethno-archaeology on the other. It is, therefore, intended to make an attempt to reconstruct the fossilised behaviour and the cultural pattern of the people once lived in the archaeological past against the backdrop of the living cultures of the ethnographic present. It is, in this sense, an ethnographically rooted regional archaeology.

The book embodies five chapters. The first chapter– Introduction- addresses itself to the aims and objectives of the study, the methodology adopted in the collection and analysis of the data in addition to the review of the literature on ethno-archaeology with the intention of gaining the theoretical background in the light of which the empirical data collected from field and the archeological data collected from the secondary source have been analysed in order to arrive at a conclusion.

The second chapter devotes to the study of the geo-ecological setting of the five Kabui villages under study in particular and the geographical background of the state of Manipur in general in order to give a picture of the relationship between the material culture of the people and their physical and biotic environment, and also a brief geographical introduction to the field sites. This chapter also depicts an enthographic profile of the Kabuis who are also known as the Rongmeis, an ethnonyme gaining recognition among both the academics and laymen alike as the people like to call themselves by the name. It deserves special mention here that they are one of the thirty six recognised Scheduled Tribes of Manipur inhabiting mainly the western part of Manipur, administratively designated as undevided Tamenglong District with a population of about eightytwo thousand three hundred individuals.

The third chapter studies the techno-material basis of the lifeways of the Kabuis on the basis of the materials collected through years of field work from the aforesaid five Kabui villages with the sole aim of giving a detailed picture of the subsistence pattern of the people. They practise agriculture as a way of life but not as a profession. Moreover, it is also a fact that gathering and hunting are still a part of their livelihood though they live with a producing economy.

The fourth chapter gives a brief but comprehensive account of the prehistoric cultures of Manipur by reviewing the presently available literatures, both published and unpublished. While undertaking the task the point in view is to gain the knowledge of the tools so far discovered from the prehistoric sites of Manipur and their functional significance in the survival of the prehistoric people.

The last chapter attempts to draw a parallelism between the archaeological past and the ethnographic present on the basis of the analogy derived from the comparative study of the prehistoric evidences and the present lifeways of the people under study.

Kh. Manglembi Devi

Acknowledgements

In bringing out the book in the present form, I got many help from my well wishers and friends who rendered valuable cooperation academically and physically whenever required.

I extend my deep sense of gratitude to my respected supervisor Professor W. Nabakumar Singh, former Dean, School of Human and Environmental Science and former Head of the Department of Anthropology, Manipur University, for his valuable and inspiring guidance, and constant encouragement without that it would not be possible on my part to complete this work.

I extend my heartiest gratitude to Dr. O. Kumar Singh, former Head, Post Graduate Department of Anthropology, D. M. College of Science, Imphal, a renowned archaeologists of Manipur, for his valuable advice.

I owe my debt to my respected teacher late Professor Harish Chandra Sharma, former Head of the department of Anthropology, Gauhati University, who inspired me to undertake my research work in the field of ethnoarchaeology.

I shall be failing in my duty if I do not express my sincere thanks to teachers of the Department of Anthropology, Manipur University who gave me inspiration and valuable suggestions in one or another way.

I owe my thanks to the village elders Thuiwang Gonmei, Khullakpa of Phungong; Dinkiu Lakpou Kamei, Khunbu of Phungong; Gaichinglung Gonmei, former Khullakpa of Marang ching; Lanthaolung Gangmei, khullakpa of Khonglong; Gaini Kamei, Khullakpa of Chingkhullong; Tomba Panmei and Manganjao Kamei, Village elders of Chingkhullong; late Lanjaichung Kamei, former Khullakpa of Konthoujam;

Khangbonlung Kamson, Khunbu of Konthoujam; Gujei Gonmei (teacher) of Tamenglong and friends Jinthui Gonmei, Agui Gonmei and Ruthan Gonmei of Tamenglong; Tunaremei Kamei, Agong Kamei and Khamchung Kamei of Konthoujam for their invaluable help rendered to me during the course of my field work.

I am also indebted to my respected teacher Dr. Kh. Shakhitombi Devi, former Head, Post Graduate Department of Anthropology, D. M. College of Science, Imphal and my colleague Dr. H. Sorojini Devi, Associate Professor of the same department, who always lent me a helping hand whenever I needed their help.

I owe my debt to my parents who gave me continuous moral support and encouragement, that stimulated me ever and anon when the momentum of my research work was in the wane.

I owe my special thanks to the members of my family for their moral support and whole hearted encouragement, with which I could successfully complete this research work.

My thanks are also due to the teachers of the Post Graduate Departments of Botany and Zoology, D. M. College of Science, Imphal, for their help rendered to me while classifying the plants and animals collected from the field.

My heart felt thanks also go to professor M.C. Arun, former Head of the Department of Anthropology, Manipur University, for his constant encouragement to publish this book.

My special thanks also go to Dr. L. Romeo Singh, Assistant Professor, Department of Anthropology, Moreh College, Moreh for extending his cooperation in computing works.

Last, but not the least, I would like to thanks Mr. M.P. Misra of Akansha Publishing House, New Delhi for publishing this book.

Kh. Manglembi Devi

List of Tables

Table	Particulars	Page
1	Rock types and age of formation	21
2	Village wise distribution of household	41
3	Frequency distribution of clan among the five villages	59
4	List of male costumes	64
5	List of male dance costumes	68
6	List of female costumes	69
7	List of female dance costumes	70
8	Patterns of subsistence economy	89
9	Techniques of fishing	123
10	Types of hoe	150
11	Agricultural cycle	154
12	Wild summer plants	160
13	Wild winter plants	161
14	Wild perennial plants	161
15	Domesticated summer plants	162
16	Domesticated winter plants	163
17	Domesticated perennial plants	164
18	Wild fruits	164

19	Domesticated fruits	165
20	Wild animals	166
21	Wild birds	167
22	Insects	168
23	Aquatic animals and fishes	169
24	Domesticated animals	169
25	Domesticated fowls	169
26	Artifact types of Khangkhui Cave	202
27	Bone artifact types of Khangkhui Cave	209
28	Stone artifact types of Nongpok Keithelmanbi Locality 2 and 3	215
29	The stone tool types of the Singtom site	216
30	Hoabinhian artifact types of Nongpok Keithelmanbi Locality-1.	219
31	Hoabinhian artifact types of Tharon Cave site	221
32	Stratigraphy of the 1985 excavation and archaeological finds at Napachik	226
33	Neolithic stone implements of Napachik	227
34	Neolithic Stone artifacts of Laimanai site	229
35	Districtwise Neolithic stray finds from Manipur	231

List of Figures

Fig.	Name of the Figures	Page
1	A ground plan of a traditional House	47
2	Pai- Paithou (Bow and Arrow)	100
3	Khunthuk-pha (Pit fall trap)	101
4	Jouki-pha (Automatic cage trap / Drop trap	105
5	Phai-pha (Feet trap)	106
6	Kagang-pha (Neck trap)	108
7	Jou-kong-pha (Porcupine trap)	108
8	Jou-pha (Monkey trap)	110
9	Sang-pha (Squirrel trap)	111
10	Rou-pha (Guinea-pig trap)	112
11	Pha-sang / Thang-pha (Bird trap)	114
12	Bourun-pha (Nest trap)	115
13	Tajic-pha (Glue trap)	115
14	Tang-bei (Bamboo clapping trap)	116
15	Single body valveless trap	127
16	A Barrier made for Catching Fishes	132
17	Stone artifacts of Songbu Cave	199
18	Flake artifacts of Songbu Cave	200
19	Core tools of Khangkhu	204
20	Flake and blade artifacts of Khangkhui Cave	205

21	Flake and blade artifacts of Khangkhui Cave	207
22	Bone artifacts of Khangkhui Cave	210
23	Edge-ground Hoabinhian artifacts of Fig.	223
24	Edge ground Hoabinhian pebble tools of Tharon Cave site	223
25	Sandstone quern and grinder of Tharon Cave site	224
26	Neolithic artifacts of the Napachik site.	228
27	Neolithic artifacts of Napachik	228
28	Neolithic stone artifacts of Laimanai Site	230

List of Photo Plates

Plate	Name of the photo plates	Page
(1)	(2)	(3)
1	A Traditional Kabui house	48
2	Tarangkai – a well decorated traditional house	49
3	Langom - a wooden bed near a fire place	50
4	Panthon, Mei (Mortar and pestle)	50
5	A hanging rack of three tires over a fire place	51
6	A small granary beside a house	51
7	A Kabui lady weaving Pheingao pheipong (shawl) in her loom	65
8	Cotton in raw : collected from the jhum field (A) and a spinning whorl (B)	65
9	Researcher observing the weaving technique at Phungong	66
10	Researcher (Middle) with the villagers at Konthoujam	66
11	An old couple wearing bead chains for aesthetic and magical value	67
12	Elders wearing Pheingao pheipong (white shawl) and Chingkhongphei pheipong (black shawl) on a memorial occasion in Gan-Ngai festival	67

(1)	(2)	(3)
13	Pheipong (A.& B.Pheingao, C. Mareipan, D. Masinpheipong (Male shawls)	71
14	A male Kabui in dance costume	71
15	Pheisoi (A. Langhu, B.Pheingao, C. Langjin, D-Phaisoi of different colours (Female loin clothes)	71
16	Dancing dresses and ornaments A. Duangh (Hd.dress) B.Phang phei, C. Langhu- pheisoi, D. Pheilak (waist belt), E. Tadan-tu (bead chain)	71
17	A Kabui Male and a lady in dance costume	71
18	Processing of pig for Gakpai-jaomei	82
19	Gakpai-jaomei- observation of spleen as an omen	82
20	Bamboo tubes for carrying rice beer	83
21	Tamcha-ponmei	83
22	Bamboo - a village deity	84
23	Taokhon - a memorial stone	85
24	Boys, collecting vegetables from the jhum field, on the way to home	91
25	Girls, collecting vegetables from the jhum field, on the way to home	92
26	A young girl collecting firewood from the surrounding hill	93
27	An old lady taking rest after collecting plantain leaves from the hill	94
28	Bui- A. A bamboo having pointed tip (reng bui) used as a spear, B. Iron tipped spear heads	95
29	A model of Keikang-bei (Rack fall trap) -	120
30	A model of Thing-dang-pha (Beam trap)	120

(1)	(2)	(3)
31	Teng-ka-pha (A)	121
32	Teng-ka-pha (B)	121
33	Tao-pha (All purpose trap)	122
34	Iron tip of a fishing spear that resembles a double barbed Harpoon	133
35	A multiple headed fishing spear	134
36	Single body valveless trap	134
37	Double body valveless trap in action	134
38	Plunge basket	135
39	Hemishperical trap	135
40	Cage trap	136
41	Cast net and net sinkers	136
42	Dip net	137
43	Bang -Dao, iron blades of different shapes	157
44	Bangkhoi- Sickle, a plain iron blade	157
45	Phu- Spade, of different sizes	157
46	Dri - axe	158
47	Phu-Hoe, different sizes of hoes (A. Lougai, B. Loupun phu, C. Nuchou/phu)	158
48	Buffalo yoke and plough	158
49	A.Jhap-Winowing fan; B.Malek -Threshing implement; C. Indhi -Umbrella; D. Thing/ tha -threshing mat	159
50	Indhi-an umbrella used by the plain Kabuis and Researcher	159
51	Village elders drinking rice beer using Goicheibung (mithun horn) and Humsaf jou-bong (bamboo cup)	181

(1)	(2)	(3)
52	Bu- wooden barrel with three legs	181
53	Ta-dop -Small gourd mug	182
54	Jou-mu -Large gourd wine vessel	182
55	Jou-lai - Earthen wine pot protected with cane strip	183
56	Jou-lai - Earthen wine pot of smooth surface	183
57	Dui-lai- Earthen water pot	184
58	Fire making with a log-Meigang and a string-Meilu	186
59	La-tai-kwak -Bamboo stirrer	186
60	Kwak dung- Wooden dishes for keeping dressed meat	187
61	Thing-nap-kwak- Wooden dish	187
62	Thing tam-kwak phai- Bowl with stand	188
63	Thing nap-kwak phai- Dish with stand	188
64	Goi-chei-jou-bung -Mithun horn-used as a drinking vessel	188
65	A & B. Kampho; C. Simpai; D. Napurrak; E. Ka; F. Kaluang	191
66	Khok – Basket for storing clothes	191
67	Khok – Basket for keeping ornaments	192
68	Nangmoi - Spindle whorl	192
69	Ku-wak -Adze	193
70	Langpa / Langom- Wooden bed and Thin piban Wooden pillow	193

List of Maps

Map	Particulars	Page
1	Manipur, at the gateway between the South-East-Asia and India	13
2	Map of Manipur showing the location of the study villages	13
3	Classification of the Forest of Manipur	15
4	Classification of the Rocks of Manipur	19
5	Classification of the Soils of Manipur	22
6	Rivers and lakes of Manipur	27
7	Geographical location of Phungong village	43
8	Geographical location of Marangching village	44
9	Geographical location of Khonglong village	45
10	Geographical location of Chingkhulong & Konthoujam villages	46
11	Map of Manipur showing the location of Prehistoric Sites	196

1
Introduction

Theoretical Orientation

No matter what we were, where we were and what we are today in the space-time continuum, we can never be outside the ambit of universal laws and principles. One such a law, among many, is that actions and reactions are equal and opposite. These two forces only hold and drive the universe together. Like body and image, none of the two never leads a single life and never goes alone. This popular law of physical science can be analogically extended without much hitch to the other branches of knowledge particularly to the study of prehistoric archaeology, for the present is the reflection of the past and both the present and the past are the foundations on which the future is built. Past will be grafted in the new facet of the present and will be observed in its new dimension.

Many scholars have expressed this universal principle in different languages and phraseology without changing its underlying significance. One such popular word is ethnoarchaeology. It may etymologically sound that archaeological method and principle will be employed in the study of living people. However, its primary concern, diametrically opposite to the etymological notion, is the use of ethnographic methods and information in the interpretation and explanation of archaeological data.

Ethnoarchaeology is now basically based on the premise

that the study of the traditional socio-cultural and behavioural patterns of a group of people along with traditional tools can lead us to the knowledge of the past cultural life of the human group. The reasoning in the case of this kind of research is based on analogy derived from the comparison of the artifacts explored in archaeological studies with the traditional artifacts used by the people under observation.

This kind of study may act as a bridge between the past and the present, that is, the inferences, resulted from the current ethnographic studies may fruitfully be employed in the reconstruction of the past human activities, and behavioural pattern by way of drawing an analogical parallel between the two. While explaining the past behavioural pattern of human activities, the ethnoarchaeological explanations are mostly based on the materials related to ethnographical present. In such a way, by studying human behaviour related to the material culture of the contemporary simple society a researcher can reconstruct the past cultural life ways, particularly the subsistence activities, established in an ecological setting. Thus ethnoarchaeologists are concerned primarily with examining human behaviour related to material lifeways and material residues in order to discover relationship between past and present of the human society. The generalisation resulted from such a study enables them to specify when and under what circumstances certain kind of behaviour may have been important to overall process of human adaptation. Ethnoarchaeological studies of the modern primitive society, thus, attempts to reconstructing the stories of early man on the basis of the tangible cultural information and associated behavioural pattern.

The reconstruction of fossilized human behaviour and the cultural pattern of the archaeological past using ethnographic methods and observations has a long history. Though the initial attempt at applying ethnographic information on contemporary simple society to interpreting and explaining archaeological facts dates back to the 17th century, the serious attempt to explore the method and the applications of ethnography as a tool of archaeology is relatively recent (Stiles: 1977).

Sir John Lubbock later known as Lord Avebury occupies a special position in the history of the development of ethnoarchaeology as he discussed the lifeways of the modern savages in his book first published in 1865 under the title *Prehistoric Times* as Illustrated by Ancient Remains, in order to "throw light on the ancient remains found in Europe and on the condition of early races which inhabited our continent" (Nagar : 1975)

The towering evolutionary thinkers who championed the old school of the evolutionary thought in anthropology have reconstructed the different stages of the evolution of human society on the basis of their knowledge of contemporary primitive societies. For instance, Tylor (1865) in his book *Research into the Early History of Mankind and the Development of Civilization*, traced the history of civilization with the help of the knowledge of living primitive societies. Moreover, Morgan (1877) too gave strong emphasis on his ethnographic knowledge of American Indians, Australian aborigines and other primitive societies in devising the stages of savagery, barbarism and civilization.

Sollas (1911) used the concept of ethnographic parallelism on an even larger scale. He drew a parallelism between the Mousterian culture and the Australian aborigines, the Aurignacian and the Bushman and the Megdalenian and the Eskimo.

Clark (1951, 52, 67), in a number of his writings, has critically used ethnographic evidence, that can be of considerable help, in reconstructing the archaeological remains, especially those relating to technology, economy, material culture and settlement pattern. He (1965) has further opined that the prehistorians learn from ethnography as to how particular people adapt themselves to their environments and shape their resources to the way of life demanded by their own culture.

Research in experimental archaeology and ethnoarchaeology gained popularity in the 1970s through some obvious studies like the tree felling power of stone axes and the cultural ecology of modern hunter-gatherer in the Kalahari desert. Binford has utilized the knowledge of the present day societies to successfully interpret the past human society and its culture to a large extent and it is he who has shown the real utilitarian usage of ethnoarchaeology in its true spirit and perspective. He (1977, 1978 and 1983) has also studied Nunamiut Caribou hunters of Alaska and the Novajo and developed cybernetic theory that explains the parallelism between prehistoric and contemporary primitive societies.

Truly speaking, ethnoarchaeology is, as an academic sub-discipline of anthropology, still in its prime. It is still in the process of expanding its academic horizon by way of formulating its own fully developed theories and methodologies. It cannot even arrive at a generally acceptable definition as different scholars have defined the term from the perspective of their own studies. It is, however, beyond doubt that a common denominator of all the definitions, offered till date, centres around the conditions of the actual field study.

Oswalt (1974), for instance, states that it is "the study, from an archaeological perspective, of material culture based on verbal information about artifacts obtained from persons, or their direct descendants, who were involved with the production".

On the other hand Stanislawski (1974) states that ethnoarchaeology is "the direct observation field study of the form, manufacture, distribution, meaning and uses of artifacts and their institutional setting and social unit correlates among living, non-industrial peoples for the purpose of constructing better explanatory model to aid archaeological analogy and inference"

Stiles (1977) opines that the two definitions referred to the above come closer in their meaning to what Gould (1968, 1974) and he (1977) have termed "living archaeology" and "archaeological ethnography" respectively. The question at issue is the crystallization into a definite name though ethnoarchaeology gains popularity over other names. It may be inferred from the fact cited above that ethnoarcheaology, though it has in it the making of a fertile academic sub-discipline of anthropology, is yet to grow in its fullest stature.

At the core of the problem of ethnoarchaeology is the extent to which the ethnoarchaeologist is able to use the ethnographic data, obtained from either normal ethnographies or archaeological ethnography or other sources, successfully in the archaeological interpretation. Stiles (1977) has suggested three possible uses of ethnographic data in arriving at a specific archaeological interpretation. They are : i) the ethnographic analogy, ii) the generation of hypothesis or models and iii) the testing of hypothesis.

The ethnographic analogy concerns itself with the comparison of a specific set of ethnographic data to an analogous set of archaeological data. The degree of similarity between the two sets of data in respect of their properties will in turn again determine the probability of reconstructing the fossilized behaviour and the cultural pattern of the people once lived in the archaeological past against the backdrop of the empirically observed and verified activity of the people of the ethnographic present. The role of time and space in the formulation of ethnographic analogy is also found to be very important, for these two dimensions have led to the distinction of two general types of ethnographic analogy namely, "Discontinous and continuous models" (Gould, 1974).

The former operates under conditions where the archaeologically observed data and the ethnographically observed activity are disparate either in time or space or both. In other words, in such an analogical studies "no connection can be demonstrated between the culture producing the archaeological traces and the culture providing the ethnographic analogue" (Stiles, 1977). The literature of ethnoarchaeology is rich in the examples of these type of analogy, for most archaeologists have profitably employed this under different terminologies in their pursuit of ethnoarchaeological studies. "New analogy" (Ascher, 1961), "general comparative" approach (Paterson, 1971), and "buckshot" method (Yellen, 1974) are the terms currently in vogue in the literature.

Similarly, "folk culture" or "direct historical" approach (Ascher, 1961), "direct historical" analogy (Paterson, 1971) are the terms synonymously used with the "continuous model" of Gould (1974) in the ethnoarchaeological research when a connection can be demonstrated in terms of time and space between the tangible remains of the archaeological past and the ethnographically observed facts.

The second possible use of ethnographic data is the generation of hypothesis and models that can be tested in the light of archaeological data thereby enabling ethnoarchaeologists to reconstruct the past culture whose authors are far removed from us in time. It is, however, to be made certain that the ethnographic information on which the hypothesis is drawn will be a potential analogy to the specific archaeologically observed phenomenon that the ethnoarchaeologist attempts to reconstruct.

In the case of the generation of models "a body of ethnographic observation may be combined to try to reconstruct and interpret a corpus of archaeological data" (Stiles, 1977). It, thus, enables one to reconstruct a section of prehistoric life by drawing a parallel between the ethnographic model build up in the light of the body of ethnographic data and the archaeological material of a specific site or culture. Thomas (1972) and David (1973) have employed this approach in the study of Great Basin Shoshone and Noallian culture respectively. Some scholars like Lee (1972, 1974) and Schrire (1972) formulate models on the basis of ethnographic information without taking archaeological data into their consideration.

The testing of hypothesis, formulated from ethnographic observation, begins with the analysis of the results of the comparison between the ethnographic data and the relevant archaeological data. One may assume that a valid analogy has been made in case "the pattern of archaeological material falls within the range of variation of the pattern of the physical traces which resulted from the ethnographic activity" (Stiles, 1977). Though no method has been devised to quantify the degree of probability, the logical reasoning leads to the generalisation that the more conditions the two situations share in common, the more the probability of the analogy between the archaeological data and the observed ethnographic fact. In the testing of the hypothesis, there is possibility of opening the hypothesis to doubt, thus "spoiling" its confirmation. In other words, the testing of the hypothesis may also lead to the invalidation of the analogy, called the spoiler method by Yellen (1974). The three methods discussed above can be and often are used together in order to arrive at a conclusion on the reconstruction of a section of the life ways of prehistoric men who left no trace of their behaviour except the artifacts they used.

It is evident from the above discussion that the ethnoarchaeological approach has made a logical linkage between the archaeological and the ethnographic activity. Stiles (1977) is of the opinion that ethnoarchaeology encompasses the concepts of both "doing" and "using": the former refers to what he calls "archaeological ethnography" that involves the collection of data for use in analogy and the latter centres around the use of the ethnographic data obtained from the written sources and field studies in the construction of hypothesis or models or comparison with archaeological data for use in analogy.

Aim and Object of the Study

The present study, theoretically rooted in the methodological correlates of both ethnography and archaeology, is based on the primary data collected from five Kabui villages situated at different geo-ecological settings using standard techniques of anthropological research and also concerns itself with the study of their subsistence pattern with a view to establishing its relationship with the prehistoric cultures of Manipur through the theoretical understanding of ethnographic parallelism, a domain of research presently in vogue in the field of ethnoarchaeology.

The first and foremost aim of the study is to formulate an ethnographic postulate about the subsistence pattern of the Kabuis inhabiting the valley and hilly regions of Manipur by way of making an ethnographic observation from a close range so that an empirical insight into how their economic activities, such as gathering, hunting and agriculture interweave with the cyclic rituals, and how the techno-material basis of their lifeways continues from their past to the present, can be arrived at. Such postulates resulted from the ethnographic observation lead to the formulation of hypothesis which will be tested in the light of the archaeological data. The study also aims at studying the prehistoric artifacts discovered from different places of Manipur at different times by different scholars in order to make a comparison with the artifacts related to the subsistence economy of the Kabuis by way of picking up relevant ones from both the domains of research. Efforts will also be made to test the goodness of fit of the two sets of data so that an ethnographic parallel may be drawn between the two. However, the relevance of negative evidence in the attempt will not be lost sight of. As the study also devotes to the study of the lifeways of the Kabuis inhabiting the three different ecological settings, attempt will also be made to look into the continuum of the subsistence pattern of the Kabuis.

One more important concern of the study is to look deeply into the relevant analogies between the ethnographic present and the archaeological past that can be inferred from the comparative study of the ethnographic and archaeological data so that a generalisation on the behavioural pattern associated with the prehistoric subsistence pattern may be arrived at. In this context two specific properties of analogy, namely, time and space are taken into consideration in order to specify the type of ethnographic analogy the study is intended to carry out. It sees fit to make a mention here that no connection in terms of space and time can be established between the prehistoric culture producing the artifacts presently available in Manipur and the Kabui culture which has been studied as the ethnographic analogue. Hence, the methods of "discontinuous model" (Gould, 1974) or "general comparative" (Paterson, 1971) or "new analogy" (Ascher, 1961) has been employed in the present study.

Methodology

The study, which is an ethnographically rooted regional archaeology, endeavours to reconstruct the fossilised behaviour and the cultural pattern of the people once lived in the archaeological past of Manipur against the backdrop of the ethnographic present drawn from the living culture of the Kabuis who live in three different ecological zones. Relevant data collection of the present study, therefore, involves the use of the different standard techniques of both ethnographic and archaeological researches.

The ethnographic materials related to the subsistence economy of the Kabuis were collected from five Kabui villages located at different geo-ecological settings. The objective of establishing a continuum in the subsistence pattern of the Kabuis speaks of the philosophy for the selection of five different Kabui villages that represent the different habitats of the people. Two villages, namely Phungong and Marangching situated at the interior and geographically isolated regions of undivided Tamenglong District, Chingkhulong and Konthoujam Kabui villages located in Imphal West District and Khonglong, a village of Senapati District at the meeting point of the hill and the valley were selected as field sites representing "Area of Relative Isolation", "Rural Areas" and "Intermediary Area" to look into the changes of the subsistence pattern of the Kabuis along with the associated technology owing to their adaptation to the specific habitat of varied ecological background.

The Kabuis of these villages were studied from a close range by staying in the field sites for more than a year. Annual cycle and associated economic activities of the people were closely observed in order to gain an exhaustive knowledge about the material basis of their life. Rituals, beliefs etc. kept alive as indigenous knowledge by handing down from generation to generation were also recorded, for the economic activities of the people always go hand in hand with them. Various techniques of data collection like participant observation, key informant interviewing, case history method and scheduled method were employed as the situation and nature of the data demanded. Basic house hold information that form the foundations of the study was collected through scheduled method by going from door to door and meeting the adult members of the family. Technical features of the culture were collected by direct observation whereas non-technical features like behaviour associated with a particular activity were recorded by way of participating in the activity as one of them. Both structured and unstructured interviewing of informants were employed for collection of the range of data varying from the household economic activities to the cyclic rituals preformed at the level of both household and community. Households of every sample village were stratified on the basis of the economic level and case histories of the stratified samples in respect of their food habits, economic activities etc. were collected in order to gain a comprehensive account of the production, distribution and consumption pattern of the economic life of the people. Cross checking of the data collected is done by collecting the same information from different informants. In practice, the techniques, sometimes simultaneously and sometimes one technique in conjunction with another were employed according to the situation in the field.

The data thus collected were processed and analysed properly using standard methods. For instance quantitative data, such as population, age, sex etc. were computed statistically to arrive at a certain conclusion. Qualitative data concerning the non-technical features of the culture had also been procured and analysed taking all the common denominators and variations into consideration so that a conclusion may be drawn. In such a way certain ethnographic postulations as to the subsistence pattern of the Kabuis of Manipur have been made for comparison with the unauthorized, prehistoric artifacts of Manipur with a view to arriving at a conclusion on the parallelism between the Kabui ethnography and prehistory of Manipur.

2

Geographical Setting and The People

About Manipur

Location

Manipur having a unique geographical feature lies at the gateway between the South-East-Asia and India. The State lies between 23·83^0 N and 25·68^0 N Latitude and 93·03^{0}E and 94·78^{0}E Longitude. Its capital city Imphal is 790 meters above the sea level (Map 1).

It is the nineteenth State of the Union of India that came into existence on 21.1.1972 under the North-Eastern Areas, Recognition Act, 1971. Prior to the merger with Indian Union on October 15, 1949 she was a small kingdom. She joined Indian Union as part-C state and then was given the status of Union Territory. She is surrounded on the north and west by the State of Nagaland, the North Cachar hills and Cachar District of Assam, on the east and south by the Kabaw Valley and its adjoining areas and the Chin hills of Myanmar (Burma). On the south west corner lies Mizoram. Manipur comprises an area of 22,327 sq. km and has a population of about 21 lakhs (the provisional census figure of 2001 is 21,66,788) of which the tribal population accounts for approximately 34 percent of the total population (the provisional census figure of S.T., 2001 is 7,41,141).

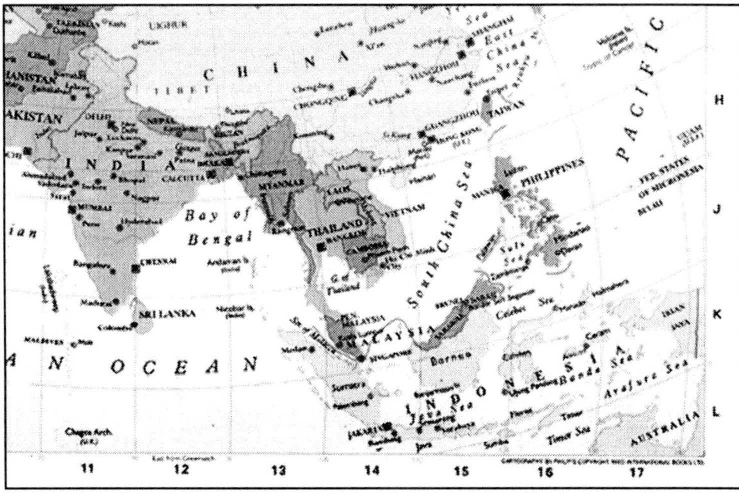

Map 1. Manipur, at the gateway between the South-East-Asia and India.

In olden days, Manipur was known to her neighbouring states by different names supposedly given by them. In Rennal's

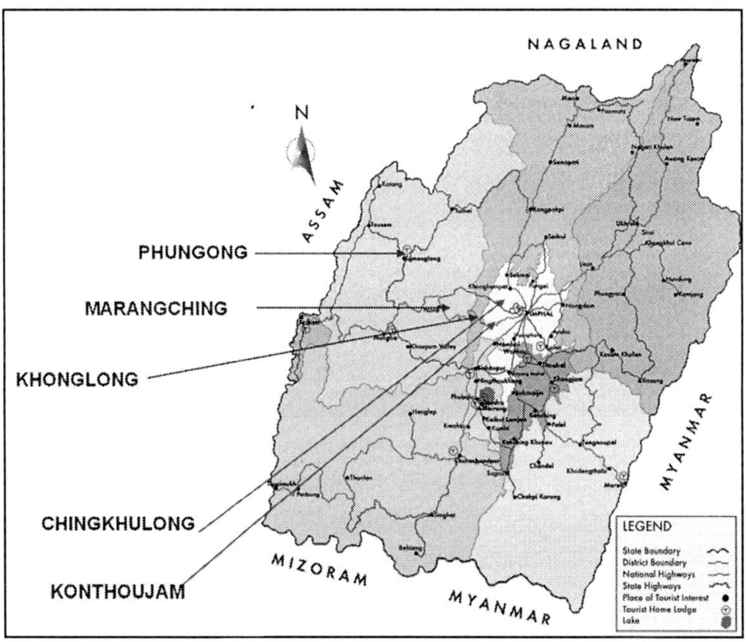

Map 2. Map of Manipur, showing the location of the study villages

Memoir and Maps of India, it was called 'Mecklay'. In the narratives of Symes and in Maps of that period Manipur was called 'Cassy'. To the Shans it was known as 'Kase' wheras to the Burmese as 'Kathe', a corruption of the same word. The Ahoms called it 'Mekeli' and the Cacharis 'Magli', while the old Assamese name for it was 'Moglan'.

Physiography

Geographically, the state may be divided into two distinct regions :

(a) The hilly region, which surrounds the oval shaped valley forming about 92 percent of the total land area of Manipur, is the homeland of a number of indigenous ethnoses.

(b) The centrally situated valley region, covering an area of about 1,820 sq. km, accounts for about 8 percent of the total land area and is an alluvial plain inhabited by different communities of which the Meiteis are the majority.

The valley region is somewhat oval in shape, wide at the centre and tapering towards the north and south. There is a decrease in altitude towards the south. As such, all the drainage and rivers flow towards the south.

The ranges of hills surrounding the valley are the extensions of the Himalayas. The Brahamaputra or Shangpo after flowing from west to east direction on the north of Himalayas makes a sharp bend and enters into Arunachal Pradesh. Ranges of mountains, however, continue its extension towards the east. The extensions or offshoots first running in a south westerly direction forms the hills of Nagaland, whereas the part of the extension running in a southerly direction forms the hills of Manipur. The ranges of hills running in the north-south direction bifurcates in the northern part of Manipur: a series running on the east of the valley and the other running on the west of the valley. These two series meet again in the southern part of Manipur thus encircling the Manipur valley.

Eastern range : The eastern hills form a compact and continuous mountain chain, and their average height is about 1,500 meters. Some important peaks in these hill tracts are Khayangbung (2,833 m), Sirohi (2,568 m), Kachoubung (2,498 m), Nupithel (2055.4 m), Chingai, Ungoching and Yomadung.

Western range: The western hills lie more or less parallel to the north south direction and stretch in the three districts – Churachandpur, Tamenglong and Senapati. The Yangpujilong, the Daimikilong, the Koubru, the Khoupum, the Nungba, the Kalanaga etc. are the important hill ranges of the western hills.

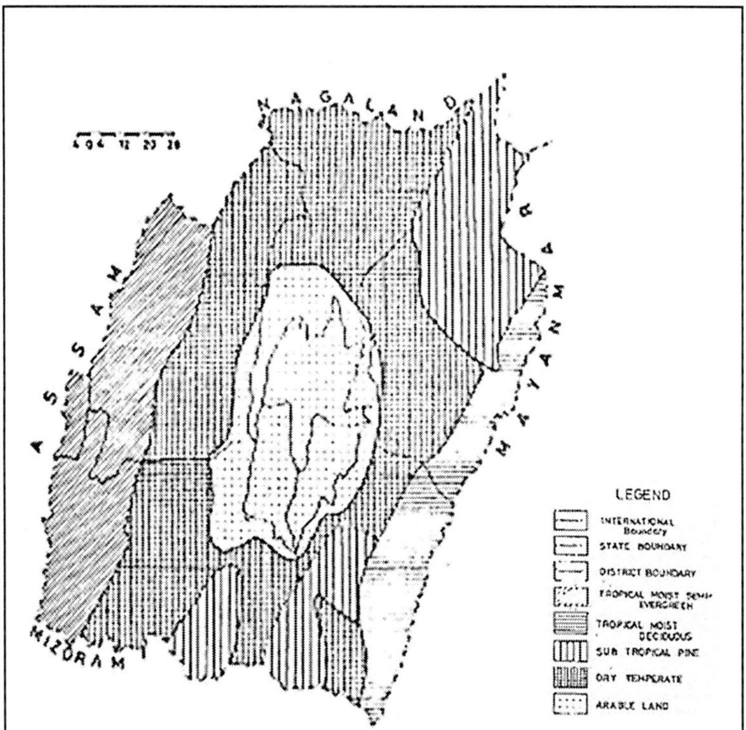

Map 3. Classification of the Forest of Manipur

Mount Iso, also known as Tanipu, is located on the north western part of Mao and is the highest peak of Manipur. It is about 2,994 meters above the mean sea level. Other important peaks are, Leikot (2,831m) Tamphaba (2,564 m), Koubru (2,562 m). The eastern slopes of these ranges are very steep. Sandstone, shale and clay constitute the rocks of the western hills. These hills measure about 50 km and 70 km in breadth in the north and the south respectively (Singh, 1982 :20).

A number of isolated hills are also situated in the valley. The Nongmaiching and the Langolching deserve special mention.

Natural Vegetation

Forest is the main important natural vegetation of the State. Forest covers an area of 15,154 sq. km. Forests are mainly confined to the hills of Manipur. The Imphal valley is used for settlement and agriculture. Four different types of forests are identified in Manipur (Map 3). They are :

(a) Sub-tropical deciduous forests,

(b) Sub-tropical evergreen forest,

(c) Tropical moist deciduous forests and

(d) Tropical moist semi-evergreen forests.

a. Sub-tropical deciduous forests : These forests exist in and around the Imphal valley, particularly in the hill slopes overlooking the valley. They have a denuded appearance because of excessive cutting of the trees to obtain timber and firewood. Various species of oak, toon (*Cedrela toona*), and chestnut are found in these forests. Towards the south of the valley, there is pine forest where oak trees are also grown. Most of the isolated hillocks are also covered with oak and chestnut.

b. Sub-tropical evergreen forests : These forests are found in the north-eastern part of the State at elevations varying from 1,200 to 1,400 meters. The colder climate of this region favours the growth of soft coniferous trees like pine. Pine is mainly confined to the higher altitudes while at lower altitudes it is mixed with oak and chestnut. The area covered by these forests is about 1,300 sq. km.

c. Tropical moist deciduous forests : These forests are located in the south-eastern part of Manipur along the international boundary with Myanmar covering an area of about 900 sq. km. The hot and moist climate of this region favours the growth of tropical moist deciduous trees such as Teak (*Tectona grandis*), Toon, *Kangin* (*Dipterocarpus tuberculates*) and the *Kheu* (*Melanorhhoea usitata*) (Singh, 1982 : 34). Teak thrives well on alluvial banks of small streams flowing from Manipur into the Yu river of Myanmar. Palm trees of areca nut are also grown here.

d. Tropical moist semi-evergreen forests : These forests are found in the western hills and the Barak basin stretching along the Manipur-Assam border within the jurisdiction of Tamenglong and Churachandpur Districts. High temperature and heavy rainfall of this region support dense vegetation. Bamboos constitute the most important vegetation and these forests contain as many as 13 major species of bamboos (Singh, 1982 : 34). Some of the important timber species grow in this forest are –Haldi (*Adina cadifolia*), Siris (*Albizzia lebbek*), Chaplash (*Artocarpus chaplasha*), Aini (*Artocarpus hirsute*), Agar (*Aquilaria agallocha*) Toon (*Cedrela toona*), Jarul (*Lagerstroemia flosregina*), Bonsum (*Phobe hensiana*), Iron wood (*Nesua ferrea*), Mango (*Mangifera indica*) etc. These forests produce cinnamon and canes in large quantities.

Geological Formation

The geological or the tectonic history of Manipur can be understood as a part of geological evolution of North East India. Some researchers have presumed that there existed a shallow sea called Tethys which provided a geosynclinal environment in this part of the world during the lower Paleozoic and Mesozoic era (Ansari, 1985). However the Shillong plateau of Meghalaya remained as a landmass since the Precambrian times.

The Tethys continued to receive sediments eroded from the Archaean rocks during Palaeozoic and Mesozoic eras. During the cretaceous period the North East India underwent Orogenic movement caused by geodynamic forces. The long accumulated sediments on the floor of the Tethys were deformed as ridges and basins. This caused the appearance of land on the one hand and deepening of parts of the Tethys on the other. It has been pointed out that the oldest rocks found in eastern Manipur belong to Cretaceous group including shales, slates, quartzite etc. This area has serpentine rocks which are younger than cretaceous rocks. The lime stones of cretaceous occur near Ukhrul and Hundung. The rock types in this area are the shales, and sandstones of the Disang series. It is said that the stratigraphy of Manipur is better understood from Eocene period (40-60 m.y.). The cretaceous formations are overlain by lower tertiary formations belonging to Eocene period. In Chandel District in South-Eastern Manipur the sedimentary rocks belong to Disang series. The Disang and the Jaintia series are overlain by the Barail series belonging to Oligocene period. This sedimentary rocks form the Barail range. The Barail series occupy a large part of Assam, Nagaland and Manipur. The Barail series consist of sandstone, siltstone, and conglomerate. The Barail covers considerable tracts of Manipur. In Tamenglong area the rock types are the shale, sandstone of the Barail series (Ansari, 1985).

Oldham (1883) of the Geological Survey of India worked out a general tertiary geological succession of India. Dark grey to green splintery shales intercalated with fine grained sandstone, occasionally carbonaceous shale belongs to the Disang series of the Eocene system. Upon them, are flaggy sandstone, coarse blended with sandy shales referable to the Barail series of the Oligocene system. The Barails are unconformably overlaid by the Surma and succeeded by the Tipam series of the Miocene period. And these deposits cover a small area in the Barak basin on the western flanks of the state. The alluvium which forms the valley of Manipur is of recent (geologically Pleistocene) origin composing mainly of sand, silt and clays. Angou (1987) has made an attempt on the quaternary studies of the Manipur valley. He has opined that this landmass was close to sea during Oligocene, Miocene period and there after successive upliftments of the hills took place during the Pleistocene resulting in the subsidence of the central part to form the present Manipur valley.

Rock formation

According to Angou (1987: 33-35), the types of rock formation are as follows (Map 4) :

(a) Alluvium

(b) Tipam series

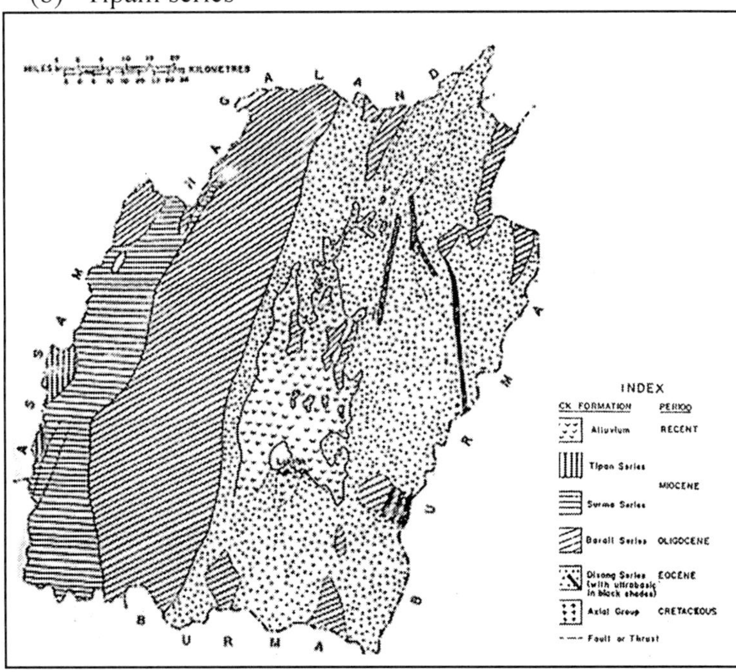

Map 4. Classification of the Rocks of Manipur

(c) Surma series

(d) Barail series

(e) Disang series

(f) Axials

a. Alluvium : Alluvium deposits consists of very fine grained sand, silt and clay. It is considered the youngest deposit and covers major parts of the valley. Occasionally, a few pockets of gravels consisting of materials reworked from the Disang series are also included. It covers a depth ranging from 200-300 m.

b. Tipam series : It is characterized by the coarse grained ferruginous, micaceous and weathered sandstones and interbedded with shale clay and conglomerate. It occurs in a small area and has a thickness of 2700 m. The age of this formation is believed to be upper or middle Miocene (Angou, 1987:33).

c. Surma series : This type of rock formation is found specially in the western part of Manipur and Assam borders. It comprises the usual alternation of sandstones and shale. It dates to lower Miocene and has a thickness of about 4000-4500m (Angou, 1987 : 33-34).

d. Barail series : Some parts of the eastern and northern Manipur are deposited by the Barail series. It consists of buff to yellow and olive colour medium to coarse grained sandstone. The age of this series is Oligocene and upper Eocene. It has a thickness of about 4000-6000 meters (Angou, 1987 : 33-34).

e. Disang series : Parts of south eastern hilly areas of Manipur and some parts of valley and hill ranges in the western side of Manipur belong to this series. This layer consists of dark, olive grey and buff colour splintery shales which are well bedded, highly cleaved, joined, folded and often intercalated with beds of fine grained sandstone, mudstone and siltstone

(Anand etal, 1968). It is dated to the geological age ranging from the Upper Cretaceous to the Upper Eocene.

f. Axials : The areas to the north and the north east of Sekpao and around Ukhrul, and the eastern part of the State are found to be composed of sedimentary rocks and these rocks which are mainly of buff colour and variegated shales, slates and siltstones with subordinate sandstone, quartzite and limestone beds, have been mapped as axials (cretaceous). A few small serpentinite intrusives which occur in the forms of dikes within the axial group of rocks are also encountered. The occurrence of forminiferal assemblages of upper cretaceous age in the limestone lenses and the closing shales has also been reported by Jha and Agarwal (1981).

Geologically, Manipur is a part of Assam–Myanmar unit in which Tertiary ranges sweep in a long curve from the north eastern corner of Assam to the cape Negrais of Myanmar. The geological succession established by Oldham (1883) is as follows (Table 1).

Table 1 Rock Types and Age of Formation

Sl. No.	*Locality*	*Rock type*	*Formation age*
1	Manipur Valley	Sand, silt and clay	Recent
2	Western Hill ranges at higher elevation and Chingai formation on the eastern side of the valley	Flaggy, sandstone, coarse bedded with sandy shales.	Barail group (Oligocene)
3	Western Hill ranges at lower elevation and the relict hills in the valley.	Dark grey to green splintery shales with fine grained sandstones and carbonaceous shales.	Disang formation (Eocene)

Soil

As per report of the exploration of the underground water by a unit of Geological Survey of India, 1969 the soil of hilly region is chiefly of unconsolidated sedentary rocks and porous red sandy loam (1.52m to 2.15m in thickness) and that of the valley is of recent and fertile alluvial filling (106.68m to 152.40m in thickness). The red silts are transported from the hill to the plains. It contains large amount of clay and plant nutrients. Captain Pemberton (1835) remarked, "*The fertility of the soil is so great that crops generally prove most abundant*". Colonel McCullock, (1859) remarked with some astonishment, "*Not a particle of manure is placed on the ground, and yet year after year good crops are raised from the same spot*".

The Indian Council of Agricultural research (ICAR), Delhi, on the basis of climate, rainfall and drainage characteristics of the state, has reported the soil of Manipur as under (Map 5).

a. Alluvial soils,

b. Lateritic soils,

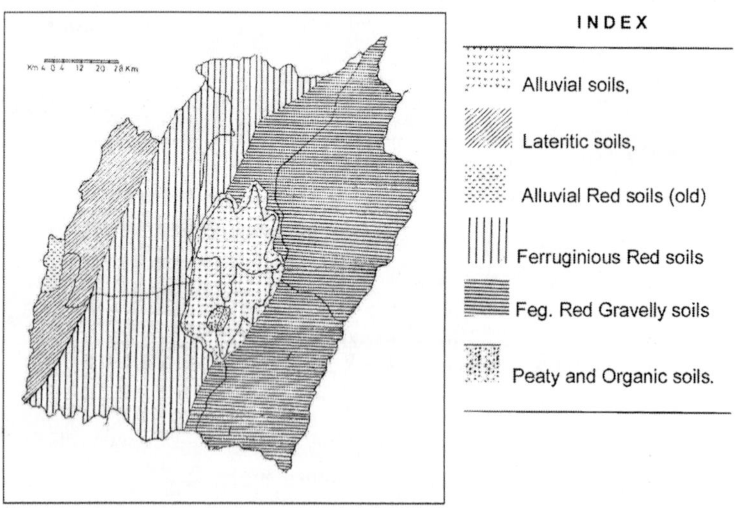

Map 5 Classification of the Soils of Manipur

c. Non-lateritic soils,

d. Mountain or forest soils and

e. Peaty and organic soils.

a. Alluvial soils **:** It covers 1,600 sq. km in Manipur valley and contributes the largest share to the State's agricultural production. It contains good proportion of potash and phosphate. These soils are formed by the transportation and depositional action of Manipur river system deriving parent materials from the surrounding hills, mixed up with organic particles.

b. Lateritic soils : These soils cover an area of about 300 sq. km in the lowland and 2,500 sq. km in the high hill regions. Generally they are red in colour containing moderate proportion of nitrogen and phosphate both in hills and in lowlands. They are found on the western slopes of the western hills of Manipur and river basins.

c. Non-lateritic soils : This type is by far the largest soil group of Manipur covering over 17,000 sq. km. These soils occur especially in the major portions of Tamenglong and Chandel Districts. Mostly the soils of the western hills of Tamenglong District are by nature ferruginous. They contain rich phosphate and potash but they lack in nitrogen. The eastern hills of Chandel and Ukhrul Districts have the nature of ferruginous red gravelly soils that contain rich phosphate and potash with fair quantity of nitrogen. These soils are generally shallow in texture and sandy loam in nature.

d. Mountain and forest soils **:** This type of soils scatter in the hilly regions of Manipur. They are characterized by the deposition of organic matters derived from forest growth. Generally, these soils are brown in colour. They are mostly found in small valleys, hillock tribulates and foothill areas. These soils are deficient in potash, phosphoric and lime but rich in humus and acid.

e. Peaty and organic soils : This type of soils are specially found in the reclaimed swampy areas of the Manipur valley and has a high humus content. It covers about 100 sq. km of area in and around the Loktak and the other lakes and marshes of the State. These soils remain under water during the rainy season. They are dark grey in colour and clayey loam in texture with high fertility. Some of these soils sometimes burn like charcoal (specially in Lamphelpat).

On the basis of relief and parent materials, Ansari (1976) has also classified soils of the State into two classes viz., Hill land of poor sandy and rocky soils and Valley land of fertile clayed soils.

On the basis of the analysis of the available geological data, Singh, (1982) has recognized the following types of soil in the State.

a. Non-laterised Red soils,

b. Laterised Red soils,

c. Alluvial soils and

d. Organic soils.

Laiba (1988) holds that the soils can be classified according to the parent rocks from which they have been derived. According to him, the soils of the State are divided into :

(i) Valley soils and

(ii) Mountain or Hill soils.

According to their mode of origin, these soil groups can be grouped again into residual soils formed in situ and those transported and deposited by water, which may be a mixture of materials of different origin.

The soil depth of Manipur depends on parent rocks, slope, nature of the vegetation and climate. The climate is responsible, to a large extent, for the nature of the soil. The moist semi-evergreen forest region having rainfall more than 200cm, the sub-tropical pine forest region having rainfall 150 to 200cm and the regions of Tamenglong, Churachandpur and south eastern hilly sections of the state have thin soils. The thick soils are found in the valley region and tropical moist deciduous forest region of low rainfall area. It comprises the Indo-Myanmar border of the State with the growth of teak, toon, *Kangin* and *Kheu* trees. The types of soils can also be identified by its colour. The largely available red and yellow coloration soils of Manipur are attributed to the presence of iron compounds, notably the oxides and hydroxides of iron. The dark colouration soils of Bishnupur, Imphal and Thoubal Districts is due to high humus content having much nitrogen.

Hydrography

Many rivers and streams traverse the mountains and the valley of the State and provide the sustenance and the other means of livelihood to the people of Manipur. Besides, a number of lakes and marshes are situated in the southern part of the valley. Manipur lies at the catchman area of the Ganga-Brahamaputra and the Chindwin-Irrawati river systems. The land lying between the plains of Cachar and Manipur forms the catchman area of the Barak river. Nearly half of Manipur lies in the Barak catchment. The eastern half of Manipur including the central plain is in the catchment of Chindwin-Irrawati system. Thus, the drainage system of Manipur can be divided into three main systems (Map 6).

(a) The Manipur or Imphal river system

(b) The Barak river system and

(c) The Chindwin river system.

a. The Manipur or Imphal river system : The Manipur or the Imphal river basin covers about one fourth of the total area of Manipur, while the Barak and the Chindwin river basins cover two fifth and one fourth of the areas of the State respectively. These important rivers and their tributaries are perennial (Angou, 1987: 51). On its way through the valley the Manipur river is joined by many tributaries, such as the Sekmai, Kongba, Iril, and Thoubal. The iril and the Thoubal are the two most important tributaries, of the Imphal river. The Iril rises in the north eastern part of Mao and flows southwards to join the Imphal river at Lilong. Thoubal river rises in the Huimi Hills of Ukhrul and flows south-westwards and joins the Imphal river at Mayang Imphal. The river does not fall into the Loktak, rather it flows to the eastern part of it. Other rivers of the Imphal valley that fall into the Loktak are the Nambul, the Nambol, and the Moirang. The Nambul and the Nambol (Maklang) rise in the Kangchup hills and the Moirang river rises in the western hills of Moirang. The Nambul river passes through the heart of Imphal town and follows a course west of the Imphal river. The water from the Loktak is drained by a river called Khordak, which in turn falls into the Imphal river. In the south of the Loktak lake the Imphal river is joined by its tributaries, the Khuga and the Chakpi. Here the river is known as Manipur river. The river crosses the southern boundary of Manipur through narrow and winding gorges and enters the Chin Hills of Myanmar. It finally falls into the Chindwin river of Myanmar.

b. The Barak River system : The Barak river is the largest river of Manipur and it rises in the northern highlands in the eastern part of Mao. Near the origin, it follows a south-westerly direction. At Karong, it takes a sharp bend towards the north. It then flows westwards and forms a short natural boundary between Manipur and Nagaland in the north west. The river now becomes broader and flows southwards through the western hills of Manipur. On its way to the south, the Barak is joined by the Makru and Irang. The Makru and Irang are the two main tributaries of the Barak. The Makru river rises in the north-western part of the Barail range. It follows southwards in the west of the Barak river and almost parallel to it. It joins the Barak at a place about five km south of the Kalanaga village in Tamenglong District. The Irang river rises in the northern part of the Yangpujilong range in the west of Karong. The river follows a south westerly course through steep and narrow gorges. It joins the Barak river at a place about 32 km north of Tipaimuk. The Leimatak and the Ijei are the two important tributaries of the Irang river. Further at Tipaimuk, the Barak is again joined by a north flowing river called Tuivai. Here, the Barak turns north and follows in a winding course. Then it is joined by the Jiri river at Jirimukh. Again the river forms the natural boundary between Manipur and Assam. It follows towards Cachar and Sylhet plains and finally falls into the old bed of the Brahamaputra near Bhairab Bazar.

*c. **The Chindwin River system*** : The rivers of the north eastern and the eastern parts of Manipur falls into the Chindwin Irrawati system of Myanmar. Thus the rivers viz. Chingai, Chamu, Lokchao, Phou-khong, Yu are the tributaries of the Chindwin system.

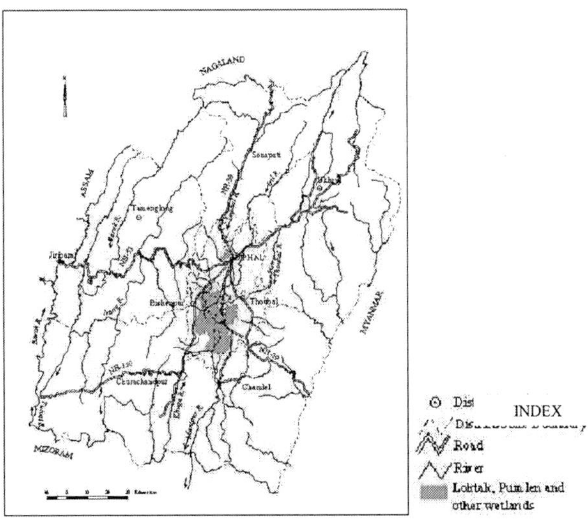

Map 6. Rivers and lakes of Manipur

Map source : Spatial Solutions, Lamphel

Lakes

Besides the above river systems there are a large number of lakes, marshes and swampy areas on either side of the Manipur river right from the central part of the valley, but specially towards the southern part. Since the level of the Imphal river is lower than that of the Loktak lake, which lies close to the right bank of Imphal river, it does not fall into this lake. In fact, the other lakes viz. Ikop pat, Kharung pat, Lamjao pat, Pumlen pat etc. are connected to the Imphal river through a number of natural waterways. Therefore the southern parts of the valley are occupied by many lakes and marshes.

Loktak lake is the most striking landmark of Manipur. This lake is the biggest natural reservoir of the valley. The general elevation of this lake is 767.3 m above the mean sea level, where water spread covers an area of 260 sq. km and varies from time to time. The rivers, such as Nambul, Nambol, Thongjaorok etc. feed this lake. This lake is also connected to the Manipur river or the Imphal river through narrow channel. The other smaller lakes that occupies the left bank of Imphal river are also connected to the river through natural channels. There are three hillocks in the southern part of the Loktak lake and they are Thanga, Ithing and the Karang.

Climate

Manipur has a Sub-tropical type of climate. The hills, being at higher altitude, are cooler than the valley region. But the westernmost part of Manipur (Jiribam) is comparatively very hot. Manipur has thus a variety of climate within its borders. Most of the places in the valley and in the hills has a cool and the pleasant climate except in Jiribam and the adjoining Cachar District of Assam and Moreh on the Indo-Burma border where there are oppressive heat in summer. Up in the heights of Ukhrul, Mao, Tamenglong and some other hilly regions intensive cold winter is experienced. The rains of the summer are provided by the Bay of Bengal branch of the south-west monsoon. The cold and dry weather of the winter is due to the anticyclonic control. However, many factors influence the climate of Manipur. They include topography and elevation, cyclones, originating from the Bay of Bengal and the South China sea and the western disturbances that originate in the eastern part of the Mediterranean sea.

On the basis of the average annual weather system the climate of Manipur may broadly be divided into three seasons (a) Cold season (October to March), (b) Hot season (April to June) and (c) Rainy season (June to September), However, one does not feel any abrupt change in the succession of the seasons. Of these three seasons, the early and the last part of the cold season are the most pleasant months in Manipur. During the cold season the wind blows from the north east direction and it lowers the temperature even up to 0^0 centigrade in December and January, which causes snowfalls sometimes back at the rate of half an inch per night at some higher altitudes, such as Koubru and Ukhrul. The average temperature ranges between 12^0C and 18^0C in this season. Skies are clear and light westerly winds also blow during this period. Such a fine weather is disturbed occasionally by the Western Disturbances which cause light winter rain in Manipur. Due to differential heating of the hills and valleys, local winds start blowing in the later part of February.

The beginning of March is characterized by a sudden increase in temperature and frequent gusty winds. Unequal heating of the hills and valleys is responsible for the windy nature of this season. The temperature over the low lying plain is warmer than that of the hill top. The hot winds of the plain being light, rise upwards and in order to fill the vacuum, cool winds from the hills blow downwards. Therefore, dust rising winds are very common during the month of March. The average temperature varies between 18^0C and 28^0C. Sometimes during April and May temperature raises up to 34^{0}C. Towards the end of the season temperature as well as the number of rainy days increase significantly.

The rainy season starts from June and lasts up to September. This is the longest season of Manipur. It is also a season of high temperature and heavy rainfall. Rainfall during the month of June is often accompanied with thundershower. By this time, the south-west monsoon provides abundant rain throughout the State. Rainfall is heavy during June and July while it is moderate in August and September. Thus floods are very common in the valley during June and July. Cloudiness, high humidity, etc. make the weather oppressive during the rainy season in Manipur. The rainfall is generally higher in the hill areas than in the valley. While the average annual distribution of rainfall at Imphal is 143.4cm, that of Tamenglong is 195.8cm, and it is 132.7cm for Ukhrul, 129cm for the Churachandpur, 224.9cm for Thanlon etc. (Singh, 1982:29).

Flora and Fauna

Manipur is gifted with rich wealth of flora and fauna because of its geographical position and climatic condition. The scenic beauty of the State charms the heart of the beholders. Different varieties of big and small trees, plants, herbs, shrubs, flowers etc. grow luxuriantly on the undulating surface.

The North Eastern hill tracts of the State are rich in different species of plants of the sub-tropical pine forest. Here pure Khasi pine (*Pinus khasya*) with patches of Oak and Chestnut are found. Siroi lily (*Lilium macklineae*) which is not anywhere in the world, is also found here.

The hills in and around the Manipur valley are covered with dry temperate forest. Here various species of Oak intermixed with chestnut are found.

Some of the worth mentioning plants are bamboo (*Bamboosa tulda*), bay leaf (*cinnamonum*) amla (*Emblica *officinalis*), banana (*Musa paradisiaca*), cotton (*Gossypium herbaceum*), mango (*Mangifera indica*), maize (*Zea mays*), potato (*Solanum tuberosum*), pineapple (*Ananus cosmosus*), papaya (*Carica papaya*), sal (*Sorea robusta*) etc.

Soyabean, paddy, wheat , pulses of various types, oil seeds (mustard, sesamum), jute, turnip, cauliflower, pumkin, squash, citrus fruits of various types, apple, passion fruit, various species of phaseolus are also found abundantly.

Among the trees of great economic value mentioned may be made of Teak (*Tectona grandis*), Toon (*Toona ciliata*), Kangin (*Dipterocarpus tuberculates*) Kheu (*Melanorhhoea usitata*), Haldi (*Adina cadifolia*), Siris (*Albizzia lebbek*), Chaplash (*Artocarpus chaplasha*), Agar (*Aquilaria agallocha*), Jarol (*Lagerstroemia flosregina*), Bonsum (*Phobe hensiana*), Iron wood (*Nesua ferrea*), etc. The important forests products are cinnamon and canes (Singh, 1982).

Another peculiarity of the flora of Manipur is the presence of various species of orchids which are found in all the forest of Manipur.

Since the state has 92% coverage of thick forest, the State is not only rich in fauna but also abounds in both wild and domesticated animals. Different kinds of bears are found in the hills. Elephants are also found in the thick forest of the Jiribam Sub-division. But they are not common now. Besides, there are mithun and varieties of jungle cats. Boar is also commonly found in almost all parts of the State specially in the hilly regions. Monkey is another common mammal found in Manipur. Varieties of deers namely the spotted deer, barking deer and *Sangai*, the brow antlered deer are found in the State. *Sangai* is recognized as the State animal of Manipur.

Besides, large varieties of birds are found both in the hills and valley. Wild ducks of various kinds and wild geese are extraordinarily plentiful. The Loktak lake, the biggest fresh water lake of North East India is also seasonally visited by different varieties of migratory birds coming even from far places like Siberia. Among the reptiles various poisonous snakes and large pythons are found in the moist warm part of the valley and in the hills. Porcupine is available in the hills.

The People

> "Manipur is one of the routes between South Asia and South East Asia and Central Asia. Various ethnic groups belonging to southern Mongoloid group , the Tibeto-Burmans, the Indo-Aryans and a sizeable section of Tai (Shans) came to Manipur from the prehistoric times down to the present day. The present ethnic groups of Manipur, viz,., the Meiteis, the Naga tribes, the Kuki Chin tribes and other Indian communities are the descendants of those migrating people. And Manipur and its central valley provided the ecological setting for building up a civilization. These migrating people brought with them varying degrees of technology ranging from the Old Stone Age roughstone tools to more refined Neolithic and potters. With the coming of metal tools mostly bronze, copper, and tin during the historical period from Thailand and Upper Burma cultural zone, the metal civilization of Manipur was developed mostly through the trade" (Gangmumei, 1991).

Manipur, by virtue of being a gateway of India into South East Asia is again influenced by her geographical situation in shaping of her history and culture development. The geographical isolation that acted as barrier in the way of cultural contact with the outside world had resulted in the preservation of much of its material and cultural wealth for the centuries. The varied arts and crafts practised by the people of Manipur as part of their lives till today, are highly interesting for study. From the ancient time onwards there have been land routes through the hills connecting Manipur with the Surma and the Brahmaputra valley in neighbouring Assam and the Kabow valley in Myanmar.

The people of Manipur may broadly be classified into three distinct groups.

a. The Meiteis, including the Scheduled Caste
b. The hill tribes and
c. The Meitei Pangans (Manipuri Muslims)

The Meiteis are the main inhabitants of the valley. The Imphal valley and the Meiteis are usually taken as synonymous. The Lois or Scheduled Caste are scattered throughout the valley interspersed with the Meiteis. The Manipuri Muslims, locally referred to as the Pangans, are found mainly on the fertile tracts of land between the Imphal river and the Iril river. The tribes inhabiting Manipur are concentrated in the hills with some few tribal pockets in the valley.

a. The Meiteis, including the Scheduled Caste

Origin of the Meitei

The origin of the Meiteis is shrouded in mystery and the study on the subject is greatly influenced by the religious faiths and the political ideologies of the Meiteis themselves, thus making the problem highly speculative and controversial. The ethnic name, Meitei, is a, "combined appelate of Siamese 'Tai' and Kochin Chinese 'Moy' (Moy Tai = Moytai = Moitai= Meitei) and that the Meiteis belong to the Moy section of the great Tai race" (Hodgson, 1853).

One explanation that deserves special mention here is that the term Meithei is derived from the blending of two words that is "Mi" means man or people and "Thei" means separate. Therefore, Meitei means separate people (Hodson, 2003). Another explanation rooted in the indigenous knowledge is that Meetei (not Meitei) is derived from the creation of man by God in His image (Mee = image : Tei = modelled after God's image).

The ethnonym Meitei is a blending of two tribes of ancient China : Mei and Ti = Mei + ti = Meiti =Meitei (Singh, 1984a). However, it is a well known hard fact that historically, the word 'Meitei' was used during the period of the establishment of the Ningthouja dynasty by Pakhangba to mean his clan or dynasty and the ethnic and social groups which were politically and socially integrated into the Ningthouja.

Of all the theories of the origin of the Meitei the Aryan origin was most enthusiastically propounded and vehemently rejected by the protagonists and their opponents respectively (Singh, 1984b). This Aryan connection was an outcome of the adoption of the Hinduism. The representatives of the Aryan elements are Manipuri Brahamins and the Nongchup Haram (those migrants from the west, i.e. India) section of the Meiteis.

Hodgson's suggestion of the Moy tai origin of the Meiteis is rejected by T.C. Hodson on the basis of Meitei being a Tibeto Burman language group and Tai being the Siamese Chinese linguistic family, though both of them belong to the Sino Tibetan Linguistic family. Though not of the Tai origin, it has been conjectured that there was a relationship between Meitei and Mon Khmer and Tai because of historical connection, both conquest and the socio cultural contacts which produced Tai influence on the language and the culture of the Meiteis. Recent archaeological findings of the excavations of the Tharon cave, Napachik in Manipur point to the existence of Mon Khmer Australoid Mongoloid people in Manipur who migrated to this land before the advent of the Tibeto Burman speakers (Singh, 1984a). This Mon Khmer elements were absorbed by later immigrants. All the archaeological and the historical evidences point to the relationship of the ancient Meiteis with the Mon Khmers and the Tai people but not of Mon Khmer Tai origin of the people. However, the absorption of many Tai immigrants into Meitei society since the 8th century A.D. and more actively since the 15th century has been recorded in the chronicles of

Manipur. The clan genealogy also indicates the assignment of clan (*salai*) and the lineage or sub lineage (*sagei*), later on Hindu gotras to this eastern (San and Burmese) immigrant who are collectively known as the Nongpok Haram (The immigrant of the east).

Grierson (1967) in his monumental Linguistic Survey of India has grouped Meitei in the Kuki Chin sub-families of the Tibeto-Burman languages. A more appropriate name of this sub family, in the opinion of many linguists would have been Meitei Kuki Chin. Based on a historical assumption that the Tibeto-Burman and the other Mongoloid groups were inhabiting the upper courses of the Yangtes and the Hoang Ho river in China in the prehistoric times, he is of the opinion that the ancestors of the Meiteis were among their kinsman who migrated from China to upper waters of the Irawadi and the Chinwin rivers of upper Burma. They lived in the Hukwak valley, the present land of the Kachin before they moved into the Manipur valley. Though the time and the manner of migration cannot be easily established, he generally presumes that the ancestors of the Meiteis were among the Tibeto-Burman speakers in south west China, Eastern Tibet and upper Burma. Hence, their affinity with the Tibeto-Burman tribes like the Nagas and Kukis who are less advanced than them.

Greatly influenced by the linguistic and cultural affinities between the Meiteis and the Hill tribes of Manipur and their folk lore, McCulloch (1859) advanced a theory that the major tribes and clans of the Meiteis appear to have been the descendants of the Nagas and the Kuki tribes.

b. The hill tribes

The tribes inhabiting Manipur can broadly be divided into two major groups – i) the Naga group and ii) the Kuki group.

i. Naga Group

It is not clear, how the name 'Naga' was derived. There have been several attempts to trace out the etymological origin of this popular ethnonym. It is hard to accept the theory of 'Naga' originating from the Sanskrit Nag meaning snake or serpent because there is no popular form of such a worship among the Nagas though there is fear and dislike for the pythons. Though no final word has been said on this derivation, it is certain that this name is given by outsiders to mean this group of people who are divided into more than two dozen tribes. Whatever the origin, this is an old name popularised by the Ahoms and later by the British. The theory of Naga coming from the Sanskrit or Hindustani Naga cannot be easily discarded.

The British military and the political officers gave the generic name to the present Nagas of Nagaland, Assam and Manipur. In Manipur, the people were known by their tribes' name throughout the 19th and early 20th century. But the British for administrative conveniences applied it to mean a group of tribes who, according to their anthropological classification, were Nagas. The Naga tribes of Manipur are the Tangkhuls, the Kolya, Khoirao or Mayangkhong, the Kabuis, the Quoirengs, the Chiru, the Marings, Mao and Maram who are all Tibeto-Burman speakers. Their migration into Manipur has been told and retold in their tradition preserved in their folklore, hymns and songs. There are legends current among the Nagas about their origin and migration. These traditions tell more about their migration and settlement in Manipur and the trans Chindwind region. It is reliably believed that these tribes were in occupation of the present habitat in the early century of the Christian era or even in the centuries before Christ. The Meitei historical and the literary works refer to the Naga tribes as having been in occupation of the hills of Manipur.

ii. Kuki Group

The Kuki (non Naga) tribes of Manipur are a branch of the great family of Kuki-Chin people. They are linguistically related to Meitei. Kuki is a generic term covering a large number of tribes inhabiting the whole of north east India and some parts of Burma. Kuki is probably a Bengali word meaning hill man. Some Kuki tribes migrated to Manipur hills in the prehistoric times along with or after the coming of the Meiteis to Manipur valley. Greater migration occurred from the eighteenth century onwards due to the great Kuki exodus which affected the demographic landscape of the hills of Manipur and the adjoining areas. The Kuki-Chin tribes are the Thadou, Paite, Hmar, Vaiphei, Gangte, Simte, Zou, Biete, Mizos. There are attempts to cover these tribes under a new blanket name Zomi.

However, officially, as per 1981 census report, the tribes of Manipur can be classified into three umbrella groups –

(i) Naga group

(ii) Chin-Kuki-Mizo group and

(iii) Intermediary category, which, strictly speaking, affiliate their identity with neither of the two groups.

(i) The Naga tribes are Kabui (Rongmei and Puimei), Kacha Naga (Liangmei and Zemei) collectively known as Zeliangrong, Mao, Maram, Tangkhul and Maring (six tribes).

(ii) Chin-Kuki-Mizo tribes are Gangte, Hmar, Lushai (Mizo), Paite, Simte, Thadou (Kuki) Vaiphei and Zou (eight tribes).

(iii) Intermediary tribes are Aimol, Chiru, Koireng, Kom (Collectively called Komrem), Anal, Chothe, Lamkang, Koirao/Thangal, Purum, Monsang and Monyon (Eleven tribes).

c. The Meitei Pangans (Manipuri Muslims)

The generic name Meitei Pangan is given to the Muslims of Manipur, for Pangan is the equivalent Manipuri word for Muslim. The term Pangan is derived from the word Bangal meaning Man of East Bangal (Jhaljit, 1965). Historical references (Brown,

1873; Ibungohal, 1963; Jhaljit, 1965; Khelchandra, 1969) trace the origin of the present day Pangans of Manipur to Silhet of East Bengal and Cachar, from where they had been deported as prisoners of war (Brown, 1873) by Khagemba, the then king of Manipur at the beginning of the seventeenth century when he repelled an invasion from the West in 1606 (Singh, 1987). They married woman particularly the Kabui and the Chakpa women and settled in Manipur. Though they adopted Meiteilon as their mother tongue they continued to practise their Islamic traditions. The Muslims who are an endogamous population, are the second largest community of the valley. They live in villages homogeneous in composition and spread over along the fertile tracts of land on the banks of the Imphal, the Iril and the Thoubal. They live side by side with the Meiteis in discrete hamlets within a village. Consequently they share similarities with the Meiteis in respect of their material way of life. Their primary occupation is agriculture though some of them are found to be engaged in different traits of occupation.

About the Villages Under Study

Location and Boundary

The present study site comprises five villages selected from the three districts of Manipur. Two villages, namely, Phungong and Marangching are located in the interior hilly areas of undivided Tamenglong District. Another village –Khonglong, located on the foothill, is from Senapati District and two other villages in the valley, Chingkhulong and Konthoujam, are located in the western side of Imphal- the capital city of Manipur.

Phungong : It is an old hamlet of Tamenglong Khunjao. It is situated at a distance of about 143 km to the west of Imphal. It occupies the hill top situated at an altitude of about 1175m above mean sea level (Topo Sheet, 1970). The parental village has a long history of 2000 years as claimed by the local scholars (Kamei, 2004).

Marangching : The village, named after the hill on the top of which it is situated, is at a distance of 60 km from Imphal to the west along the National Highway 53. It is situated at a height of about 1271m above mean sea level (Topo sheet, 1970). It lies in Tamenglong Sub-division of Tamenglong District. The market nearest to the village is None Bazar from where one has to climb a distance of about 4 km to reach the village.

Khonglong : The village is situated on a hillock to the western side of Imphal city at a distance of about 21 km along the National highway 53. It measures a height of about 840m (MSL). The nearest marketing centre is Keithelmanbi, situated at the junction of the hill and the plain. From the market the distance of the village is about one and a half km to the west. Leinganglok river flows from west to east direction at the foothills of the settlement area. It is in Sadar Hills Sub-division of Senapati District, Manipur.

Chingkhulong : The village is located at a distance of 8 km to the west of Imphal in Imphal West District along the Imphal Kangchup road. The village, bounded on the east by RDO Office and the Lamdeng hills (Langol Ching), on the west by Lamdeng Khunou road (Mayang Langjing road), on the north by Lamdeng Khunou and Laingam Khul, on the south by Lamsang bazar, is under the jurisdiction of Lamsang Police Station. Luwangli river flows through the village and joins the Nambul river.

Konthoujam : It is situated at a distance of about 12 km to the south west of Imphal along the National Highway 53. It is bounded on the east by Konthoujam Mamang Leikai, a Meitei village; on the west by paddy field, Nongloubung Meitei village and Maning Leikai Kabui Khul ; on the north by Konthoujam Lairembi, Konthoujam Meitei Khul and Sagoltongba and on the south by paddy field known as Yarou field and Machin Manao Ching.

The selection of the field villages has been made with a methodological reasoning that is appropriate for the present study that attempts to reconstruct the subsistence pattern of the prehistoric people who are believed to have settled in Manipur in the light of the knowledge of ethnographic analogy drawn from the study of the Kabui lifeways. Phungong, a hamlet of Tamenglong Khunjao, the core culture center of the Kabuis has been selected taking its remoteness and tradition-ridden lifeways that still remain untouched by waves of modernity into consideration. Their material ways of life is still at subsistence level and whatever they have practised for their livelihood has been practised as a part of their way of life but not as a profession. Shifting cultivation, hunting and gathering are their economic pursuits for gaining the livelihood. Marangching is also a Kabui village situated at a relatively isolated place. The people of this village still earn their livelihood by engaging themselves in shifting cultivation, hunting and gathering. Though they are a bit exposed to the outside world they are yet to escape from the strong bondage of their tradition. The reason why this village is selected lies in its location, both cultural and geographical, in the intermediary position between the hill top and foot hill habitation of the Kabuis.

Khonglong is selected as a field site because of the fact that the village is situated at the foot hill and represents a hybrid cultural life of the hill and the plain Kabuis earning their livelihood by practising both wet and shifting cultivation. The other two villages, namely, Chingkhulong and Konthoujam have been selected as model Kabui villages of Manipur valley as the material life ways of the people of the two villages may be regarded as the microcosm of the larger Kabui society of Manipur valley. One more important fact that needs explanation is the selection of five Kabui villages from the hill and plain areas of Manipur. It may be explained in terms of the objectives of the study that endeavours to explain a holistic picture of the lifeways of the Kabuis by selecting the villages at different ecological and cultural settings but yet in a continuum.

Table 2 Village wise Distribution of Household

District	*Name of Village*	*Household*
Tamenglong	Phungong	53
	Marangching	18
Senapati	Khonglong	30
Imphal West	Chingkhulong	41
	Konthoujam	27
Total		169

Settlement Pattern

The Kabuis settle in three habitational zones-(i) hilly zone, (ii) foot hill zone and (iii) valley zone.

A. Hilly zone :

It represents the villages lying in the interior hill, far away from the valley. The people living in these villages usually construct their houses on the top of the hills quite separated from the neighbouring villages as well as from their jhum fields. It is for their security specially from the enemy and the jungle fire. Each village has two main gates – one known as front gate and the other as back gate.

Those who settle for a long time on the higher altitudes usually tend to adapt to the tropical moist semi evergreen environment. Thus their way of living, sources of income, and pattern of subsistence have undergone some significant changes as compared with those in the other ecological zones. Two villages- Phungong and Marangching selected for the present study belong to this zone. The Kabuis living in these two villages get advantage from the terrain formed by the junction of two different slopes or two different types of relief, easy availability of water, etc. The usual site of such a settlement is generally selected taking the optimum conditions for to and fro movement from the abode to the work place into consideration.

***B. Foot hill zone* :**

Under this zone, come the villages which are on the foothills. The people of this zone enjoy both hill and valley traditions, particularly in their subsistence economy. Such a zone is characterized by the full of slopes. It is difficult to find a tract of flat piece of land in this zone; land with gentle slope is, however, put to cultivation. The springs supplying water are usually located at the foothills. The water point is at a distance of about a half km from settlement site and the onerous task of collecting water is shouldered by the womenfolks. The village selected from this zone for the study is Khonglong.

C. Valley zone :

In this zone the villages lie in the plain and the cultivable lands are also located around the villages. The farmers practise wet cultivation. Chingkhulong and Konthoujam are the villages selected for study from this zone. The Kabuis living in this zone are the ones who have experienced the greatest exposure to the outsiders because of their continuous interaction with the plain people, particularly the Meiteis.

House type

There are three types of houses among the Kabuis – traditional, slightly modern and modern. The traditional houses are of two types, one for the common people and the other (*Tarangkai*) for the rich people, constructed after offering a series of feast to the villagers. The house of common people are smaller and usually consists of two rooms-sleeping room (*Keijao*) and kitchen (*Keinong*) - one open verandah (*Keimasak*), three doors - one larger door in the front and two smaller doors on either side of the back room or kitchen of the house without any window. The framework of the traditional houses is made of timber and the roof is covered with thatch or straw. The walls

Map 7.
Geographical Location of
Phungong Village, Tamenglong District

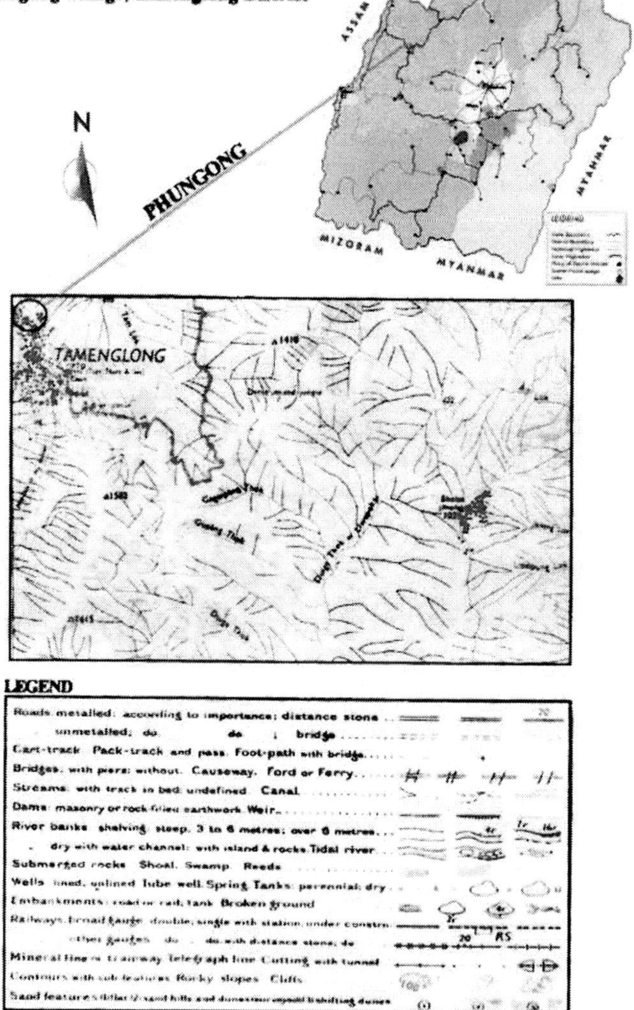

Courtesy from Govt. of India, 1974; Sheet 83, H/9

Map 8.
Geographical Location of Marangching Village, Tamenglong District

(Not to scale)

N

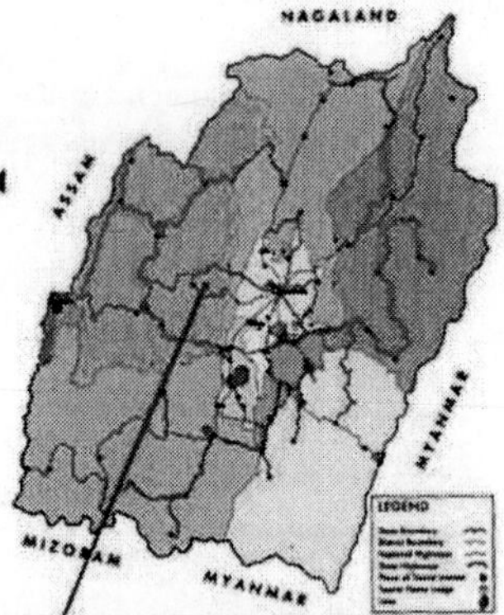

Courtesy from Govt. of India, 1974; Sheet 83, H/9

Map 9.
Geographical Location of Khonglong Village, Senapati District

(Not to scale)

N

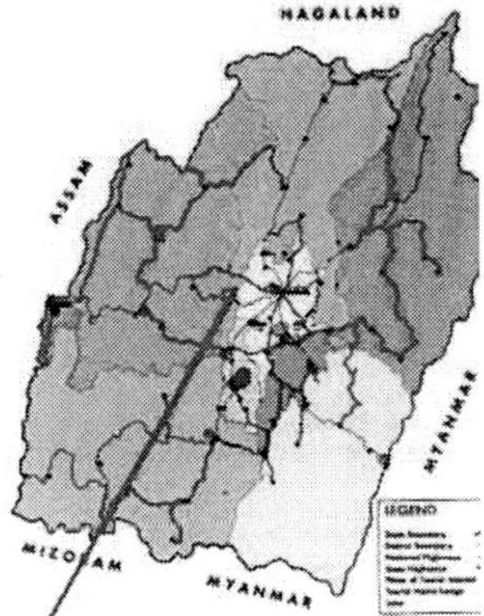

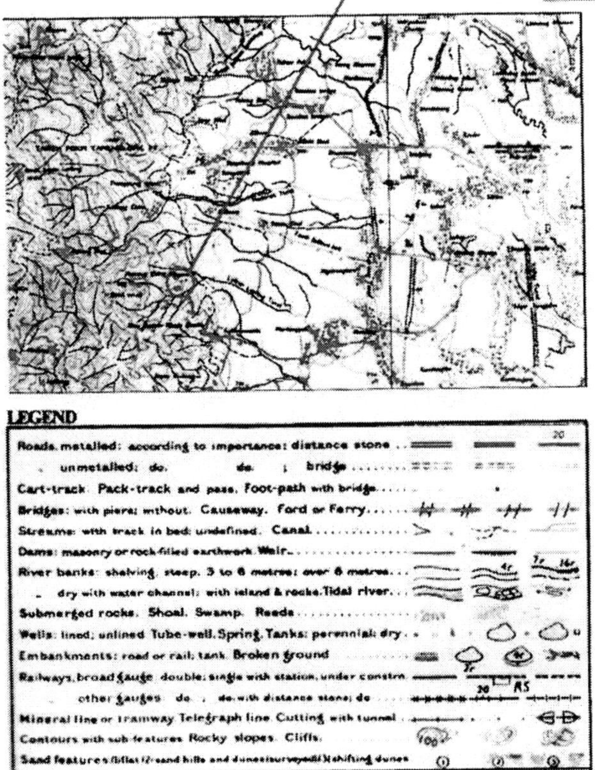

Courtesy from Govt. of India, 1974; Sheet 83, H/13

Map 10.
Geographical Location of Chingkhulong and Konthoujam Villages Imphal West District

(Not to scale)

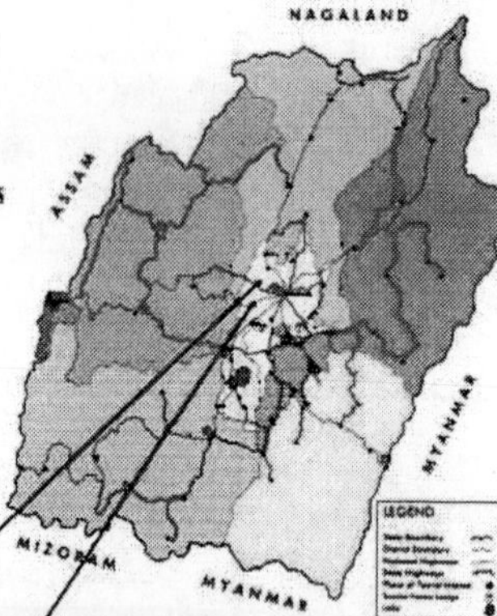

Courtesy from Govt. of India, 1974; Sheet 83, H/13

are made of either mud-slabs or the reed/bamboo mat plastered with the mixture of mud and cow dung or the naked bamboo mat. The partition inside the houses are normally of bamboo mat (Plate 1). The *Tarangkai* has almost similar number of rooms with that of the common traditional houses but the differences are only in materials, size, decorations, adorning of animal heads, weapons etc. The building plan is usually rectangular in shape and the houses have open verandah on eastern or southern side for more sunlight. The houses are furnished with furniture, domestic utensils, mortar and pestle, winnowing fan, and broom (Plate 2).

A traditional house :

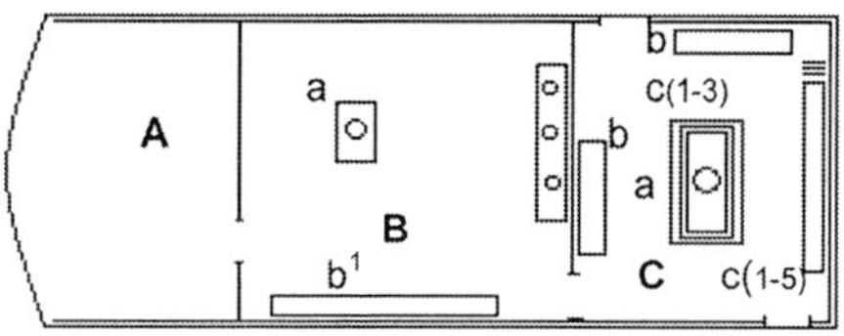

Fig. 1. A ground plan of a traditional House

LEGEND

A Verandah (*Keimasak*)
B Sleeping room (*Keijao*)
C Kitchen (*Keining/ Keinong*)
a Fire place (*Meimang*)
b^1 Plank use as bed (*Langom*)
b Bed (*Langphai*)
c (1-3) Hanging Rack of three tiers
c (1-5) Wall Rack of five tiers

The houses are distributed on either side of the main road facing the latter. However in the case of Kabui villages situated near the Meitei villages the houses generally face towards the east.

In most houses long wooden bed (*Langom*) measuring about 3m and 1m in length and breadth respectively are placed in the first room and used as bed (Plate 3) A long wooden mortar (*Panthon*) and pestle (*Mei*) having three holes for pounding is also placed at the inner sid• of the room (Plate 4). One fire place (*Meimang*) with three stands of stone is also present.

Next room is kitchen cum sleeping room. The backmost portion of the room is decorated with bamboo or wooden racks of four to five tiers. The lowest is for storing water pot and the topmost for keeping baskets. The middle ones are for keeping dish, utensils, and *Joumu,* a big rice beer storing pot made from bitter gourd, etc. A permanent fire place with a hearth of three stands of stone is situated either at the center or towards the backside. Above this fireplace, three racks *Keikang*, *Kangchong* and *Kangseng* are kept hanging one above the other (Plate 5). *Keikang,* the lowest is meant for drying meat, paddy, etc. and the other two for storing dry leaves, seeds, fermented liquid of mustard leaves, meat, dry skin, baskets, hoe handles, hoe, etc.

A small granary and a shed for storing firewood are generally constructed near the side of the house (Plate 6). Most households rear pigs and cows but they have no sheds. Pigs roam here and there in search of food. No household has separate latrine because the waste materials are consumed by these pigs. Fowls are reared keeping in a coop at one corner of the verandah.

Plate 1 : A Traditional Kabui House

Plate 2 : Tarangkai - A well decorated traditional house

Plate 3 : *Langom* - a wooden bed near a fire place

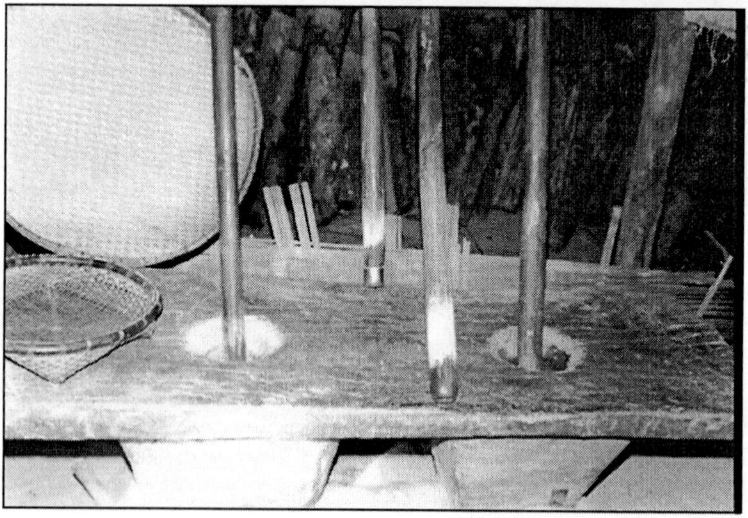

Plate 4 : *Panthon-Mei* (Mortar and Pestle)

Plate 5 : A hanging rack of three tires over a fire place

Plate 6 : A small granary beside a house

The Kabuis : A Brief Ethnographic Profile

Origin and Migration

The Kabuis are one of the thirtythree scheduled tribes of Manipur. Their habitations are found in both the hills and the plains of Manipur. The general concentration of the Kabuis is on the western hills of Manipur. The Kabuis are also known as Rongmeis meaning southerners. Together with Zemei, Liangmei, and Puimei, the sister tribes of the North, they form a unified ethnopolitical group known as Zeliangrong.

The Government of India recognizes Rongmei and Puimei tribes as Kabuis and Zemei and Liangmei as Kacha Naga. (Z.N.U. 1985). The Kabui tribe is the third largest tribe among the officially recognized 33 tribes of Manipur. It is, however, worth mentioning that some still prefer to be identified themselves separately as the Rongmei, the Liangmei, the Zemei and the Kabui, instead of integrating themselves as the Kabuis, as recorded in the Tribal Benchmark Survey of West District, 1983. The survey shows that none wanted to be identified himself as the Puimei or Cacha Naga.

As regards the original habitat of the Kabuis Colonel McCulloch (1859) stated that "Songboo tradition gives, as the place of their origin, the mountain towards the south of the valley named Thungching (now Thangjing). They state themselves to be at present located on the sites of the villages at one time occupied by the southern tribes, who are, they say, the elder branch of the family of which they themselves are the middle and the Manipourees the younger branch". R. Brown (1873:22) further reported that "the Munniporees place their origin at Kayboching, near the Aqui route, north of the Government road, from whence they spread to the south". T.C. Hodson (1982:14), in support of the aforementioned views, remarked that " I myself was informed at the village of Aqui that there is a split stone in the north from which they came.

Long-ding-yong is the name of the place, and the meaning of this is the place where the thick jungle weed grows".

McCulloch (1859: 42) reported the habitation of the Kabuis as follows :

> "The Koupooees occupy the hills between Cachar and the valley of Munnipore in the whole breadth, a direct distance of about forty miles; and from 25^0 North Latitude, they formerly extended over nearly an equal distance to the south". As reported by Brown (1873 :22) " the Kowpoi tribes chiefly inhabit the hill tract lying near the Government Road leading from Cachar to Manipur. Formerly their villages were to be found some three or four days' journey south of the road, but on account of Lushai raids they have been evacuated, and now the farthest off is only some three or four hours' journey distant from the road in a southerly direction. To the north they extend for about three or four days' journey, and abut on the Jatik and Koyla tribes. There are several villages of them settled in the Manipur valley, where they employ themselves in cultivating, and also in carrying firewood and acting as coolis. On account of Lushai disturbances, chiefly of late years, number of Kowpois have also settled in the Kachar District in Lakhipur, Chandrapur, Baskanti, and also in the tea gardens ; they employ themselves in the gardens, and also in bringing firewood from the jungles". The Kabui, being a major tribe of Manipur, never escape from the academic report of the British administrator anthropologists, who devoted their time to the study of the various ethnoses of Manipur. "The Kabui Nagas are now restricted to the hills immediately north of the Cachar road. There is ample evidence, historical and traditional, to show that their expulsion from the hill to the south is comparatively recent. I have stumbled across ruins of large villages in the jungles south of Nungba, and learn that there

were ruins of Kabui villages that had been destroyed either by Kukis or by Manipuris in the early part of last century. There are small villages of Kabuis in the valley of Manipur which are in a semi-survile condition" (Hodson,1982:4).

Historically, the homeland of the Kabuis is the western hills of Manipur stretching from the Barail Mountains to the confines of Chin hills of Burma and Mizoram. The Rongmei had migrated to Assam and Nagaland (M. Kamson, 1976; T.C. Hodson, 1982). In Manipur they are mostly found in Tamenglong and Senapati Districts. They are, however, found scattered in several districts including Imphal valley (R.K. Jhaljit 1965).

Brown (1873) described three sub-divisions of the Kabuis – the Songbu, the Koiveng (Koireng), and the Kowpoi (Kabui) and further mentioned the Songbu as the strongest sub-division. But, the Koireng is recognized as one tribe and not a sub-tribe of the Kabui (Directorate of Economics and Statistics,1985). The Songbu presently remain as the Rongmei. Though the origin of the Kabuis is lost in mystery, their folk tradition points to Makhel in North Manipur, as a place of earliest settlement during the course of their migration from the South-West China, through Burma and islands of South-East Asia to Manipur and then to Northern Manipur, before branching out to their respective present habitats (Kamei, 2004 : 28).

Moreover, the entire life of the Kabuis is rich in legends and folk lores that explain either their origin or a pattern of social behaviour; the people has had a story to fall back on. The Kabuis, following their folk traditions, believe that they had come out from a cave (Mangthoi Thaimei, 1976; Meijinlung Kamson, 1976; Marulung Remei, 1981; Gangmumei Kamei, 2004). It gives an ample hint that the ancestors of Kabui were cave dwellers in the remote past. As the stories go, a mithun removed a large boulder that blocked the mouth of the cave called Mahou-Taobei (Mahou is the name of a hill, *Taobei* is the boulder) which is said to be located near *Ramting kabin*. In our present state of knowledge it is, however, rather difficult to give the exact location of the cave as well as the area though the tradition seems to point its finger to a place somewhere near Makhel or Makhal Village in the present Mao area of Manipur.

Geographically, the hill areas of Manipur share a common boundary with Burma on the east and south east, Assam on the west and Mizoram on the south west. The land routes connecting Manipur valley with Burma, Cachar District and Nagaland run across these hills. Thc communication system connecting different regions of different hill districts on one hand and the hill districts with the valley district and the neighbouring states on the other is still poor. This is, to a large extent, responsible for geographical isolation of the people living there.

Family and Marriage

The Kabui society, is socially divided into four exogamous clans, namely, 1. Kamei (Pammei), 2. Gonmei (Newmei) 3. Gaangmei and 4. Longmei. A boy of Kamei clan can marry either a girl of Gonmei, or Gaangmei or Longmei clan.

Though they follow monogamy, polygyny is also permissible. Patrilocal is the existing form of residence and father is the head of the family. Women are subordinate to male. Cross cousin marriage (MBD) is the most preferable type of marriage. Nowadays people particularly the youngsters prefer to make their mate selection not from amongst the marriageable cross cousins. Parallel cousin marriage is strictly prohibited among them. They, as a tradition, practise levirate.

The following marriage types are found among the Kabuis of Manipur.

(a) Marriage by engagement and solemnization called *Thanmei Noukao / Khamthan / Noushonmei*

(b) Marriage by elopement called *Samtunmei /Charai noukao / Jaipakmei.*

(c) Marriage by force called *Nimjaimei / Nimjaina Kaomei.*

(d) Marriage by service called *Noumangmei*

a. Engagement

It is the most ideal type of marriage. The first step of this marriage involves presentation of a pot of wine with one tilling hoe (*Lougai*) to the parents of the girl by two or three elderly men and women. It is followed by repeated persuasions from time to time from the boy's side through the elderly go-betweens for settlement of the marriage. This initial stage is called *Nouthanmei.* The settlement takes a long time generally two to three years. The parents of the girl, after taking consent of the girl, (without consent of the girl in earlier days) accept the marriage proposal in case they like it and negotiation for bride price has been made as a social mark of agreement between the two parties. This arrangement that has brought the two parties to a binding relationship is known as *Manthing remmei.*

The bride price customarily consists of a traditional shawl, a spear, a dao, two hoes and one jar of wine. Two mithuns/ buffaloes are also paid to the bride's family as bride price. However, it may be mentioned that rich families may organise it in a grand way by providing the bride's family with more than the minimum items.

The day of the marriage ceremony is fixed after the payment of the bride's price to the girls parents. The parents of the bride never sent their daughter empty handed but with different items of things that she generally needs in running her family. The gifts thus given varies from society to society as the needs vary from society to society according to the standard of living of the people.

In the bygone days or societies living in far isolated places the gifts which may also be referred as dowry consists of the following items.

(i) Cloth for father-in-law, husband, mother in-law, and sisters

(ii) Salt packets

(iii) Bitter gourd (*mu*)

(iv) Hoe (*Lougai)*

(v) Carrying baskets for fire collection *(Ka)* and paddy (*Kalong*)

(vi) Weaving materials (loin loom)

Besides these, cows or pigs are also given by the rich families.

Customarily, the marriage ceremony is performed at the residence of the bride groom. On arrival of the bride at the house of the bride-groom, she is received by the parents, relatives and friends of the groom.

Before the marriage ceremony begins, she is asked to remove the ornaments, such as armlets and wristlets. This process is known as the *Taa-tu lokmei*. Then the ceremony is initiated by a local priest (*Taku*) by holding a cock in his hand and simultaneously reciting the rites-*Raagang mailaak soi.* During the process, two ends of the clothes of the bride and bridegroom are tied together and the bride and the bride groom are asked to place one of their feet over a *Laogai paak* (a tiny tilling hoe) till the ceremony is over as a mark of promise. This ritual process is known as *Mailakmei*.

In the case of marriages other than the engagement, there is no much consideration regarding the bride price, dowry etc. However, the couple at least has to pay a grand feast to their parents as a mark of gratitude to the bride's parents. This is associated with a rite, called, *Duiluiduk loukaimei* celebrated to purify the unholy union of the spouses and to neutralise the embittered relation between the two parental families.

In the Kabui society a spouse is entitled to seek divorce from his or her partner by bringing the matter to the notice of the council of village elders. If a man desires to divorce his wife on a condition considered reasonable by the council of village elders he can do it without making any kind of payment. In case, the condition is found unreasonable by the council of village elders, he at least has to pay one buffalo, or a bull or a mithun and a big brass vessel to the divorcee. But if the divorce is due to the fault of the wife, she has to pay back the bride price to the husband.

Clan Structure

In the Kabui society clan system is the basic framework of the social structure. From the insiders point of view a clan is an intricate association of people of both sexes, membership of which is determined by unilineal descent. The clan members cannot trace their descent back to the founder ancestors. Generally these clans are exogamous and enjoy equal social status in the society. However, in some villages the head man of the village is selected from the Kamei clan. The social system

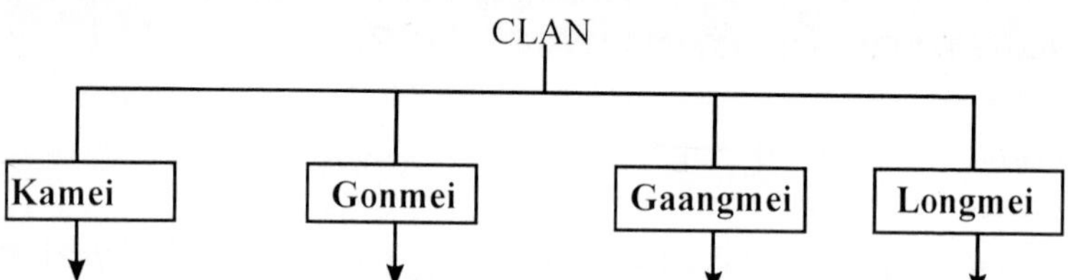

(Sub-clans)	(Sub-clans)	(Sub-clans)	(Sub-clans)
(a) Khandangmei	(a) Gonthangmei	(a) Pheigagangmei	
(b) Marangmei	(b) Remmei	(b) Sidougang	
(c) Phaomei	(c) Panmei	(c) Jukhaogang	
(d) Pammei	(d) Thaimei		
(e) Kamson	(e) Maringmei		
(f) Marangpongmei	(f) Danghangmei / Dhatngmei		
(g) Singgongmei	(g) Gondaimei (Gonthangmei)		

of the Kabuis is one of the most well organized systems. The Kabui society consist of four exogamous clans, viz. Kamei, Gonmei, Gangmei and Longmei along with their sub clans except the last one-Longmei. However, as revealed by the field study, no Longmei is found among the people of five villages under study. They are given below in a tabular form.

In the distribution of clans among the villages, the higher frequency of Kamei is observed only in Konthoujam village being 77.78% while Gonmei is observed as a major clan in three villages viz. Phungong (64.15%), Marangching (44.44%), and Chingkhulong (58.54%). Gangmei is observed in three villages of which the higher frequency is observed in Khonglong village being 63.33% (Table 3).

Table 3 Frequency distribution of clan among the five villages

Clan	*Phungong*		*Marang-ching*		*Khong-long*		*Ching-khulong*		*Konthou-jam*	
Kamei	19	35.85	4	22.22	9	30.00	10	24.39	21	77.78
Gonmei	34	64.15	8	44.44	2	6.67	24	58.54	6	22.22
Gangmei	-	-	6	33.33	19	63.33	7	17.07	-	-
Longmei	-	-	-	-	-	-	-	-	-	-
Total	53	100.00	18	100.00	30	100.00	41	100.00	27	100.00

One important point that deserves special mention here is that there is a divide among the Kabui scholars as to the sub-clan structure of the Kabuis.

According to Kamson, (1977) Kamei clan is composed of seven sub clans. However, there is no sub-clan of Gangmei and Longmei as below :

Thaimei, (1995) is of the opinion that Gangmei clan has been classified into four sub-clans such as Kamhang Maigang,

CLAN

Kammei	**Gonmei**	**Gangmei**	**Longmei**
(Sub-clans)	(Sub-clans)	(Sub-clans)	(Sub-clans)
a). Kamei	a). Gonthangmei	a). Pheigagangmei -	
b). Khandangmei	b). Remmei		
c). Marangmei	c). Panmei		
d). Phaomei	d). Thaimei		
e). Pammei	e). Maringmei		
f). Kamson	f). Danghangmei/Dhangmei		
g). Singgongmei			

CLAN

Kammei	**Gonmei**	**Gangmei**	**Longmei**
(Sub-clans)	(Sub-clans)	(Sub-clans)	(Sub-clans)
a). Marangmei	a). Gonthangmei	a). Pheiga-Gang -	
b). Marangpongmei	b). Gondaimei	b). Seedou-Gang	
c). Phaomei	c). Remmei / Maremmei	c). Jukhaogang	
d). Pammei	d). Maringmei	d). Kamhang Maigang	
e). Khamdangmei	e). Dhangmei		
f). Kamson	f). Panmei		
	g). Thaimei		
	h). Gon-Gangmei		

Jukhaogang, Pheiga-Gang, Seedou-Gang etc. He, however, agrees with Kamson (1977) that there is no sub-clan of the Longmei clan. But the Gonmei clan, as contended by Mangthoi

Thaimei, has eight sub clans, such as Dhangmei, Gondaimei, Gonthangmei, Gon-Gangmei, Maringmei, Panmei, Remei / Maremei, Thaimei.

Each clan has food taboos. The members of Kammei, Gonmei and Gangmei avoid to eat bul bul (*Ahuina*), nightingale and tiger (*kamang*) respectively. The sub clans have their totems as they are named after particular birds, trees and animals.

Property and Inheritance

The property usually consists of both movable and immovable possessions. Property may be earned by oneself or it may be inherited from the forefathers. The movable property may consists of money, agricultural implements, weaving implements, weapons, musical instruments, different kinds of precious ornaments, utensils, domestic animals like buffalo, cow, pig, dog, cat, poultry and so on and so forth. The immovable properties include land, like house site, reserved forest and cultivable land both wet and jhum field etc, buildings and any other super structure, such as memorial stone, etc. Property is generally owned by man, while woman does not own property, except a few movable items like clothes and different kinds of ornaments.

One can give all the movable properties to whomever he chooses. In the case of immovable properties one cannot dispose of them as he pleases. Though he has got the right of ownership over both self acquired and ancestral property, he cannot dispose of the immovable property without the knowledge of the clan members. If a man wants to dispose of any immovable property to avoid complicacy and misunderstanding among the clan members, he must ask some of his nearest adult male members to do the needful on his behalf. The entrusted persons will then ask the clan members if they are interested to buy the immovable property that is put on sale. Any interested persons of the clan may purchase the same without any objection. But, if there is none from the clan, the entrusted party may sell it to any person outside the clan.

Succession and inheritance among the Kabui community are patrilineal and ultimogeniture. The headship of the family, lineage, clan and the village is always passed onto the male descendants. A Kabui father has the right to distribute his properties among his sons. If a man having three or four sons, died without saying anything about properties as to how they would be distributed, the mother may distribute it or if the mother died earlier, the nearest relatives may take the responsibility, otherwise the eldest son may take the full responsibility of the matter. If a son is born posthumously, he also should get his share because the death of the father had established his right. Under such circumstances the eldest son must take the sole responsibility of the new born brother. In case a man dies having no male issue, the nearest male relatives will inherit his properties. The daughters have no right to inherit their parental properties.

Dress and Ornaments

The Kabuis have their own costumes woven at their traditional loin-looms (Plate 7). There are varieties of clothes meant for chieftain, men, women, unmarried persons, children and even for the deceased.

Nowadays the traditional clothes are used on ceremonial occasions especially by the women. However, in day-to-day life, the Kabui woman wear clothes similar in fashion with that of the Manipuri women. The younger generations prefer modern dresses to traditional ones and follow the modern trend of fashion.

When we look into the past McCulloch (1859) refers to the scanty clothes of males and comparative over-clothing of females. "The man ties a cloth round his waist, the end of which hangs down in front to conceal his privates, otherwise he is quite naked".

Those villagers living in the interior hills are less aware of luxurious dresses and ornaments. The elders hardly change new clothes for years together. They manage anyhow with whatever they have in their possession. But the children change their dresses specially during festivals. Occasionally, they go to market for purchasing or selling. But it may be only once in a year.

The traditional dresses of the Kabuis are quite similar with that of the Zemei, Liangmei and Puimei.

The technique of making the clothes is quite simple, that is, loin loom technique and the implements of weaving are also made of wood, bamboo, reed and the skin of cow or mithun. The yarn has been prepared from the cotton grown in the jhum field (Plate 8, 9). So in the early days, people living in the plain used to purchase cotton from the hill people. Now a-days, they purchase woolen thread from the market and weave in their traditional loin loom.

They are still practising dyeing of yarn from the locally available plants. The black colour is obtained from the leaves of a herb called *Khim* and red colour is prepared from the bark of a creeper called *Gui*. Yellow and green colours are also prepared from the locally available orchids and grasses. Almost all the Kabui girls have the knowledge of weaving (Plate 10).

The Kabui people adorn a number of traditional ornaments at the time of dance during festivals. In day-to-day life also old people of both the sexes use necklaces of semi precious stones with conch shell and ivory. Imitations of semi precious stones are still used as necklace in day today life by the people. The people have attached aesthetic and magical values to their ornaments as the latter enhance their beauty as well as protect them from wild animals and evil spirits (Plate 11). Some of the ornaments are also the symbols of the status of a person in the society as well as the stages of life.

Table 4 List of Male Costumes (Plate 12, 13)

Name of the cloth and type	*Used by*	*Colour of the cloth*
Sineiphi or *Senei-pheipong- shawl*	Young boys who start walking.	White colour with red border and small simple designs.
Inthem Phei or *Themphei- shawl*	Boys who start herding cattle.	White colour with red border. / Black colour with four or six yellow small stripes.
Mareipan- shawl	Youth going to dormitory.	White colour. The side borders are decorated with red, yellow, black and white broad strips.
Pheingao - shawl	Matured or senior youth including the married.	White background with multiple stripes of red, yellow, and green.
Langhu Pheingao shawl	Old people	Almost similar with *Pheingao* but design differs.
Koukhram Pheingao shawl	Old people	Black background with small white stripes.
Chingkhong phei Decorated shawl	Prominent men of higher status.	Black background with red borders and yellow and green stripes.
Masinphei- shawl	The old people.	White background with green stripes.

Plate 7 : A Kabui lady wearing Pheingao pheipong (Shawl) in her loom

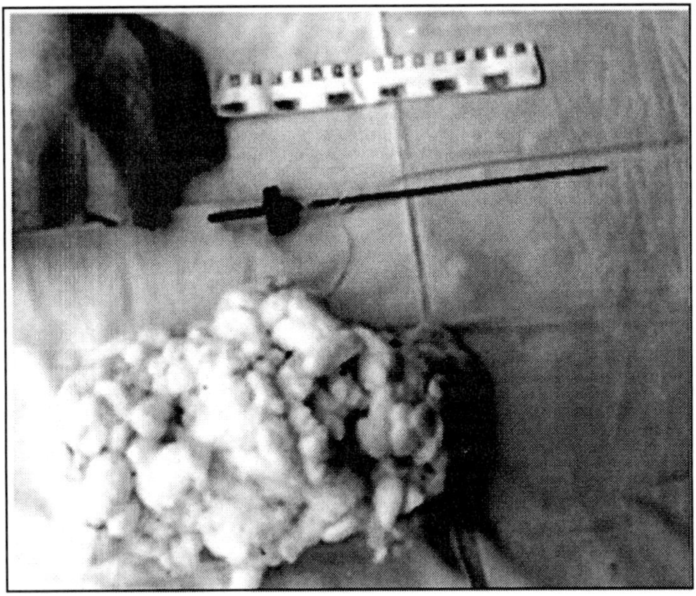

Plate 8 : Cotton in raw, collected from the jhum field (A) and a spining whorl (B)

Plate 9 : Research observing the weaving technique at Phungong

Plate 10 : Researcher (Middle) with the villagers at Konthoujam

Plate 11 : An old couple wearing bead chains for aesthetic and magical values

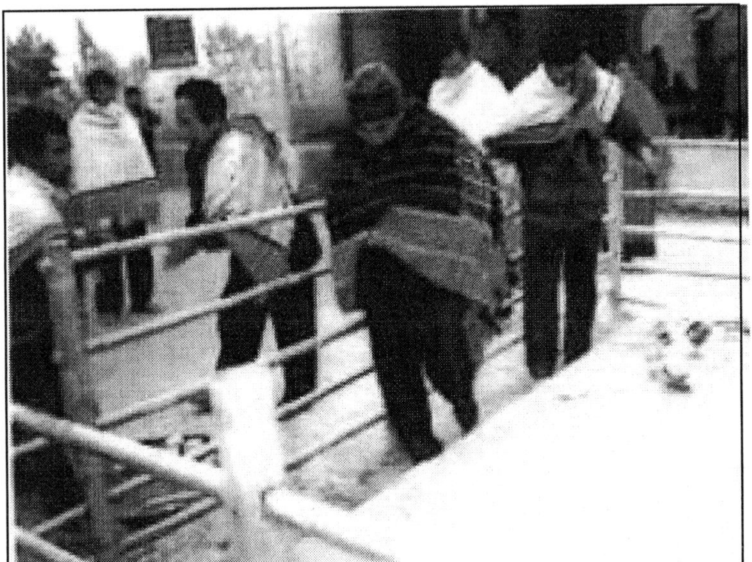

Plate 12 : Elders wearing *Pheingao pheipong* (white shawl) and *Chingkhongphei pheipong* (black shawl) on a memorial occasion in Gan-Ngai festival

Table 5 List of Male Dance Costumes (Plate 14)

Name of the cloth and type	*Used as*	*Colour of the cloth / material*
Lenglan / Renglan	Lower dress	Red colour.
Shianlam / Sellem	Waist belt	White background with green border.
Laangsem	Shouldered belt	Folded *Mareipan* used as shawl across the shoulder.
Chei and Langton	Head dress	Made of bamboo, shape is like the horn of mithun or buffalo.
Pikam	Head dress	Made of bamboo and horn bill feather.
Jeisu	Ear dress	Made of blue feather of *Jeipui* bird.
Peikam	Calf belt / calf cover	Made of bamboo, either black or white in colour.
Tadantu	Bead chain	Made of semi precious stone of red and yellow colour.
Vei-tu	Bead chain	Bead chain with one large white elephant tusk.
Gangkam	Necklace	Made of conch shell.
Phaisang	Armlet	Made of cane.
Gokneilaa	Armlet	Made of canine of pig.
Taidu	Bracelet	Made of copper.
Beithingrem`	Ear dress	Made of copper.
Bang –Chakiu	Decorated dao	Aluminium dao or knife.

Table 6 List of Female Costumes (Plate 15)

Types	*Name of the cloth and type*	*Used by*	*Colour of the cloth*
Shawls	*Sinei phei*	Girl	White background with red, yellow and green stripes.
	Pheingao-themmei-phei	Women	Almost similar with *Pheingao* but small in size.
Lower garments	*Lengli pheisoi / Lenglam pheisoi*	Baby girls	Black and white background.
	Pheingao pheisoi	Adolescent girls	White background with red border.
	Langhu-pheisoi	The girls, bride, and women at the time of dance and marriage.	Black background with white stripes and decorated with hanging yarns.
	Langjin-pheisoi	Women	Yellow or greenish background, red border with arrow design.
	Pheisoi	Females	Varying colours and designs for day today use.

Table 7 List of Female Dance Costumes (Plate 16, 17)

Name of the cloth and type	*Used as*	*Colour of the cloth / material*
Phang phei	Blouse like black cloth covering the upper part of the body	Black colour, decorated with hair of horse dyed with red colour. Dried yellowish orchid stem called *hung* is also used to wrap the hair of the horse.
Langhu Pheisoi	Female wrapper lower garment	Black background with white stripes.
Pikhim	Head dress	Made of bamboo without fur.
Pidoung	Head dress	Made of bamboo with fur.
Duangh	Head dress	Decorated head dress.
Pheilak or Bunkam	Waist belt	White with red border.
Beithinglem	Ear ring	Decorated earring of beads.
Tadantu	Cornelian bead chain	Red, yellow, and white colour.
Vei-tu	Bead chain	White colour made of elephant tusk and red and yellow beads.
Gangkam	Chain	Made of conch shell.
Taa / Tadu	Bracelet	Metal bracelet / armlet.
Konru	Ear dress	Made of orchid.

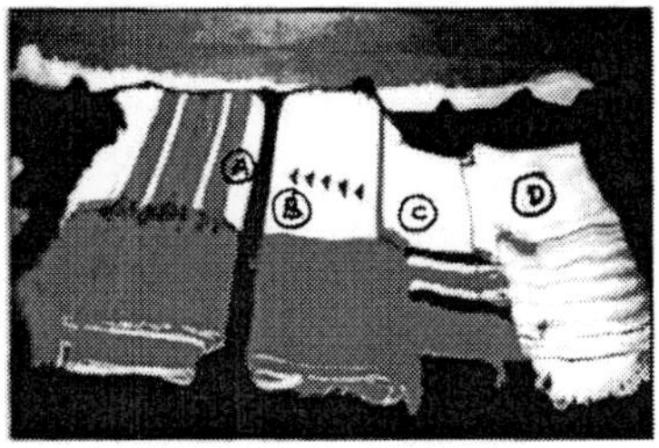

Plate 13. Pheipong (A & B. *Pheingao*, C. *Mareipan*, D. *Masinpheipong*) (Male shawls)

Plate 14 . A male Kabui in dance costume

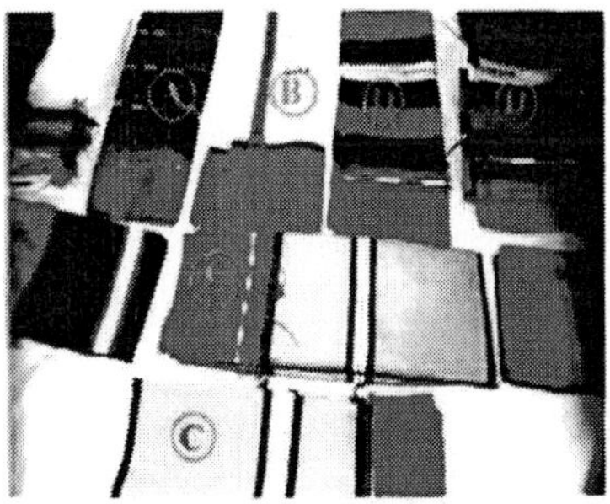

Plate 15. *Pheisoi* (A. *Langhu*, B.*Pheingao*, C. *Langjin*, D. *Phaisoi* of different colours (Female loin clothes)

Plate 16. Dancing dresses and ornaments
A. *Duangh* (Hd.dress) B.*Phang phei*,
C. *Langhu- pheisoi* . D. *Pheilak* (waist belt),
E. *Tadan-tu* (bead chain)

Plate 17. A Kabui lady in dance costume

Festivals

The Kabuis celebrate a number of festivals locally known as *Ngai* in connection with their cyclic economic activities, sometimes to please the deities who are believed to have control over the activities and sometimes to seek an omen or prediction about the economic activities and sometimes to herald the coming of a particular season associated with a particular economic pursuit. All festivals are found to be associated with rituals performed at the level of either the household or the community. They follow a lunar year in observing the festivals. Most of the months of a year have one or more festivals and the days of celebrating them are decided by the village elders. So there is variation in time and period from village to village in the celebration of the festivals. Gangmumei (2004) also supports the view. Besides these festivals a number of rites and rituals connected with agricultural activities are also performed. Some to the important festivals of the Kabuis are :

(a) Chaga-Ngai
(b) Phuton gudui-Ngai
(c) Pukpha-Ngai
(d) Gan-Ngai
(e) Katoi-Ngai
(f) Chakak-Ngai

(a) Chaga-Ngai :

Chaga-ngai which is also known as *Rih-ngai* is celebrated in January and is one of the most important festivals mainly connected with war, hunting, fishing and agriculture.

It is celebrated for seven days. This festival is becoming less important nowadays particularly among the valley people as their life is far removed from the activities of fishing, hunting and war. It is performed together with *Gan-ngai* in valley villages. It is exclusively for the males. So males themselves prepare their food separately in their respective houses with the new fire of the festival. Even the conjugal relation between husband and wife is avoided during this festival.

The important events are making of fire; cleaning and sharpening of all kinds of fighting weapons publictly; rededication of all able men collectively to the God for the defence of the village; procession of youths in full armour from one end of the village to the other end with the shouting of Ho in chorus. Jumping, singing and victory cry challenging the enemies are the characteristics of the procession. Target spear throwing, shooting to the wooden or plantain human effigies, statue of human figures, recitation of warrior talks, war hymns, war rites by elderly men are other events.

The first day is marked by the announcement of the inauguration of the festival by *Tinku* -the village priest. It is followed by *Chaga-jouphao-puni*, the preparation of rice beer for the festival by individual households. Males are also tabooed from eating creepers as well as drinking of rice beer on the bamboo cup on this day.

The preparation of rice beer continues till the end of the second day.

On the morning of the third day new bamboo cups are made by individual households for use for the whole year. *Gakpai-jaomei* - observation of spleen of pig as an omen - is performed in the evening at *Thoubei*- a meeting place for the village elders (Plate 18, 19). It is followed by *Mei-lap-mei* (making of new fire by friction) at *Khangchu* (boys' dormitory). The new fire is made available to every household of the village by the members of *Khangchu.* The villagers have to prepare food by the fire and have to offer the food to the spirits of the hunted heads buried at the front gate for the welfare of the villagers. It is known as *Tathe-phai-mei.*

The fourth day is *Rang-kap-mei* which means making

of two male and female effigies either from wood or stem of plantain. One is kept at the front gate and another at the back gate of the village. Target spear throwing is performed for seeking omen of war, hunting, crop production, fertility etc.

The fifth day is known as *Jang-pangu-mei-tingmik* - means day of hunting, either individual or group. After coming back from hunting, they, in the evening, move round the village singing songs about the bravery deeds of the villagers and drink rice beer from the long bamboo tubes.

The sixth day is known as *Jang-charuk-mei-ting-mik*. On this day, *Joupon-long-mei,* that is, competition in the quality and quantity of meat (*Jang-kok*) and wine (*Jou*) brought by the members of *Khangchu* is performed. Those persons who carry the best meat and wine are selected by the council of village elders. The people then go to the respective households of those selected persons and pray to God uttering *Hoi* in chorus for the physical welfare of the latter. The host in turn offers wine and meat.

On the seventh day *Inchi-dansan-mei* – ritual of observing omen with the help of a bamboo is performed at the village playground (*Chum-Chn-Jang*).

(b) Phuton-gudui-Ngai :

Gudui-ngai is an important festival performed in the month of *Gudui-bu* (April), to mark the completion of sowing of seed in the field. The particular day of the festival is decided by the village elders. It takes place in the month of May in the valley. Formerly, it was celebrated for three/four days. This festival is also known as *Phuton gudui-ngai* and *Maleng-ngai* as it celebrates the ceremonies of *Phutonmei* (throwing out of *phu*) outside the village gate by *Taku* indicating that sowing of seed for the year is completed and *Malengmei*, a ceremony of calling back of food grains lost during sowing of seed. Every family performs *Malengmei* ceremony in which an offering of a cock, rice beer and *Gutam* (salad of ginger and chilli) is made to *Apou-ragwang* (Plate 20). In early days, either pig or cattle was sacrificed to *Apou-rag*wang. Even *Taku* made a symbolic sacrifice of himself to evil spirit for more food production. Another important item of this festival is *Gudui-jangmei* – drinking of soup of ginger and meat of pork or chicken with the belief that the juice of ginger will replace the energy lost due to long hard work in the field. Merry making with songs and games like tug of war between the boys and girls, males and females also form important parts of the festival. The day after the festival is observed as a taboo day of the doing any work.

***(c) Pukpha-Ngai* or *Kha-Ngai* :**

This festival that continues for five days is celebrated in the month of July for the good harvest when the early crops are about to ripe and ready for harvesting. On the first day a pig or cattle is sacrificed by *Tinku* to *Apou-ragwang* for blessing with plenty of crops and vegetables.

Preparation and repairing of village path towards jhum field are the important activities of the fourth day. This part is considered as *Tun-ngai* festival in the valley. Among important items of this festival is to give or present rice beer, dry meat, dry limb of cow to the daughters who have fulfilled the obligation of the payment of the bride price.

(d) Gan-Ngai :

Gan-ngai, celebrated about a week, is an important festival of the Kabuis. It is generally performed when the agricultural products are in the granary. As the harvesting season of the shifting cultivation comes earlier, this festival is performed in the hill, where shifting cultivation is practised, usually in the month of October whereas it is performed in the early part of January in the valley.

The main theme of the festival is merry making by the villagers, thanks giving to God, farewell to the deceased persons who died in that year and *Nanumei,* social - recognition of children born in that year. *Nanumei* is also performed as a separate festival for one day among the valley Kabuis usually in the month of March.

(e) Katoi-Ngai :

It is a festival of testing sesame. It is celebrated in November and continues from one to many days. On this day every family prepares the curry of sesame and gives a little of it each to neighbours and kinsmen.

During the period of this festival the villagers customarily perform marriage ceremonies and construct their *Tarangkai.* One of the special features of this festival is the performance of a dance called Matui dance by the members of boys' and girls' dormitory. Therefore, the period of the festival varies from year to year depending on the number of wedding to be celebrated and the number of *Tarangkai* to be constructed.

(f) Chakak-Ngai :

This festival, celebrated in December, relates to the construction of *Taokhon* (memorial stone) by the villagers for their deceased relatives and resting place, *reeng nhew,* outside the village gate. Large flat stones are selected by the individuals for erecting the commemoration stones in memory of their relatives. Competition of long jump, short put among the *Khangchu* members, selection of winner by the *Thoubei* and prayer to *Apou-ragwang* in the house of those winners uttering 'Hoi' in chorus by the male *Khangchu* members are also the important features of the festival.

A ceremony to drive away the evil spirits from the village and a ritual known as *Dongjao*, that is, the offering of pig, rice beer to *Apou-ragwang* by the rich villagers mark the end of the festival. Now a-days, as *Dongjao* is observed as a separate festival in the valley.

The change of habitat, conversion into Christianity and

modernization in the lifeways greatly affect the performance of the traditional festivals particularly among the valley inhabitants who came down from the hills long back in the historical past. However, they are still following the ritual processes of the festivals, though symbolic in nature, with a slight change in the degree and time of the performance of the festivals.

Religious Beliefs

The Kabuis are animists and polytheistic in their religious belief wherein *Apou ragwang* - king of the Gods who created the earth and all things in the universe is considered the patron God. *Keipa Bamboo* (Male God) and *Keipi Bamboo* (Female God) who are believed to have protected the villagers from physical sufferings are important deities. A boulder generally portrays the image of the god (Plate 22). They generally worship gods and goddesses either in the form of prayer or sacrifices with a strong belief that the deity will help them and fulfill their wishes. The sacrifice consists of offerings of vegetables, grains, cocks, animals like pig, cattle, meats etc.

At present, many of the Kabuis specially residing in the interior hilly regions have converted into Christianity. As a result, many of them have abandoned most of those traditional beliefs and practices.

Age grading system and grading of social status

The social system of the Kabuis is one of the most well organized systems based on age and sex. The age grading system of the Kabuis consists of three sub-groups known as *Khangchu*, *Gangchang-kaibang*, and *Banza-kaibang*. Each male member of the village is generally a member of one of these institutions in different stages of his life.

Khangchu **:** The *Khangchu* (primary institution) is further sub-divided into three sub-divisions, such as the *Gana*, the *Ganpi* and the *Khangbon*. The *Gana* forms the juniormost of the three grades and consists of only unmarried young men.

Next higher grade is the *Ganpi*. *Khangbon* is the highest section of the *Khangchu* organization and members are middle aged men. Year by year, the members of the juniormost section, namely, *Gana* are usually promoted batch by batch, according to seniority in age, to the next higher grade *Ganpi*. In the same way the members of *Ganpi* are also promoted to next higher grade, namely, *Khangbon*.

The seniormost member of *Khangchu* are promoted batch by batch to *Gangchang-kaibang* (house of the junior village elders). Similarly, the members of the *Gangchang-kaibang* are promoted to the *Banza-kaibang* (house of the senior village elders) according to their seniority. The *Bnaza's* are the authorities in religious and spiritual matters. They also act as village priests. The seniormost of them is called *Taku* or *Tinku*.

Village polity

Thoubei **:** The council of elders of the village is known as *Thoubei* or '*Pei*'. It is the highest grade of the male group. Generally it consists of at least six members elected from among the clan heads of the village. They are *Khunbu, Khullakpa, Luplakpa, Mantri*, *Lambu* and *Changloi*. When they are in the council the said elders are known as *Peikhang Peiru*. This council is the highest court of the village and as such it has distinctive roles in the sphere of religion and administration, and in enforcing a high moral discipline among men, women and children of the village.

This council has strong administrative and judicial power over the inhabitants of the village. In fact, this council is the guardian and custodian of the traditions of the people. There is no separate house for this institution. Therefore, all the duties or functions of this organization are performed at the house of *Khullakpa*

Khullakpa is the head of the village council. In matters of religious ceremonies,such as crises rituals and cyclic festivals he functions as a priest (*Taku/Tinku*). The post of *Khullakpa* and *Khunbu* is not hereditary but elected. He is assisted by the other members of the village elders' council in all the administrative and religious matters. As the administration of the village lies in the hands of the elders, the Kabuis have gerontocratic form of government.

Like the male members of the society, the female members also have their institutions based on age. They are :

(a) *Luchu* or , *Tunakailiu*

(b) *Mathenmei* or *Meipuikailiu*

(c) *Kengzapui* or , *Kerapuikailiu* etc.

Tuanakailiu **:** It is the institution consisting of the unmarried girls. The main function of the institution is to organise dance during the festivals.

Meipuikailiu **:** A married woman automatically becomes a member of *Meipuikailiu.*

Kerapuikailiu **:** This is the largest age based institution of the women comprising old women. The main function of *Kerapuikailiu* is to serve the villagers. They take the main responsibility at the time of *Nanu ngai* (ear boring) festival.

Burial System

It is believed that the soul after the death of a man goes to *Taroiram* –the land of dead. Right from the moment of the departure of the soul, an old man informs the villagers about it and asks them to stop all the duties. It is followed by *Kahomei* - chanting of 'Ho' by the villagers.

A man customarily holds the head of a dying man and chants loudly "*Ho-Ho-Aow-We*". A dead man for whom this invocation has not been done at the right moment gets a slightly different treatment in burial rituals. The body is then washed, dressed in full customary dresses and kept inside the house. During that period the relatives of the deceased are informed and the dead body is kept even for two days inside the house so that his or her relatives who are living outside the village can pay their last homage to the departed soul.

During that period the family members offer rice, *zou* (rice beer), dry meat of beef and other items to the deceased by digging a pit near the dead body inside the house. When all the relatives arrive, one of his or her nearest male kin starts digging of burial ground -*Keiphun-phumei* with *lougai,* a tilling hoe after offering *zou* by an old man. Thus, *lougai* plays an indispensable tool in the burial rites among the Kabuis.

On the second day, a simple feast is made with his or her relatives, near and dear ones and then ready for bringing the corpse in a coffin (*Tanku*) to the burial site with packets of food and drinks, clothes, utensils and some other household items, such as - hoe, dao, axe, spear, carrying basket, bead chain, one set of loin loom, one piece of wristlet, a pair of earring, one set of pointed thornful weapon for the purpose of defending the deceased from the attack of his/her enemies. In case of a dead man whose body cannot be traced out a log of wood or a stalk of plantain has substituted for the dead body and due rites are performed.

Selection of burial site depends on the nature of death of a man or a woman. In case of normal death they use to bury the corpse within the village area, usually in the northern side of the courtyard while in the case of abnormal death, such as hanging, drowning, accident, child birth etc. it is customary to bury the corpse outside the village gate.

A trench of about five feet long, five feet broad and four feet deep is dug in such a way that an inclined niche for the encashment of the coffin is made at the side of the trench. The mouth of the niche is closed with sticks, by the kins nearest to the deceased in order of inheritance. Thus farewell is given to the deceased. Normally, a flat stone is kept over the burial ground for his /her memory.

In Kabui language there is a word *Tao-khon, Tao*-means stone, *Khon*-means memory. So, *Tao-khon* is the memorial stone erected in memory of a dead person (Plate 23). It may be erected on or near the place where the dead body is buried. In some cases, before the death of a person according to his or her wish *Tao-khon* may also be constructed. It is known as *Tanku-daomei. Tanku* means-wooden frame for placing the dead body and *daomei* means cutting or preparing. It is also believed that construction of *Tanku-daomei* either lengthens one's life span if luck favours him/her or shortens in case luck does not favour him/her.

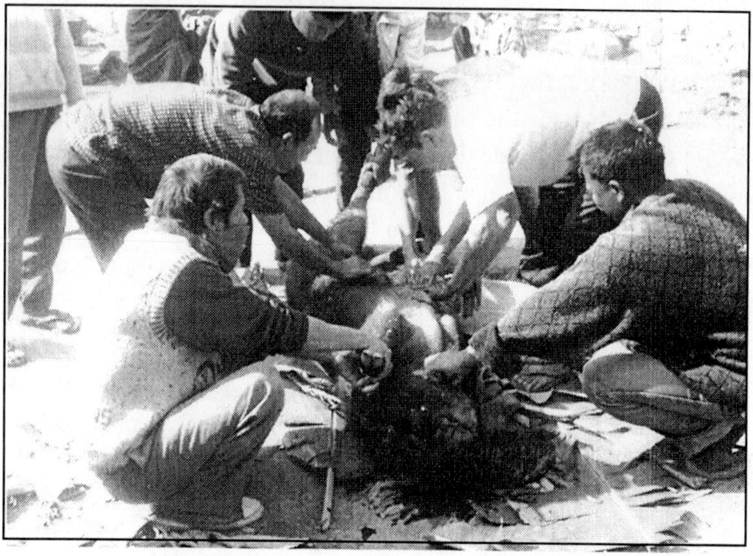

Plate 18 : Processing of pig for *Gakpai-jaomei*

Plate 19 : *Gakpai-jaomei*- observation of spleen as an omen

Plate 20 : Bamboo tubes for carrying rice beer

Plate 21 : ***Tamcha-ponmei***

Plate 22 : Bamboo – a village deity

Plate 23 : Taokhon - a memorial stone

3

Material Culture And Subsistence Pattern

Gathering and Production of Food

Material culture is an aspect of culture. While culture may be defined as the sum total of people's different ways of life which means what they do and think and how they behave. Tylor (1913) defined 'culture as that complex whole which includes knowledge, belief, art, law, morals, customs and any other capabilities and habits acquired by man as a member of society'. To explain more clearly about that complex whole, it may be said that culture is a whole which is an integrated unit, that includes various aspects of man's works, thoughts and behaviour that is both the physical or material aspects and the intangible or non material aspects of culture. The objects which are man made and used for the purpose of getting food, shelter and clothing are generally termed as material culture (Herskovits, 1974).

Again, according to Das (1989), there are various needs of man besides his three primary needs, such as food, shelter and clothes. Whatever he makes and uses to meet these needs is termed as material culture. So material culture comprises tools and implements, weapons, cookery, dress and ornaments, houses, transport devices, etc. These items of material culture differ from society to society and from one community to another community. The material products of the mankind are made in relation to their habitat. As for example, people living in the high altitude use hoes, dao, small spade, carrying baskets, for digging the soil and for carrying the products on the steep slopes of the hill. But in case of the plain areas, these materials are shaped in a different way.

By studying the material culture, we can understand the material way of life of a group of people, specially with reference to their subsistence economy, cultural change, social organization, technology, habitat, etc.

Various methods have been conceived and developed in the mind of man for making different weapons, implements, tools, etc for using in different ways. This cultural knowledge about the manufacture and use of tools which helps man to survive is called technology (Das 1989). Thus technology reflects economic activities of the people. The economy of the nonliterate people is mainly concentrated on food collection, gathering, hunting and fishing activities. These economic activities are the main characteristics of the subsistence pattern which is found in simple societies because they fall in the broad categories of subsistence economy (Majumdar etal, 1987). As the subsistence economy is characterized by the absence of surplus production, distribution system among the simple societies is found in the form of reciprocity. Primitive economy, thus, orients primarily towards meeting subsistence and hence differs from market economy.

Sustenance of human life has depended upon the gifts of nature from the very early days. Vegetables, fruits, soil products, fish and meat, still remain the same basic items of human diet as they were in the prehistoric past when the first man began to walk on this earth. Even today, when man has reached the highest peak of his mental development he has not yet been able to create a substitute for this basic food stuffs.

Human food exploitation is still based on the old traditional practices of his forefathers. Like them, man is still dependent upon the plant and animal kingdoms for his livelihood. Today, as millenniums ago, the tilling of the soil and the art of animal husbandry are the bases of human food. Modern man, like his forefathers, cannot overcome the hazards of the climate. The availability of the different items of plant and animal foods depends mainly on the climate. Human life is thus shaped indirectly by the influence of climate; so man has to adjust himself to his habitat and also his material needs to the condition of climate in which he is born. Man had no knowledge of plant cultivation or animal husbandry during the Palaeolithic period so it was perhaps possible for him to subsist on whatever nature offered to him. Similarly the economic pursuits of simple non literate societies show well marked relation to the different climatic condition of their respective habitats. Lack of stability in their lives due to scarcity of food is the main feature that compels them to exploit large territories, which again forces them to make continuous migrations. This very rudimentary stage of social development, is even characterised by the division of labour. The womenfolks are mainly collectors and gatherers of vegetable products like roots and tubers and fruits from the jungle, while man hunts on lands for meat and also in water for fish. The women's tool to break the soil and to get tubers, is the digging stick, while man uses various types of tools, such as spears, bows and arrows, etc. Man is really inventive when he comes to the full exploitation of plant food. As soon as one area has been exhausted new areas are taken up, until the whole forest region, sometimes covering several kilometers, has been totally exhausted. The gathered food items change with the change of season.

Men's technical skill of hunting and gathering, their knowledge of making and using of weapons like spears, bow and arrow, traps, etc. and lastly their use of fire for cooking are the evidences of a long history of their development. The contemporary primitive people who live on hunting and gathering are the adherents of the oldest form of subsistence economy.

The primitive subsistence economy may broadly be classified into two stages – food collection and food production which again may broadly be divided into gathering, hunting and fishing under the former stage and pastoralism, horticulture and agriculture under the latter according to their main economic activities. The main divisions and sub-divisions of subsistence economy are given below in a tabular form.

Division of Subsistence Economy (Table 8).

Table 8 Patterns of Subsistence Economy

<table>
<tr><td rowspan="6">Subsistence Economy
Subsistence economy</td><td rowspan="3">Food production</td><td>Agriculture</td><td>By using Plough and fertilizer</td></tr>
<tr><td>Horticulture</td><td>By using Simple tool like hoe and digging stick</td></tr>
<tr><td>Pastoralism</td><td>By rearing Cattle, Pig, Fowl</td></tr>
<tr><td rowspan="3">Food collection</td><td>Fishing</td><td>By using Bare hand, Spear, Hook, Trap, Net, Poison, barrier</td></tr>
<tr><td>Hunting</td><td>By using Weapon, Trap, Trained animal</td></tr>
<tr><td>Gathering</td><td>Digging and picking</td></tr>
</table>

The Kabuis, particularly those who are still living in the remote and isolated villages in the hill districts of Manipur are still leading a life dependent, though not entirely on nature and moreover they are yet to escape from the mercy of the nature as regards their livelihood for their economy is still at the subsistence level. In such a way different types of food collection play a vital role in their economy. The subsistence pattern of the Kabuis as evidenced from the study of the different Kabui villages situated at different habitats is described below.

Food Collection

The Kabuis engage themselves in the economic activities of

gathering, hunting and fishing either as secondary activities as found among valley inhabitants or as a way of life as revealed by the life ways of the Kabuis living in remote, hilly region. The former practise the activities to supplement their food whereas the latter practise the same to get their livelihood.

Food gathering : (Plate 24-27)

As family is an economic unit, its members are responsible for the collection of edible plants and they, either in individual or groups, go in search of edible roots, tubers, etc. The males are usually responsible for collection of woods, reeds, thatches, etc. which they generally use in the construction of their houses. Buffalo sledge is occasionally used in the transportation of the wood. Collection of wild bees and honey comb is also a task of the males. Females, on the other hand, are responsible primarily for the collection of vegetables, such as tuber crops, cucurbitaceous crops, fruits, root crops, legume vegetables, leafy vegetables, and bulb crops. They also help the males in the transportation of firewood, charcoal, etc. with the help of carrying baskets which they generally carry on their back. The Kabuis residing in both the hill and valley regions also collect, in addition to plants and tubers readily available in their natural surroundings, insects like the beetles, larvae of bee, termites, grasshoppers, etc.

The comparative study of the Kabuis located at three ecological zones reveals that those living in the interior villages gathered more seasonal vegetables, fruits and tubers for their daily consumption than those living in the plain. However, the plain dwellers still retain the habit of gathering as well as consuming wild plants.

People sometimes use pointed sticks for digging purpose. For the collection of fruits and buds from higher branches of trees, they use long bamboo poles. Besides, they are expert in the collection of honey comb. From the nature and the mode of

Plate 24 : Boys, collecting vegetables from the jhum field, on the way to home

Plate 25 : Girls, collecting vegetables from the jhum field, on the way to home

Plate 26 : A young girl collecting firewood from the surrounding hill

Plate 27 : An old lady taking rest after collecting plantain leaves from the hill

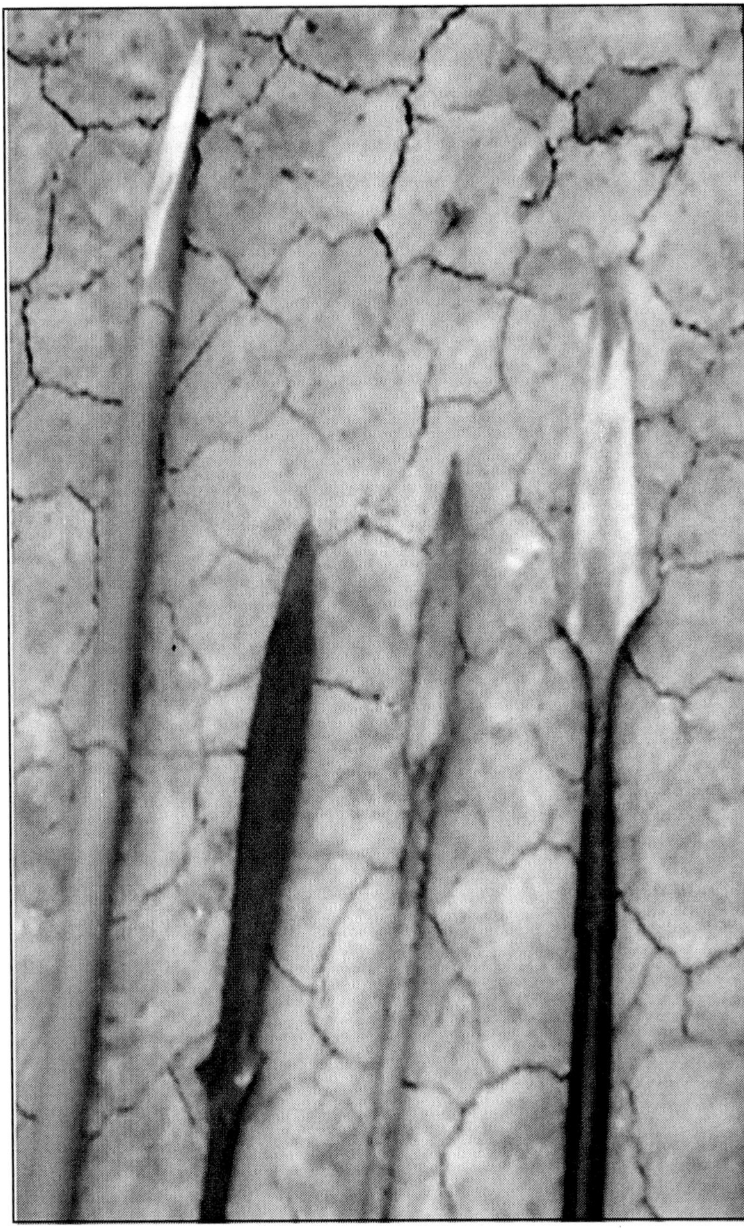

Plate 28 : Bui- A. A bamboo having pointed tip (reng bui) used as a spear B. Iron tipped spear heads

flying of the bees, they could ascertain the location of the nest. At the time of the collection of honey comb, they usually expel the bees through smoking. They burn the skin of the python to protect from being bitten by the bees. Generally bees having nest under the ground have larger nest. For collecting such a large honeycomb and larvae they inject the smoke of burned chilli through the entrance hole with the help of bamboo tubes.

They collect a variety of fungi grown on rotten wood and make them dry for their future use. Those living in the plain consume different types of dry fungi by purchasing from the market. They make mats of bamboo strips, baskets of cane and bamboo, mortar and pestle of wood, wooden barrel, etc. from the materials collected from the nearby jungles for their own use.

The implements used by the Kabuis in the pursuit of their gathering activities are digging stick, bamboo poles, dao, axe, hoes, etc. and different types of baskets are also used by them for carrying and transporting the materials they have collected from different places of their habitat.

Hunting

The antiquity of the hunting gathering way of life in India goes back to the Middle Pleistocene and possibly even earlier than that (Nagar *et al,* 1994). By the beginning of the Holocene, Stone Age hunter gatherers had extended their settlement into almost all parts of the country. The hunting gathering way of life started undergoing modification when knowledge of agriculture began to diffuse during the Neolithic period. However, such a kind of lifeways has not disappeared totally. Tribal societies practising some forms of primitive agriculture continues to supplement their subsistence by hunting and gathering.

Like other tribal societies, the Kabuis also practise different types of hunting. It is another means of getting food in villages under study. This, however, is rarely practised at Konthoujam and Chingkhulong for want of thick jungles abound with games. Nonetheless, they have the habit of hunting wild animals. Even the people of Konthoujam hunt small animals at Machin Manao Ching, a hillock to the southern side of the village at a distance of about 1km. The villagers of Chingkhulong also practise hunting at Langol hill situated about one km to the north eastern side of the village. Whereas to the people of Khonglong, Marangching and Phungong, it is a way of life. They hunt many times in a year or on any day whenever favourable conditions smile on them. But the best season of hunting is from January to March. However, they hunt a number of wild animals during the month of July and August from the Jhum field when the animals come to eat the crops like paddy, maize, arum, chilli, bean, etc. Wild animals like deer, boar, etc. often cause heavy damage to the standing crops and they have to guard against these animals. Wild boars turn up the soil of the jhum field in search of tubers. Birds are also a menace to the crops when the paddy begins to ripe. In order to protect their crops they kill the wild animals and consume them.

They considerably use traps and snares in order to catch them easily. While hunting they carry dog, club (*thing-dang*), bamboo spear (*rang bui*), bow and arrow (*pai–paithou*), catapult (*gulen*), pallet bow (*sairong*), spear with iron blade (*bui),* dao (*bang*), axe (*dri*), etc.

Both individual (*sugoimei / sukhoimei /su-chonmei*) and group (*suilaimei*) hunting are practised by the people. Literally, *sugoimei* means waiting for animals by one individual and *suilaimei* – means chasing or hunting in group. In the case of individual hunting they sometimes carry dogs to locate the games at the midst of thick jungle. Whereas in the jhum field they never use dog. During the rainy season, when the crops grow luxuriantly in the jhum field, animals like deer (*asan*), wild pig (*chabom*), and sambar (*chakhang*) come regularly to the field to eat beans (*Karu, biloi*), brinjal (*pantho*), chilli (*tingsaisu*) king chilli (*sahib-tingsaisu*), paddy (*nap-nang*) and arum (*bi*). By that time they kill such animals with spear or club according to their convenience. Generally traps are also used in individual hunting.

In group hunting (*suilaimei*), a few people with dogs will drive down the animals towards the foothills and some other people will wait for the game at the foothills particularly near the source of water, such as river or spring and kill the animal when it comes for drinking water in exhaustion as well as for bathing to regain strength. It happens in case of deer hunting. The most primitive type of trapping is to drive the animals into a dangerous place.

Hunting by chasing is the most primitive type which is being continued since the Palaeolithic period and it is still followed by the people.

The hunting practice can be grouped as follows:

(a) Hunting by weapon

(b) Hunting by trap and

(c) Hunting by tamed animals

(a) Hunting by Weapon

The earliest weapon of hunting was a branch of a tree or a lump of stone. The hunting implements used by the Kabuis of the villages under study are as follows :

i. *Thing dang* (Club) **:** It is a mere log or a branch of a tree of reasonable size and has no specific shape and size. Usually the smaller end of the log is used as handle and the thicker as the working end. Sometimes the handle of the axe is also used as club. This implement is used when the game is very close to the hunter, for instance, when the hunted is trapped or about to die as a result of earlier injury made with implements like spear.

ii. ***Dri*** (Axe) : It has an iron blade with slightly convex sharp cutting or working edge fitted to a wooden handle. It has used for hitting the game when the hunter and the hunted come to a close encounter.

iii. ***Bang*** (Dao) : It is a large knife having an iron blade with a bamboo handle. The bamboo handle is encircled with cane strips to make the grasping function more effective as well as to fit the blade tightly to the handle. It is comfortably used when the game is at a closer distance. The iron blade is about 25cm in length and 9cm in breadth. The handle measures about 20cm to 30cm in length with the diameter of 3.5cm.

iv. ***Bui*** (Spear) : This implement is used at the time of war and hunting as offensive as well as defensive implement. Bamboo spear (*rang bui*) with sharp pointed end is also used as a tool for hunting. The sharp pointed end is made by slanting on one side of the bamboo pole of a suitable size and the hollow area present near the sharp working end is filled with grasses. Usually the shaft is about 231.5cm long. An iron spear, however, consists of three parts, i.e. iron blade, wooden shaft, and iron butt end. The length of the blade is about 42.3cm and breadth at the broadest part is about 6cm. The uniformly rounded wooden shaft has a length of 113.5cm and a diameter of about 2.2cm at the middle. The pointed butt end is made up of iron. It has a length of 24cm. The lower end of the butt end is pointed. Different designs of iron blades are prepared locally and used by the villagers (Plate 28).

v. ***Pai- Paithou*** (Bow and Arrow) **:** Bow (*Pai*) made of bamboo and cane string is a common implement used in both war and hunting. Normally the bow is made of a slendered bamboo strip stringed with cane strip. Two types of bow are found among the Kabuis – one is the bow used with the pellet and the other with an arrow. In pellet (*sarong*) bow the string is provided with a small strap of cane which facilitates the pebbles for shooting. A *sarong* measures about 118cm in length, 4.5cm in breadth, 12.8cm in between the string and the bamboo handle with a thickness of 1.5cm. Usually it is used in the hunting of small games specially birds. In the case of bow used with an arrow, a grip of about 14cm long is tight with cane at the middle of the bending shaft. The bow measures about 118.5cm in length, 4.5cm in breadth and 2cm in thickness. There is a gap of about 15.8cm in between the string and the bamboo handle. The arrow (*paithou*) is usually made of bamboo shaft hardened by charring the pointed tip. It sometimes has an iron tipped head. The bamboo shaft is also provided with feathers or leaves. The head of the arrow is of two types-single barbed and double barbed. They smear the tip of the arrow with poison extracted from the plant products or poisonous snakes (Fig. 2: A-C).

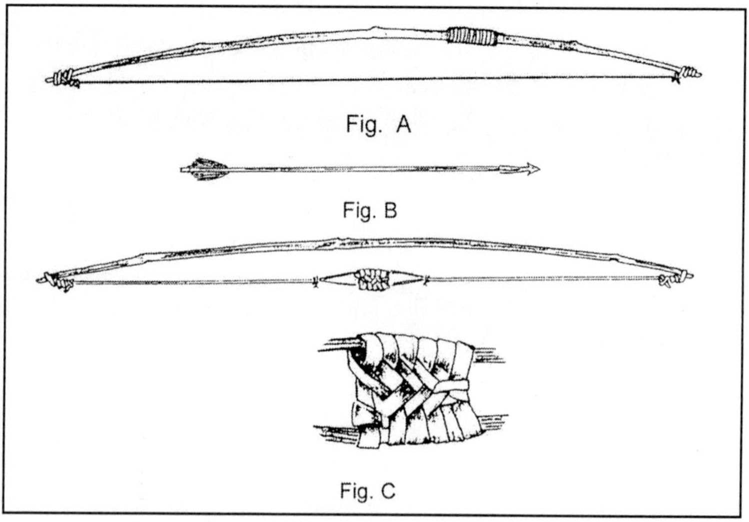

Fig. 2. A. *Pai* (Bow); B. *Paithou* (Arrow); C. *Sarong* (pellet)

(b). Hunting by trap

Some of the traps used by the Kabuis of the field villages are enumerated below :

(1) Traps for animals

(i) Khunthuk-pha (pit fall trap)

(ii) *Keikang-bei* (rack fall trap)

(iii) *Thing-dang-pha* (beam trap)

(iv) *Jouki-pha* (automatic cage trap/ drop trap)

(v) *Phai-pha* (feet trap)

(vi) *Kagang-pha* (neck trap for deer)

(vii) *Joukong-pha* (neck trap for porcupine)

(viii) *Sak-pha* (automatic spear trap)

(ix) *Jou-pha* (monkey trap)

(x) *Sang-pha* (squirrel trap)

(xi) *Rhou-pha* (guinea pig trap)

(2) Traps for birds

(i) *Teng-ka-pha* (leg trap)

(ii) *Pha-sang / Thang-pha* (noose trap)

(iii) *Bourun-pha* (nest trap)

(iv) *Tajic-pha* (glue trap)

(v) *Tang-bei* (bamboo clapping trap)

(vi) *Tao-pha* (all purpose trap).

i. *Khunthuk-pha* (pit fall trap) : It is the most common type of trap, prevalent among the Kabuis, to catch big animals. Literally, *Khunthuk* means a pit and *Pha*-means trap. Hence the name of the trap (Fig. 3).

t

Fig. 3. *Khunthuk-pha* (pit fall trap) :

It is essential to dig a large pit on the way where large animals are frequented and it is covered with light twigs or bamboo so that the unscrupulous animal may fall into the pit and be killed with spear. It varies in tune with the size of the animals they want to hunt. For boar, fox, and deer large pit ranging from 2m to 6m deep is dug. However, they generally dig a pit of about 2m each in length, breadth and depth respectively.

The pit is designed in such a manner that the mouth is narrower than the bottom and the mouth of the pit is valved with bamboo poles and long pointed bamboo sticks are piled at the bottom of the pit in order to make the animal unable to escape after falling into the pit. In order to make the valve and to protect the falling or sliding of earth from the wall and mouth of the pit while making valve, two long wooden blocks are placed on one or both sides of the pit before covering it with grasses. It is one of the most traditional and common types of trap used by the Kabuis inhabiting the interior villages.

ii. *Keikang-bei* (rack fall trap) : It is a trap working on the principle of lever release system. The name of the trap is derived from the structure of the trap itself. Literally, *Keikang* means a plane rack of woods and bamboos, usually placed above the fire-place and *Bei*- means a trap. The size and strength of the trap vary depending upon the targets to be killed. The main components of the trap are – a plane rack made of wood or bamboos, a horizontal wooden or bamboo bar slightly shorter than the length of the rack, a vertical wooden post of about 2m to 3m high having a fork at the top, two bamboo / wood posts of about 1m high piled vertically upside down about 31cm apart from each other so that their forked branches can be used as hooks, two other horizontal bamboo bars slightly longer than 30cm, the upper one is fastened to the hooks of the post whereas the lower one is left movable so that it may slide on the post when the bait tied to it is pulled down by the animal, a piece of cane made into a ring around one of the mid wooden bars of the rack and a trigger stick.

The wooden post is erected with the horizontal bar resting on its fork. One end of the bar is connected with the trigger stick through a string made from *thang*, and the other end is put slightly inside the cane-ring that connects the rack and the bar. The size of the ring allows the rack hanging about 60cm below the horizontal bar. The rack, whose weight is considerably increased by putting boulders and logs after laying the trap, is made inclined at about 45^0 to the ground.

The entire weight of the rack is transferred to the horizontal bar through the cane ring which is balanced by the *thang* string tied to the trigger stick hooked to the upper fixed bar. The length of the string serves to keep the bar horizontal. When the animals disturbs the lower movable bar in taking the bait, the trap works with its entire force releasing upon the unfortunate game (Plate 29).

iii *Thing-dang-pha* (beam trap / dead fall) : It is also a kind of trap, but it is not that sort of the trap used to catch an animal by the leg or by the neck using noose. *Thingdang-bei* means a log laid in wait to fall. Here a heavy log is laid on the path of the prey to fall upon it.

It consists of : (i) a heavy log about 4m long placed at the mid point of an opening, through which an animal is supposed to pass, of a fence made at a suitable place. (ii) five bamboo/ wood poles about 2m long, at least two of them must have strong branches on their top or if the bamboo poles do not have strong branches at their tops a suitable branch of trees having 'V' shaped joint is to be inserted into the internode of the bamboos, (iii) three bamboo/wood bars about 1m long of which one is slender , (iv) a strong circular loop made from the fibre of *thang* or cane splits whose radius depends on the size of the log used, (v) a short bamboo strip tied at one of its end with a string which is used as trigger and (vi) a few strings and bamboo splits or small trees.

Two wooden or bamboo poles having the 'V' shaped forks are erected, keeping the heavy log in between them, at one side of the fence and two other shorter poles are also erected on the same side but nearer to the fence. One of the horizontal bars is put across the 'V' shaped joints and another bar is securely tied to the other two shorter poles below their nodes. Free end of the string which is tied to the trigger is again tied securely to one of the remaining longer poles. The end of the log inserted into the circular loop is lifted while the other end rests on the ground. The longer pole now that passes over the horizontal bar is then inserted into the loop. This bar is pull down by the trigger string that passes over the fixed horizontal bar making an 'U' shape in between the shorter end of the trigger and the string. Upward motion of the longer end of the trigger is checked by putting a slender bar parallel to the fixed one.

In order to unlock the trigger, another string is tied to the movable bar that lies near one of the bamboo poles and the other end is tied to the opposite pole near its foot. A few bamboo splits or small trees are placed over the string but across the opening to make a bridge.

When the prey tries to cross the bridge, it unlocks the trigger. The log then falls on the animal and kills the game (Plate 30).

iv. *Jouki-pha* (automatic cage trap / drop trap) : *Jouki-pha* is a two chambered cage-type trap made of wood and bamboos to catch tiger, wild cat, and animals smaller than tiger. The name *Jouki pha* is derived from the name of a wild cat called *Jouki* and *pha* means trap. It measures about 120cm by 60cm by 90cm in the middle and is securely fixed in the ground. Two strong sticks about one and a half meter long which act as bolt of the door, are also erected about 1m apart from each other. The space between the poles and cage trap should be sufficient to hold the thickness of the door (Fig. 4).

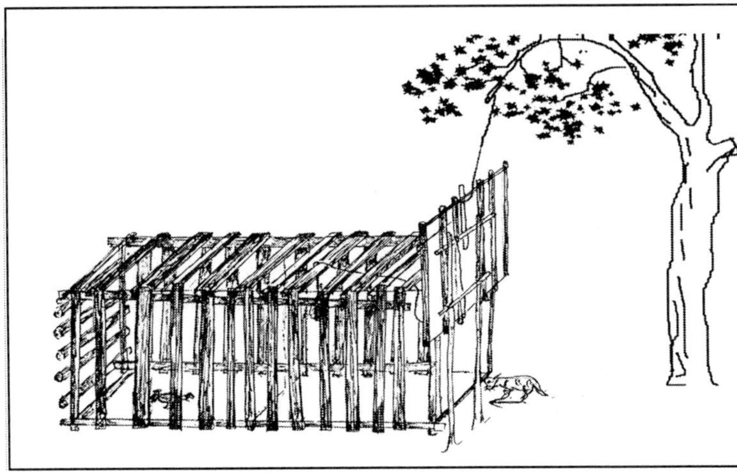

Fig. 4. *Jouki-pha* (automatic cage trap / drop trap

A resilient wood or bamboo pole, similar to the one used in *Joukongpha* is erected in a line with the two poles but at a farther point in such a way that the end of the pole after bending is vertically above the middle of the door. A rope made of *thang* is securely tied at the end of the pole and its free end is also tied to a trigger about 15cm long near its head. The upper side bar of the door is placed in between the rope and the shorter end of the trigger forming a 'U' shape. Trigger is locked by checking upward motion of the longer side by a movable horizontal bar. Another bar is also fixed below the movable one which acts as a pulley. A piece of meat which is tied to one end of a rope is hung at a height of about 60cm from the ground near the partition wall of the outer chamber. The free end of the rope passes vertically upward and then over the roof. It is finally connected to the movable bar after passing the pulley bar from below. A chick is also set free into the inner chamber to allure the animals. When the animal pulls the real bait, the trigger is unlocked and the door falls with a thud.

v. *Phai-pha* (feet trap) : It is a type of trap used to catch the animals at the foot. The name of the trap is derived from the part of the body of the animal where it is traped. Literally, *phai* means foot and *pha* -trap. Usually, such a type of trap is constructed on the narrow way where animals are frequented. A convenient branch of a tree is used to hang the trap when it is laid. If the suitable branch of the tree is not found, the trap can be laid by pilling a green wood on the side of the way.

It essentially consists of a pit having an area of about 30 square cm and 20cm deep, a string or strong creeper or a rope made of the fibre of a tree called *thang* and a few small bamboo sticks.

One end of the rope is tied to the branch of a tree at a suitable height from the ground. The rope is also tied to one end of a small stick of about 15cm long. The length of the rope should be shorter than the height of the branch to which it is tied. The stick is used as a trigger for the entire game plan (Fig. 5).

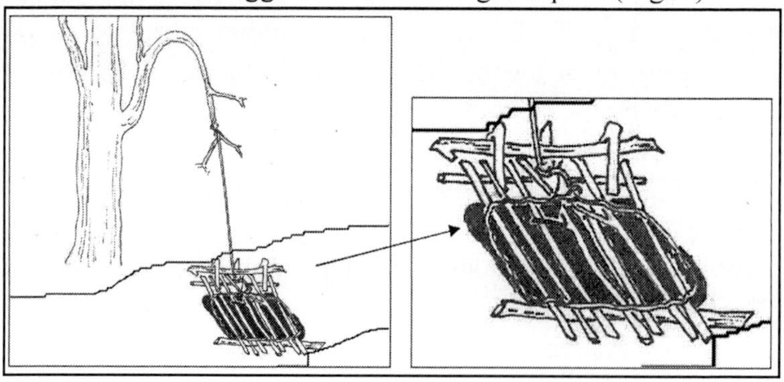

Fig. 5. *Phai- pha* (feet trap) A close up view

Two small bamboos or trees about 45cm long are piled vertically upside down parallel to the way about 30cm apart from each other within the pit so as to use their forked branches as hooks. A horizontal bar placed in proper position on the hooks support the downward pull of the rope. The shorter end of the stick, with the rope above it, is placed below the horizontal bar. The longer end of the trigger stick has a tendency to move upwards and this is checked by a similar shorter horizontal bar, balancing against the two vertical bamboo piles. This shorter bar is placed within the pit and it can fall freely within a vertical groove up to the bottom of the pit. A few small sticks are also placed horizontally on this shorter bar within the pit. The free end of the rope, has been made into a small fixed loop within which the rope can slide freely. A much larger loop, equivalent to the size of the pit is also made by passing the rope within the smaller loop. In short it is a noose. The larger loop is placed around the pit and it is hidden with grass covering above it. When the foot of the prey presses the sticks within the pit, the shorter horizontal bar falls on to the bottom thereby pulling up the animal with a tied knot on its foot. Small as well as large animals are caught by this trap.

vi. *Kagang-pha* (neck trap): This trap is usually laid near a stream where animals are frequented either for drinking or crossing the stream. It catches the game by the neck, hence the name *kagang-pha*, (*Kagang*-means neck, *pha* –means trap). It essentially consists of a string or a strong creeper or a rope made of the fibre of a tree called *thang*. One end of the string or the sturdy creeper or the rope is tied to a log of wood with branches erected by the side of the passage at a height of about 2m whereas the other end of the string is made into a noose. Nowadays, instead of that creeper iron wire is also used. However, it is covered with grasses or plantain leaves to camouflage it from the incoming prey. When the prey enters the loop, the loop automatically narrows its dimension to strangle the prey.

While using the trap, the height of the lower border of the loop varies according to the size of the animal which the hunter wants to trap. If he likes to trap a deer, the loop is placed at a height of 5cm to 10cm above the ground because deers always walk quickly looking downwards. But for the mithun it is placed at a height of about 60cm above the ground so that the neck of the mithun may easily go to the loop. This method, though widely prevalent in the bygone days, is still practised by the Kabuis (Fig. 6).

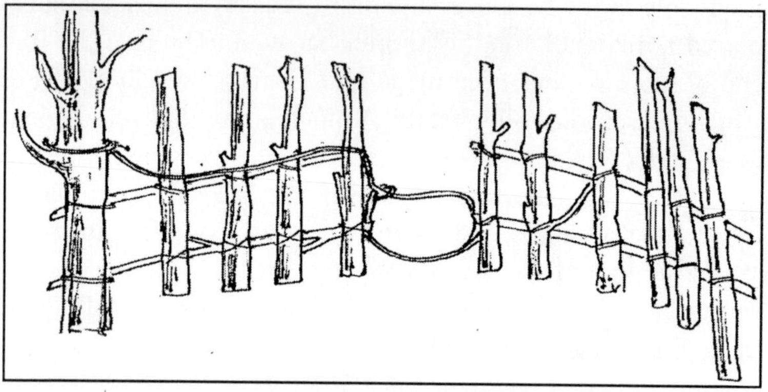

Fig. 6. ***Kagang-pha*** **(neck trap)**

vii. ***Jou-kong-pha*** (Porcupine trap) : It is a trap which strangles an animal by the neck and is used by and large for trapping small animals. The free movement of an animal is restricted to a narrow gate by fencing on both sides of its way. A strong resilient wood or a bamboo capable of bending is erected near the fencing but away from the narrow gate. Vertically below the end of the bending wood/ bamboo, a suitable stick is erected upside down so as to make a hook with its branch just 45cm above the ground (Fig. 7).

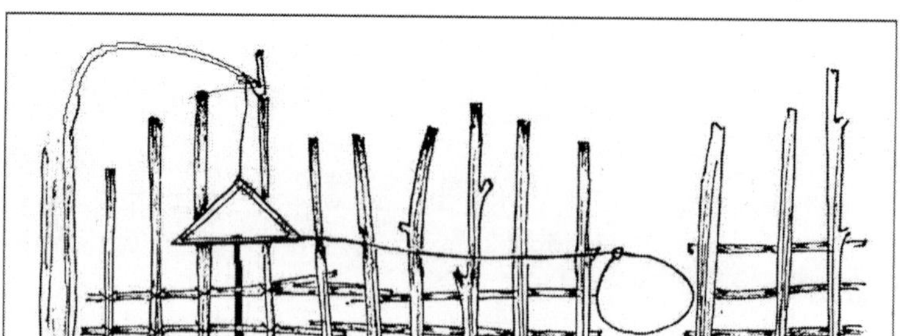

Fig. 7. ***Jou-kong-pha*** **(Porcupine trap)**

One loose and freely movable circular noose which is made of the bark of a locally available fibrous tree known as *thang* is laid through the narrow gate. The free end of the circular loop is fastened to one corner of the triangular loop which is made of properly twisted bamboo strips whose upper corner is connected to the end of the bending wood or bamboo by a rope, made of *thang*, of suitable length.

The resilient wood / bamboo has been made bended in such a manner that the base of the triangular loop, whose plane is parallel to the plane of the fencing, is put below the hooked branch which is suitably made shorter. When an animal passes through the circular noose it unlocks the triangular loop thereby pulling up the animal by the neck. As the entire force of bending of the wood/bamboo is delicately balanced at the middle of the base of the triangular loop, it is highly sensitive. This trap is more effective when the animal comes from the opposite site of the trap.

viii. *Sak-pha* (automatic spear trap) : *Sak-pha* means a trap of spear. It is a type of transfixing trap. In this type of trap an arrow or bolt is made to be released. The arrow or bolt thus released pierces or stunts the game. Sometimes human beings are also attacked by this type of trap. Nowadays, using of *sak-pha* is not allowed.

ix. *Jou-pha* (Monkey trap) : The literal meaning of *Jou-pha* is a trap of monkey (*Jou* means monkey, *Pha* means trap). These traps are laid in numbers in a place where there is regular crossing of monkeys. There are two types of traps under the generic name *Jou-pha* (Fig. 8).

The first type consists of a number of sharply pointed bamboo sticks fixed in the ground just vertically below the branches of trees which the monkeys generally use in crossing their way. The branches of the tree are suitably cut deep so that when the monkey jumps from the branches to the other or while trying to jump to the opposite branches, the branches may break down under the weight of the monkey whereby making them to fall over the pointed sticks and get themselves pierced.

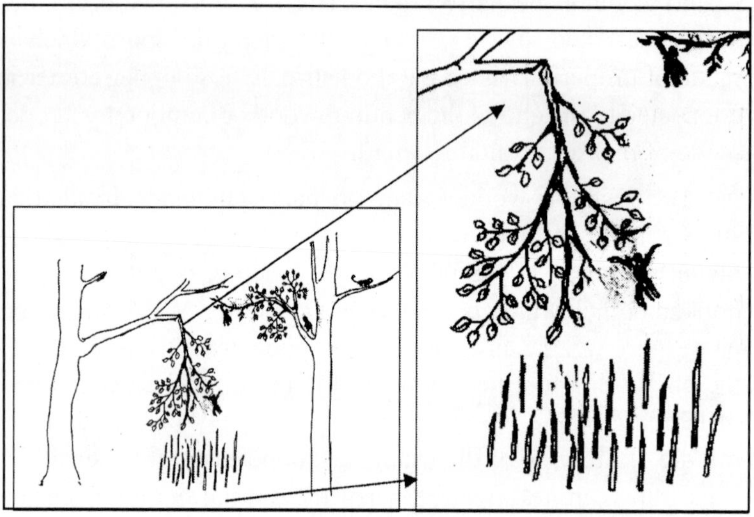

Fig. 8. Jou-pha A close up view

The success story of the second type lies in the fact that monkeys sleep together in groups at night over the large boulders preferably at the higher ups of the hills. When all of them go up for night's rest, empty eggs filled with locally made glue are placed properly on their path. They come across the allured eggs when they come down in search of food in the morning. While trying to see the content and taste it, they get their hands first smeared. It is further extended to their whole face making them blind folded. The hunters may take the advantage of the situation and kill them.

x. *Sang-pha* (Squirrel trap) : It is a trap used to catch small animals like squirrel and rat. It consists of a hyperbolic shaped frame made of bamboo strips. The base arm of the frame is about 16cm long and the two ends of the arm are tightly fastened to two sticks erected for the purpose. One end of a piece of rope made from the fibres of *thang* is made into two loops of a single noose in the form of an elongated '8' and the noose is placed in position vertically along the base arm but between the more or less parallel arms of the hyperbolic shaped trap. The rope, a few cm away from the end of the noose, is again tied to one end of a small stick which acts as a trigger and it again puts the trigger stick in a firm position at the bottom meeting point of the two arms. The upward motion of the longer end of the trigger is checked by putting a horizontal bar which rests on the other two arms of the hyperbola. A few vertical strings are made hung from the horizontal bar to touch the base arm. The free end of the rope is securely fastened around the tip of a bending pole or the end of one of the bending branches of a tree as the case may be according to the convenience (Fig. 9).

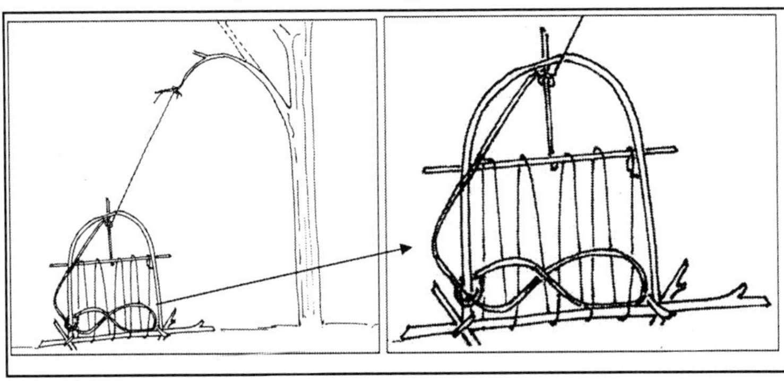

Fig. 9. *Sang-pha* (Squirrel trap) A close up view

Whenever the prey crosses the lower arm and when it moves forward, the vertical strings bring down the horizontal bar triggering the trap into action. It catches the pray by the neck. By making two secondary loops, effective area coverage of the trap is increased. But, if the prey happens to cross near the constriction of the two loops, the trap does not work.

xi. Rou-pha (Guinea-pig trap) : It is exclusively used to trap *Rou* – a rodent, burrowing at the roots of the bamboos and trees. It consists of a resilient wood or bamboo pole 2m long, a string and a small piece of bamboo strip about 15cm long. The trap is laid just a little inside the burrow through a hole made across it. One end of the string is made into a noose. The radius of the noose is made exactly equal to the radius of the burrow so that *Rou* does not disturb the noose when it comes out of the burrow (Fig. 10).

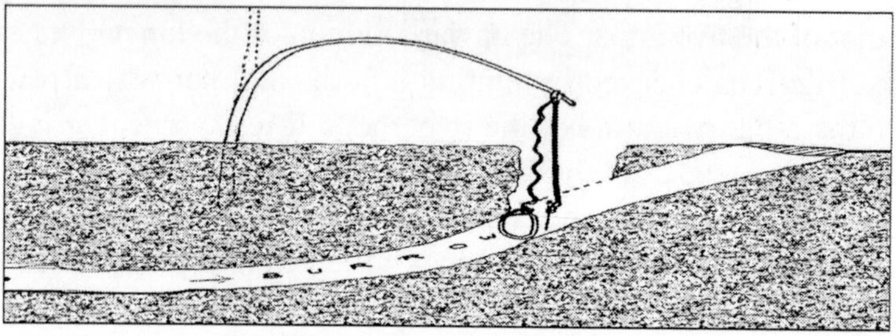

Fig. 10. *Rou-pha* (Guinea-pig trap)

Free end of the string is tied near one end of the bamboo strip and other end of the bamboo strip is again embedded into the middle of the burrow about 5cm away from the noose. A wooden / bamboo pole is erected a little distance away from the hole in such a way that the end of it is just vertically above the hole when it is suitably bent. The middle free portion of the string is tied securely to the tip of the wooden / bamboo pole so that the string may remain tightly stretched. When the rodent comes out in search of food, it finds the bamboo strip in the middle of its way. While clearing its way by cutting the strip, it was caught by the neck and hung in the air.

2. Traps for birds

i. Teng-ka-pha (Leg trap) : It is a 'U' shaped small trap used to catch birds by the leg. The two arms are made from the bamboo strips. It is tightly fastened to a branch of a tree or a stand at about the bottom of the 'U'. Two threads are securely tied together at one end of the arm and the other two ends of the threads are also tightly fastened around the middle of a thin, short stick that passes through a small hole made near the top of the opposite arm. By pulling away the stick from the arm, the two tips can be made to touch each other. Another stick which is slightly greater than the size of the hole and about 15cm long is placed between the hollow arm and the short stick so that it may hold the thread under tension and fall freely when the bird sits on it. A small thin stick is also placed between the two strings at right angle to the free stick to make the tension of the string lighter by pulling apart the two strings in the shape of a rough circle. The manipulator needs a delicate manipulation and adjustment to make the trap working effectively (Plate 31).

ii. Teng-ka-pha (Leg trap) : There is another type of *Tengkapha* working on the same principle but with a slight modification in its framework.

It consists of i) a bamboo pole of two meters long split into two halves of about 60cm long at its upper end and it is erected. ii) a strong string is fastened tightly around the point where the split ends to arrest further splitting. iii) a long bamboo strip slightly shorter than the height of the pole with one of its ends inserted into a hole made on the pole iv) two strings which are securely tied together at the other end of that long bamboo strip while the free ends of the strings after tying at the middle of a short bamboo strip of about 4cm long passes through a hole made in the top of one half of the bamboo splits, leaving the other half free, and v) two small sticks measuring about 15cm and 7cm respectively.

The smaller sticks is now inserted in between the two halves just to keep them apart. The two strings are pulling up in between the two splited bamboo halves, forcing the long bamboo strip bent.

The longer stick whose size is slightly larger than the size of the hole is kept push in such a way that it may hold the strings so long as it remains undisturbed. It may also fall easily on slightest disturbance.

The two strings are separated to form a loop along the longer stick when the short bamboo strip to which strings are tied is placed on it. The trap works when a bird sits on the longer stick (Plate 32).

iii. Pha-sang/Thang-pha (Noose trap): This trap is generally laid on the tip of branches of small trees bearing small fruits. It catches a number of birds by the neck at the time while they are trying to eat the fruits.

It essentially consists of a number of strings about 30cm long which are made from the fibre of *thang*. Each end of the strings is tied onto a bamboo strip of about 15cm long, whereas the other ends of the strings are made into small loops. The number of strings used in one piece of bamboo strip varies according to the requirements. The bamboo strip is securely tied to the tip of the branch where there is abundance of fruits. The strings are spread evenly over the fruits (Fig. 11).

Fig. 11. *Pha-sang / Thang-pha*

iv. Bourun-pha : It is used to catch birds specially when they lay eggs. The trap is laid on the nest itself. It consists of a hemispherical cap shaped structure made from bamboo strips or canes. The size of the circular ring is very nearly equal to the outer rim of the nest. Two bamboo strips - bent in the form of semi circles are tied on the ring thereby dividing the ring into four equal parts. Four pieces of strings made from *thang* are also tied securely to the four feet of the bent strips. The free end of each of the strings is made into noose. Each noose is then placed over its quarter curve surface of the hemisphere. When the bird enters into its nest, it is cornered but not strangled. When it flies out, the noose strangles it by the neck (Fig. 12).

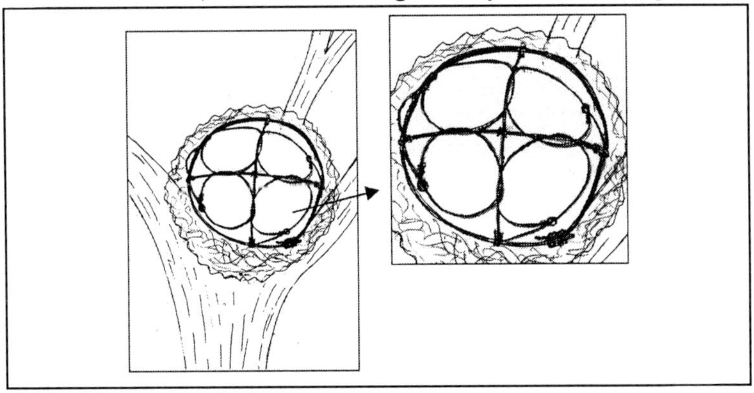

Fig. 12. *Bourun-pha*

v. ***Tajic-pha*** (sticker/glue trap) : It is a simple technique used to catch birds with the help of glue which is prepared locally by boiling the bark of *Tanat* (rubber tree), with the fruit of *Tamson* (urei). A small quantity of glue is smeared on the stones and sticks surrounding the spring having tasty or salty water. When the birds come for water, they were stuck on the glues (Fig. 13).

Fig. 13 . *Tajic pha* (sticker/glue trap)

vi. Tang-bei (Bamboo clapping trap): This trap is used to catch at most a bird at a time and it needs to reset if the manipulator likes to catch another prey.

It consist of : (i) a strong vertical bamboo pole, erected on the ground with at least two internodes above the ground, which is cut longitudinally all along the internodes about 3cm wide, (ii) three bamboo strips or halves, which are about 1m long and made with one hole each at one of their ends. One is made smaller and slender than the either two. (iii) two strong strings made from *gankheng* and (iv) a fourth bamboo strip of the same length as the first three (Fig. 14).

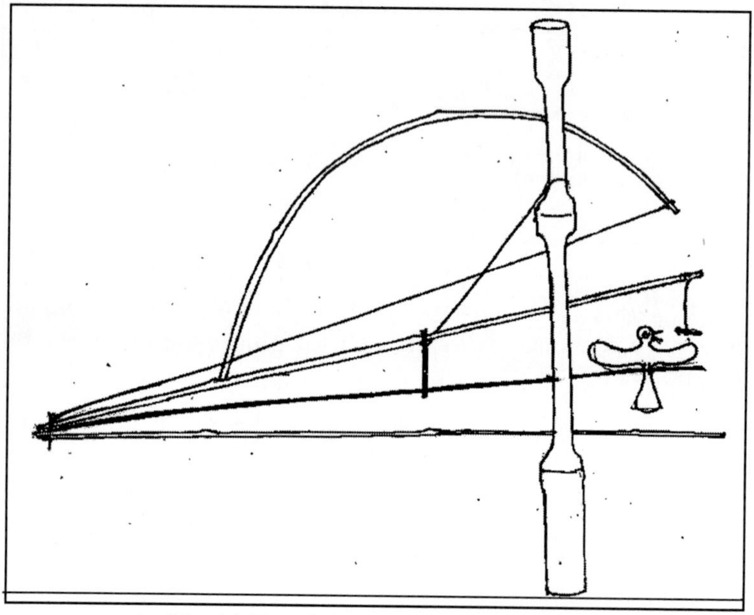

Fig. 14. *Tang-bei* (bamboo clapping trap)

The three bamboo strips, keeping the slender and smaller one in the middle, are tied together with a knot at their ends having holes with a rope that passes through the holes in such a way that the free ends of the bamboo strips are uniformly kept apart from one another. These free ends are again inserted into the first internode hole made by cutting longitudinally on the side of the vertically erected bamboo pole. One end of the fourth bamboo strip is fixed at a small cut made in the uppermost bamboo strip at a distance of about 30cm from the knot by way of inserting through the second internode hole of the bamboo pole. The free end of the rope is again tied to the other end of the fourth bamboo strip which is bent suitably in the form of a bow.

One end of another string is tied around the vertical pole above the second node whereas the other end is tied to the trigger which is placed interlocking the upper bamboo half and the middle slender bamboo split by way of adjusting the tension of the string. When a bird accidentally perches on the middle slender bamboo split, it will fall down under the weight of the bird thereby releasing the trigger. The release of the trigger consequently makes the upper bamboo half fallen above the middle one kills the bird (Fig. 14).

vii. Tao-pha (all purpose trap): It is a very versatile trap used to catch varieties of preys – snakes, pythons, small animals, birds which usually walk but seldom fly, specially wild cocks and white breasted water hen (*urourian*). The unique feature of this trap is that it has two triggers, one setting the other into a very sensitive and effective action.

It consists of i) a horizontal bamboo strip about 2m long and 3cm wide; the dimension of which may vary as necessity demands, ii) a strong string made from the fibre of *gankheng*. iii) two small bamboo strips, one about 30cm and the other 5cm long, which serve as triggers, and iv) another smaller bamboo strip twisted in the form of the two arms of a near isosceles triangle about 30cm high whose base is formed by the horizontal bamboo strip. Above all, a fencing line similar to that of *Joukipha* is used to restrict the path of the prey.

One end of the horizontal bamboo strip is split in the middle about 30cm long through which one end of the other smaller bamboo strip is inserted overshooting by about 5cm. The free end of the strip, after forming inner arm of the isosceles triangle, is again twisted downwards thereby forming the vertex and the outer arm of the triangle and then passes through the split horizontal bamboo strip near its end. It further makes a knot around the end of the horizontal strip and moves upward parallel to the outer arm of the triangle. It is again twisted near the vertex and comes down parallel to the inner arm thereby making the triangle double arm. The end of the strip is again inserted into the split horizontal bamboo strip and twisted slightly so that it may be fastened tightly to the horizontal strip with a cane strip. The two base junctions are strengthened enough with cane splits.

The main string is tied securely to the tail end of the horizontal bar and its free end is tied again to the longer trigger at about 10cm from its tail end leaving the string about 60cm long whose end is again tied securely to the horizontal bamboo split near the foot of the inner arm of the triangle. In such a way, the length of this string is almost equal to the length of the horizontal bar. Another short string is tied near one end of the shorter trigger and its free end is again tied near the head of the longer trigger. To activate the trap, the head of the horizontal bar is fastened firmly at two points on the ground and is made bent by pulling the longer trigger strongly. The main string passes through the gap between the two inner arms forming a near circular loop within the triangle. The tail of the longer trigger is now hooked to one of the upper vertexes and outward pull of its head is checked by hooking the head of the smaller trigger tó one of the inner arms. The resulted upward force transfered to the tail of the smaller trigger is now finally checked by inserting a small bamboo strip in between the two longer arms. This bamboo strip is about 6cm above the base arm of the triangle when the trap is laid (Plate 33).

C. Hunting by tamed animals

Hunting by tamed animals is also an old practice. This method is still widely prevalent among the Kabuis of Manipur inhabiting in the hill areas. They depend on dogs who render sincere services to the hunting of deer, boar, fox, etc.

Champei, the goddess of birds and beast, is worshiped when they are about to start a hunting. It is firmly believed that without the favour or blessings of the goddess one will not succeed in hunting wild games. So, before going to a hunting they have to seek the blessing of the goddess by making an offering of either eggs or chicken for a fruitful hunting.

On the eve of group hunting the oldest person offers ginger and egg to Bamboo (Village deity) who is believed to have presided over the village gate of every village and seeks omen.

Distribution of meat of the games: If the killed game is a deer the person who first speared the game gets head of the game and the remaining portion is distributed among the villagers. In such a case he offers one pot of rice beer to the village elders and can take meat of the game. But in the case of bear, tiger, or wild boar the killer cannot partake of the meat. He has to offer a pig to the village elders and the village elders will perform an omen seeking rite with the spleen of the pig. They also worship god uttering '*Hoi*' in chorus at the house of the person who killed the game. The meat of the game is distributed among the villagers as well as among his sisters and all the sisters in turn will present meat to their brother. On the day of the death of such a person, a pig is customarily offered to the villagers for the performance of *Riman-tumei.*

Fishing

Fish is an important food item of the Kabui. Fishing is, therefore, another means of getting food among them although it is not a regular practice among the people living in the interior villages located on the top of the hills for want of fishing sites in those villages. They, however, fish in the rivers or streams running in the nearby foot hills. But, this is a common practice for the people living in the plain area. Fishing is done in the

Plate 29 : *A model of Keikang-bei* (Rack fall trap)

Plate 30 : A model of Thing-dang-pha (Beam trap)

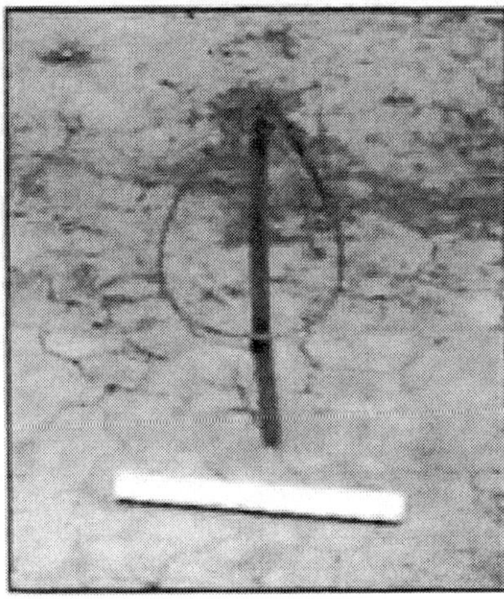

Plate 31 : ***Teng-ka-pha*** **(A)**

Plate : 32 ***Teng-ka-pha***

Plate : 33 *Tao-pha* (all purpose trap)

nearby rivers, ponds, ditches as well as in the paddy fields during wet cultivation. It is a common experience that fishing in shallow water is more convenient than fishing in deep water. It is always more difficult to fish in deep as well as in large volume of water when one uses mild poisonous plants. With this intuitive knowledge, people generally fish only during lean season at suitable places. Fishing by implements may be practised all the year round even though it is found more effective during the lean season.

The Kabuis practise both individual and collective fishing. Individual fishing is an informal type of fishing done by one individual on any day whenever his or her conscience dictates it. Collective fishing takes place at two levels. First, the entire village may organise fishing and it may be performed in a well organized way by fixing a day and distributing the work among the members of different age groups. Secondly, informal groups are formed from time to time for fishing according to the convenience of the persons concerned.

Fishing by poisoning and fishing by making barrage of stone, bamboo and wood are the common methods practised by the people living in interior villages. The informal and formal type of collective fishing by poisoning are known as *puretmei* and *khasoumei* respectively. Collective fishing at village level by making barrage of stone and bamboo across the river is known as *Dem-ding-mei.*

The method and technique of fishing practised by the people of five villages under study are given below in a tabular form.

Fishing techniques

Table 9 Techniques of Fishing

	Technique	*Types of implements*	*V1*	*V2*	*V3*	*V4*	*V5*
a	Fishing by bare hand		+	+	+	+	+
b	Fishing by spear	i. Single headed spear	+	+			
		ii. Multiple headed spear				+	+
c	Fishing by hook	i. Hook and line (angling)	+	+	+	+	+
d	Fishing by trap	i. Single body valve less trap	+	+			
		ii. Double body valveless trap				+	
		iii. Plunge basket				+	+
		iv. Hemispherical trap				+	+
		v. Automatic spindled shaped valve trap				+	+
		vi. Cage trap				+	+
e	Fishing by net	i. Cast net	+	+	+	+	+
		ii. Seine net				+	+
		iii. Dip net				+	+

f	Fishing by poisoning	Individual	+	+	+		
		Collective	+	+	+		
g	Fishing by barrage/ dam		+	+	+		

V1–Phungong; V2- Marangching; V3-Khonglong; V4-Chingkhulong; V5-Konthoujam

a. Fishing by bare hand : It is the most primitive technique of fishing. This method is practised both by hill and plain Kabuis. In Chingkhulong and Konthoujam villages this type of fishing is practised in the nearby streams, ditches, ponds, etc. during dry season when the volume of the water in different water bodies is reduced. However, in Phungong, Marangching and Khonglong, two temporary barriers are made about 7m apart across the stream in order to check free movement of the fishes and fishes are caught by bare hands. Generally, it is done in the month of September and October. Although, it is the high time for harvesting, they do fishing during the night, as the fishes are running up the streams during these months. It is convenient to perform fishing in the streams, in between the slopes of the hills, that connect the main river. Fishes moving up the stream during night are caught by this method. As observed in the villages under study this type of fishing is practised once or twice a year. At sunset, the villagers come to the spot and measure the width and depth of the stream. They then construct two temporary barriers made of bamboos across the stream to encircle an area where the fishes are supposed to be abundant. One person comes near the stream to observe the probable stock of fishes running up the stream by sitting silently near the stream. When he informs that the running up of fishes has been completed they make one barrier across the stream at about midnight. Then they are waiting silently at a place to see the fishes again running towards the river. As their path had already been blocked by a barrier, the fishes gather at the foot of the barrier. Then, they make another barrier across the stream to check the back running of the fishes. When all the fishes are believed to have gathered between the two barriers, they start fishing by bare hand.

b. Fishing by Spear : Spears are used for fishing purposes. Bigger fishes living in the midst of big boulders of the shallow water are caught with fishing spears, These fishing spears, which are of two kinds, are made of bamboo and iron (Plate 34).

One is the single headed spear with a long bamboo shaft and the other one is a multiple headed spear. It has a long shaft about 200 cm in length. The length of the multiple heads tipped with the pointed iron tips is normally about 60cm in length (Plate 35). The number of heads may vary from two to nine according to requirements. Double headed spears with a short handle is also used to catch eel fish from the holes present on the sides of the ditches or tanks. They are smaller in size. The heads are generally covered with iron tips of varying shapes. Both conical and arrow types are very commonly used. In the absence of iron tips, they made these shapes on the forked shaft itself.

c. Fishing by hook and line : It is found to be more common among the valley inhabitants. The rod is made of a branch of a particular type of bamboo which grows in abundance in their villages. This type of bamboo is suited for this purpose on account of its elasticity. The line is usually made of twisted cotton yarns which they use for weaving clothes. The hook is made of iron and purchased from the market. However, sometimes they also make it locally. The technique is to allure a fish to swallow the curved needle to which bait is attached. The baits attached to the hook are generally earthworm or grasshopper or larva of warps. Sometimes a float is attached to the lines in order to keep the bait suspended in a certain depth and to give an indication about the timing of action. In shallow clear streams, the float is not used. As soon as a fish swallows the bait in the hook, it gets entangled and imbalanced. Therefore, it can be turned out easily from water.

d. Fishing by Trap : Different types of traps like single body valveless trap, double body valveless trap, plunge basket, hemispherical trap, automatic valve trap, and cage trap are found to be in use among the Kabuis.

i. Single body valveless trap : It is only used by the Kabuis of Phungong, Marangching and Khonglong. This type of trap is locally known as *buan* and *khasai*. *Buan* is of two types.

One is made of a single piece of bamboo and the other is made of bamboo splits interplaced in the form of warp and weft. The length of the trap is about 100cm with a diameter of 30cm. The mouth portion is wider than the body and tappers towards the closed distant end. The former is made out of a single bamboo piece having two or three internodes. The lower end is closed by the node itself whereas the mouth is wider by splashing the bamboo in the form of radials which are tied by cane strings. The trap is placed against the current after making barriers. The trap is tied to the walls of the barrier by means of a rope made of *gankheng* (Plate 36).

The second type of single body valve-less trap is locally known as *Khasai*. It is a large sized trap made of bamboo poles having a total length of about 3 to 4 meters with a diameter of one meter. The largest diameter is found at the mouth region, which is kept open. The end is tapering and kept closed. During the rainy season such a type of trap is used for catching large sized fishes. The trap is tied to fix bamboo poles by means of strong cane strings. While using, the posterior end is kept at a slightly higher level formed by piled up stones and the mouth is kept against the current by making a passage through a barrage made of stones (Fig. 15).

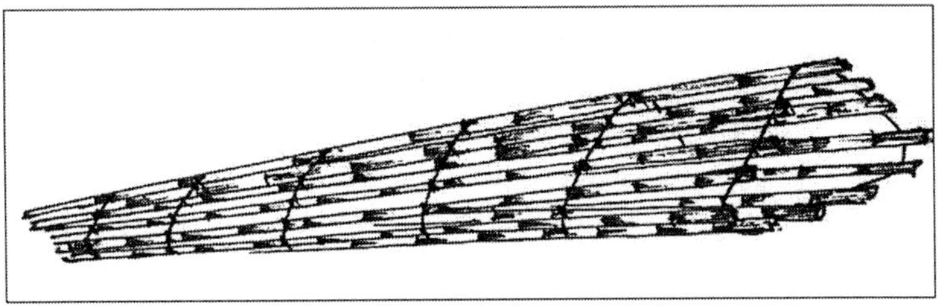

Fig. 15. Single body valveless trap

ii. Double body valveless trap : It consists of two parts. The first part, which is larger than the second part, has a wider opening with a tapering end which is again inserted in to the mouth of the second part. The distal end of the second part is closed. The second part is tightened to the first part by means of a rope. The second part is pulled out to collect the trapped fishes. The manipulation of this trap is similar to that of single body valveless trap (Plate 37).

iii. Plunge basket : This implement is made of bamboo strips and cane strings. The height of the implement is about 55cm. Its anterior opening is provided with a ring like collar which is about 14cm in diameter. A large number of bamboo strips form the radial pattern of the body of the trap.

The radial patterned body is again provided with cane rings at regular intervals to make the body sturdy. The space between bamboo strips is made narrow enough so as not to make the trapped fish escaping. By holding the collar region, the basket is plunged into shallow water to catch medium to large sized fish by the plain Kabuis (Plate 38).

iv. Hemispherical trap : It is a hemispherical shaped shallow water fishing trap made of bamboo splits. The outer rim which is the mouth of the trap has a wider bamboo ring which is fastened to the body by cane strips at regular intervals.

The diameter at the mouth is about 50cm with a depth of about 60cm. It is used in the plain (Plate 39).

v. Automatic spindle shaped valve trap **:** This kind of trap is used for fishing, specially in the running water. This trap is made of bamboo strips and cane strings. It is a spindle shaped trap having two tapering ends, one of which is tightly closed while the other end is open. At the middle of the trap there is a valve attached from the internal cavity of the trap. When it is kept in the current water, the mouth of the valve should be opposite to the running water to enable the fishes to enter into the trap. The diameter and length of the trap are about 25cm and 60cm respectively. It is used in the plain region only.

vi Cage trap : It is made of thin bamboo strips tied together with cane strings in the shape of a rectangular box. There is a vertical opening, provided with the pointed interlocking bamboo sticks loosely fastened by cane strings, on one of the longer sides of the trap. Due to the presence of these pointed interlocking sticks fishes once entered cannot get out. This type of fishing is found among the Kabuis of Chingkhulong and Konthoujam village (Plate 40).

e. Fishing by net : It can be correlated with the Neolithic or the later stage. The different types of nets used by the Kabuis are cast net, seine net, rectangular deep net, etc. Cast net is used both in the hill and in the plain. However, seine net and dip net are used only in the valley.

i. Cast net : Cast net is a hand operated net having a conical shape. It sinks with the help of the sinkers, present along the edge. When the net is cast, it spreads in a circle on water. The net is woven into a mesh pattern by thread and sinkers are made of iron or lead. A rope is tied to the conical end to make it convenient to pull up after casting the net. The broader distal end is made folded to form a long circular pocket for storing the fishes in the net and the sinkers are also tied along the mouth of the pocket at regular intervals. The net measures 2 meters in length. It is rather a difficult task to catch fish by cast net where there are big boulders at the bed of the streams. For casting the net, they prepare the fishing area in day time by shifting the big boulders across the stream to make an even surface and to maintain a steady current of the water. Some rice grain is also put as bait (*napkhuang*) in that area, At night they catch a large amount of fish by casting the net. It is a common practice at hill. They themselves make the net (Plate 41).

ii. Seine net: It is a long net provided with floats along the upper edge and sinkers along the lower edge. Such a type of nets is used by the people of Chingkhulong and Konthoujam.

iii. Dip net : It consists of three parts – a rectangular net made of cotton yarn having an area of 3x2sq. m, two bamboo strips having 4cm in breadth and 4m in length which are placed crosswise and tied with a piece of rope at the center at which a bamboo pole having a length of 4m and a rope of about 6m in length are again tied. This net is used in stagnant as well as shallow running water in the valley. The people of Chingkhulong and Konthoujam use this type of net (Plate 42).

f. Fishing by poison : Fishing by poisoning is the most common fishing method used by the people living at the interior villages. They use leaves, stems, roots, and fruits of certain wild plants as poison. Roots and barks of climbers locally known as *guwang*, *seng-nai*, herbs/ shrubs, namely, *kongsu*, *lanki*, *geng-jit*- barks and leaves or trees, namely, *Joukung-thai noang / Gurathai-noang* and fruits of a tree *Rongkhan* are used as poison for fishing.

Fishing by poisoning has two types - *Puretmei* and *Khasoumei*. *Puretmei* is the informal fishing by poisoning, making a barrier or dam by pilling up stone across the stream at the place where the stream bifurcates into two courses of water. Such a place is selected in order to divert the water of one course to the other. Leaves of a tree locally known as *Joukung-thai-nong* grown wild in the hills is mainly used for poisoning in this type of fishing. It is mainly done in winter on any day whenever they wish to do it. These poisonous plants are carried and placed on the dyke of boulders and made into pulp with a piece of wood. The pulp is dipped into water at regular intervals. When the juice of the plant is made thoroughly mixed with the water, the fishes become excited. They then become intoxicated and start floating in muddy water. The fishes are caught with bare hands. The catches are distributed among the participating members. In early days distribution was made on the basis of seniority. The old ones got more fish than the young ones. However, now-adays, the catch are distributed equally among the participants. *Khasoumei-* is a large scale type of group fishing by poisoning at the village level, mainly in winter season without making barrier or barrage. It is done once or twice in a year. Sometimes it takes place only after the lapse of a number of years. As informed by the villagers *Khasoumei* continues to take place even upto five days.

The movement of the fishes and the marks on the moss that gathers on the stones are regarded as the sign that indicates the stock of fishes in that area. Interested villagers also try to find out whether enough poisonous fruits or plants are available in the neighbourhood to poison the water. After making these initial observations they informally propose to the village elders for organising *Kha-sou-mei*. If a good number of persons agree, a date is fixed for the purpose by village elders. Generally two days are necessary to complete the *Kha-sou-mei*. On the morning of the first day, all the groups are entrusted with the work of collection of poisonous plants and fruits. The members of the older age group go to the river and find out the area where fish is likely to be plenty. They decide the length of the river or stream to be poisoned.

g. Fishing by making barriers : In this process, barriers are made by putting big boulders across a river to control the flow of water. Moreover small holes are also made in the barrier to allow the water run down through them. Behind these openings in the down stream a number of 'Y' shaped traps made of split bamboo are fixed so that water may pass through them. When the fishes enter in it, they are beaten to death with wooden club or dao. Thus they collect fishes. In the plain area these barriers are made of bamboo instead of big boulders.

In Khonglong, *Kha-shou-mei* is generally performed on the day of *Lao-khao-nu,* the day immediately following forest firing, if the *Thoubei* (council of village elders) decides to do so. Strong persons of the village are engaged in collecting poisonous plants *(yai)* from the forest while some others are engaged in constructing bridges of bamboo over the stream from which fishes are to be caught.

In the given sketch, numbring, 1, 2, 3, 4, A and B represents bridges for men and women. Bridges A and B are made a bit higher and the poisonous plants to be crushed by striking with sticks are placed in position on these two bridges, C, a fence made of plantain, is constructed between A and B in such a way that people in the bridges may not see each other. The bridge marked as 1 is constructed on the up stream and is meant only for the leading *Luchu* members. Similarly the bridge marked as 2 is meant for the leading *Khangchu* members. These leading *Khangchu* and *Luchu* members are selected for a year at the close of *Gan-ngai*, the biggest festival held at the end of harvesting season. They are collectively called " *then-dong-mei*". The boys of the *then-dong-mei* will give company to the girls on all occasions of the year. There are four leaders two each from the leading *Khang-chu* and *Luchu* institution (Fig. 16).

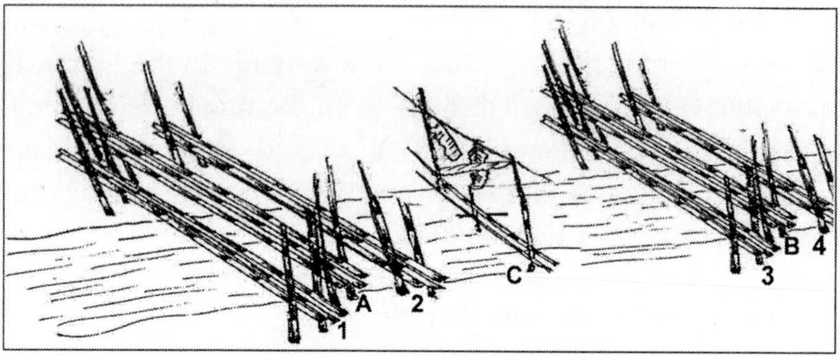

Fig. 16. A barrier made for catching fishes

Other members of the village may sit on the bridge marked as 3 and 4. These two bridges accommodate as many members of the village as they can. They are collectively called "*Then-dong-mak-mei*". By sitting on their respective bridges they crush the *Guwang* plant and sing folk songs.

After a while the girls of *Then-dong-mei* leave their bridge and go for fishing down the stream. If their catches are large, they will take a part of it for their families and rest will be offered to *Luchu* to which they belong. And if the catches are little, they will offer whatever they catch to *Luchu*. Other members of the fishing group will take whatever they catch on that day as their own.

The four leaders of *then-dong-mei* pay a visit to the house of the leading members of *Luchu* in the evening by singing songs and taste the fish curry cooked at the respective residences of the latter. The songs sung on this occasion are called *Lu-chen-mei.*

As evident from the field study at Marangching, people stand in the knee deep water and smash the *guwang* poison. The fence "C" is also not there. There is no different arrangement for their position in water. They may stand wherever they want to stand.

Plate 34 : Iron tip of a fishing spear that resembles a double barbed Harpoon

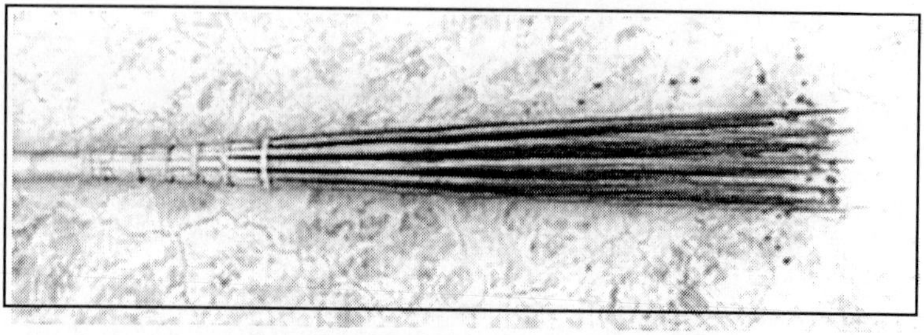

Plate 35 : A multiple headed fishing spear

Plate 36 : Single body valveless trap

Plate 37 : Double body valveless trap

Plate 38 : Plunge basket

Plate 39 : Hemishperical trap

Plate 40 : Cage trap

Plate 41 : Cast net (A) Net sinkers (B)

Plate 42 : Dip net

Old persons who can not go for fishing are also entitled to get their share. It is taken from the catches of *Thou-bei*.

Members of both the institutions of *Khang-chu* and *Luchu* give some fishes from their catch to the family of their respective institutions at the place of fishing while fishes caught by the *Thoubei* members are taken for themselves. Members of *Luchu* in turn go to their institution in the evening for tasting the fish. In case the quantity of fish is less, then the head of the *Luchu* kills either a pig or some chicken for the *Luchu* members. Dry meat is also offered if available. Two leaders of *Luchu* and another two from *Khangchu* have joined the feast. Some other grown up girls of the village may also join the feast.

Food Production

Food production is a revolutionary changeover in the history of mankind. There was a time in human history when people remained dependent on nature. With the passage of time, they acquired a great deal of control over the natural processes by domestication of plants and animals. Although the

Mesolithic people had shown an aptitude for domestication, it was the Neolithic people who actually learned the art. Food collection was replaced by food production and it had become a predominant mode of subsistence. However, by and large, food production has been classified into two major divisions as - horticulture and agriculture. Pastoralism, as a transitional phase, is identified between the stages of food collection and food production.

Pastoralism

It is a subsistence technology which is higher and finer than food collection and associated with the domestication of animals. This type of ecological adaptation that is found in the geographically marginal areas where natural resources permit neither the hunting and fishing nor the agriculture. As a consequence, the inhabitants adopt livestock breeding and lead a nomadic life. But most of these people are bound to maintain a barter relationship with the neighbouring sedentary agriculture groups.

It is believed that the domestication of plants and animals went hand in hand. Domestication of animal implies breeding and rearing of animals under human control. It debars the animals from reproducing in natural condition. The evidence that the earliest domestic animal is the dog was obtained from the Azilian stage of Mesolithic period around 9000 B.C. to 8000 B.C. in Denmark. Neolithic man had possibly pick up this specialized knowledge. Domestication of cattle, sheep and goat became familiar in Neolithic cultural phase as archaeological records came from the middle east, Nile valley and Switzerland lake settlements. Gradually people in different parts of the world realized the economic value of the tamed animals both as food provider and as beast of burden. The animals which are commonly reared by the contemporary simple societies are dog, pig, cattle, buffalo, etc. of which the domestication of the latter two animals can be traced back directly to the Neolithic age (3000 B.C.). The Egyptians and the Babylonians were fed on the milk of cow at that time (Roy, 2003). The Vedic Aryans regarded cow as sacred animal as milk and butter were the chief item of their food. Cows and buffaloes were employed to draw the plough for the cultivation of the land as done in present day India. The Todas still depend on the buffaloes for their food items. On the other hand, in many places bullocks are used for drawing the carts. Even the dung of this animal is used as fuel. The domestication of goats and sheeps also can be traced to the Neolithic period.

Domestication of Animals

The animals which are commonly reared by the Kabuis of the study villages are cat, dog, pig, cattle, buffaloes, and fowl. They are delicious food for them. However, pig, dog and fowl are also used for religious offering. Cows and buffaloes are employed for the cultivation as well as for drawing carts. However, buffaloes are commonly used for ploughing and drawing carts in the hilly areas. The people of interior villages seldom keep the cattle, buffalos at home as the animals are allowed to stay in the nearby jungles all day long. When the owners need their services, they will collect them from the jungle. Sometimes, the animals come to their owner's house at regular intervals during night time to eat salt offered by the owner. The owner can avail of the opportunity to detain the wanted animals. The animals usually bear identification mark on the ear or belly or tail made by their owners.

The cow dung is also used for plastering the wall of their dwelling house. The skin of the cow and buffalo is used for making drums and also used as, sitting mat and mat for drying grain. Buffalo horns are used as musical instrument.

Recent archaeological discoveries suggest that pigs have been domesticated first in India and China. Domestication of pig can again be traced back to the Neolithic age. Pigs are the sources of flesh. The Kabuis rear pigs for their flesh. In some places of the world, offering of pigs elevates the pride and prestiges of the person, who makes the offering. No exception in case of the Kabuis, as they also offer pig to their gods and goddesses at the time of celebrating a number of rites performed in honour of their gods and goddesses.

Dog's meat is a delicious food to some tribal people, such as the Polynesians, the Angami Nagas, who hunt wild dogs for meat. The Santals, Mundas, and Oraons also highly rely upon the dog hunting expedition. The Veddas of Cylon hunt deer with the help of tamed dogs. In New Zealand dogs hair is utilized in making the cloaks. The Kabuis keep dogs for flesh as well as for using them at the time of hunting different wild animals.

Domestication of birds and fowls is an ancient practice. Some wild varieties are still domesticated in Assam, Chittagong and Burma. The Aboriginal people of Assam and Chottanagpur use fouls not only for food but also for the purpose of divination and cock fight. Domestication of poultry birds like hens, duck, dove, pigeon, etc. is very popular among the Kabuis to obtain the flesh and eggs.

Horticulture

Horticulture is a kind of farming carried out with relatively simple tool and methods. Only a small amount of land can be brought under this farming at one time, as tilling of soils is done with simple tools without the help of draft animals. Three kinds of horticulture are practised by the people of the villages under study. They are : –

(a) Extensive or shifting cultivation,

(b) More or less continuous cultivation of roots and tree crops, and

(c) Sedentary or settled hoe cultivation

(a). Extensive or shifting cultivation is also called slash and burn method of cultivation. It is locally known as *Pamlou.* Shifting cultivation operation begins with the clearance of a plot of land by cutting down small trees, herbs and shrubs grown in that area. They are left for some time to make them completely dry. They are then burnt down before the onset of monsoon. Seed is sown in the rich layer of ashes covering the soil with the help of digging stick with the onset of monsoon rain. The ashes add fertility to the soil and rains help the seeds grow quickly. The ashes and rains in combination make the plants grow luxuriantly.

Shifting cultivation is undertaken generally on the hill slopes. In this region it is difficult to keep the water stored, even though there might be plenty of rainfall. So the fields for cultivation has to be changed repeatedly. The field once cultivated is kept fallow for some years, sometimes for more than five years, as the fertility of the soil exhausted. Then, a new plot is to be selected for the purpose. Cultivation generally continues in the same plot for two and more years if the soil is found suitable for another crop. Thus the cycle continues in rotation. That is why shifting cultivation is often called half nomadic cultivation.

The field for shifting cultivation is selected by the elders of the village after making a divination by the priest for the purpose. The crops produced by means of shifting cultivation are not adequate to meet the requirements. That is why they supplement their food largely by hunting undertaken generally by males and collection of wild growing vegetables by females. When population grows, pressure on land increases and under this circumstances fallow period of the land has to be made shortened.

(b). In addition to shifting cultivation they also practise continuous cultivation of roots and tree crops, such as oranges, lemon, *Parkia-roxburghi,* etc. They are cultivated on the hill slopes as well as around the residential area.

(c). The sedentary or settled hoe cultivation may also be termed as terrace cultivation. In this case steps are cut on the slope and farming is done on these steps. Beds are constructed compulsorily at the edge of each step. This allows the rain water to stay in the steps since water is urgently needed for cultivation. The main implements used in this type of cultivation is tilling hoe which is locally known as *lougai*. Some of the villagers of Phungong and Marangching practise such type of cultivation on the lower portion of the hill slopes.

Shifting cultivation and associated rituals

Shifting cultivation played and continues to play an important role in the economic life of the Kabuis who are living in the hill. This traditional agricultural practice is still in vogue among the Kabuis though there are slight variations at the regional/village level. The changes of faith, in the case of those people who have embraced Christianity, has brought about transformations in their cultural beliefs and practices. Hence, their traditional ways of life, though have been relegated to the past, still remains in the minds of elderly people of the community.

The different stages of shifting cultivation and accompanying rituals that constitute the annual agricultural cycle of the Kabuis are as follows :

Preparation of Field and Sowing

Needless to say, more so in shifting cultivation, that selection of sites deserves undivided attention of village elders for as much is dependant on the suitability of fields to raise good crops. Besides there are shortage of sites vis-à-vis the cycles of shifting fields.

They propose a site after thread bare deliberations upon its fertility and suitability of cultivation. It is then tested ritually for the devine approval. The process is known as *Chi-dan-san-mei* (*Chi* is a type of bamboo). In free translation *Chi-dan-san-*

mei means an omen taking from bamboo. It is performed by two village elders (*Taku,* the priest and another village elder) in the month of December or early part of January in *Chagangai* festival as decided by the village elders. Two youths are also selected to collect two bamboos from the forest. These four people are prohibited from talking with friends, sleeping with their wives the night before the ceremony. They bathe and put on new clothes to keep their body and mind clean and pure. The two youths collect the two bamboos in the night of the appointed day and hand over the same to the two villagers who are waiting for them at the village gate. One of the bamboos is split lengthwise into two equal halves. If the two halves are equal in size, it can be used for the ceremony and if the size is not equal, then the second bamboo is split again. The two village elders stand face to face holding the two bamboo halves by each hand around their waist and say to the bamboo halves, – "You please reply and give the direction of our paddy field otherwise your roots will be destroyed by *apauk* (rat)". If the two halves press each other inwards at the middle, it is a bad omen and if the two halves bend away from each other, it is considered a good omen approving the selection of field site by the divine power. In the event of bad omen the village elders rethink for a change of the selected site, if possible, from among the fields in their commands. But Colonel McCulloch (1859) observed that the selection of field is fixed and known before hand.

The number of persons involved in holding the bamboo halves in *Chi-dan-san-mei,* as evidenced from the field study, varies from one to two persons.

Selection of site is followed by demarcation of individual's area of occupation known as *Lao-phu-mei* which is done by erecting two bamboo, one each with a split top horizontally crossed by another split bamboo, at the beginning and the end of the field area. It is followed by *Lao-dou-mei* that continues for months together. During this stage the villagers clear their fields by felling herbs, shrubs and small trees and looping branches of big trees. It deserves special mention here that the clearance of field is interrupted, customarily in the beginning, by one day rest locally called *Lao-phe-nei-mei*. After that people start their work in full swing. During this period a local priest known as *Taku* performs a ritual (*Napkao-bangbi*) at the gate of the village for more production. Small packets of paddy, pig and a pot of rice beer are offered to *Apou-ragwang* in this ritual.

Drying of cleared jungle, *Pampihao-mei,* continues for about 2/3 months. After which the council of the village elders *Thoubei* decides the day of the burning of the fields and makes it known to their people as well people of the neighbouring villages. As a sign of caution, the villagers put one wooden plank coloured with red prepared from the leaf of *Sing-chagu* tree at the entrance of the road leading to jhum field. They prefer to say *Chakhang-alai-nithe* means hunting of deer instead of *Mei-lao-mei* (burning of field) in the belief that if they say *Mei-lao-mei*, rain will come and the burning of field will remain incomplete. If they burn the shifting field, automatically the animals and deers in the jungle will come to the side where there is no fire. On that side they watch and kill the games. After worshiping *Apou-ragwang* with ginger, *Taku*, the village priest, the villagers set on fire the field laying at the lower level. While burning, they take great care of the fire so that it may not bring harm to the habitat site as well as people. Next day is *Nei-mei*. On this day villagers are prevented from going to field.

Construction of field house (*Bam-kai*) and patches (*Changlang*) start from the next day of *Nei-mei*. Generally a hut measuring about 5m and 3m in length and breadth respectively is constructed at the middle of the field. The size of the hut varies depending on the size of the field. It is a granary cum rest house. Patches of 50cm wide are made by placing unburned wood or bamboo on the side. It helps in the retention of water and protection of the plants from the people while going up and down for weeding and harvesting. It may be inferred that their long experience and observance help them in developing the indigenous knowledge about the conservation of soil and water. The remaining unburned materials laying here and there in the field are collected and burnt to ashes. That is known as *Lao-tuimei or Cho-khon-mei.*

Selection of seed is done by winnowing the unwanted seeds. Sowing of seed (*Lao-phun-mei*) is customarily initiated with a ritual called *Ban-raoba*. In *Ban-raoba*, a small paddy field imitating the shifting field is prepared just outside the village gate. The village elders (*Khumbu, Khullakpa*) worship *Apou-ragwang* by offering the blood of a cock, cutting it by the neck, and rice beer. The blood is put to each and every villager. Then the villagers start working in that small paddy field with a "*Phu*" , a hoe without iron blade. They spit twice/thrice in the belief that all the wrong deeds they did last year will be removed from this moment and they are ritually pure and can go to field for cultivation. If one goes without joining this ceremony, it is believed that insects and rats will attack the plants. So it is a very important traditional ritual performed in the belief of protecting the plants from insects. Again, the use of bamboo or wooden hoe without iron blade in this ceremony is the symbolic reflection of the fact that they might have used hoe without iron blade in the early days.

On the next day of *Banraoba* either a pig or cock is again offered individually by the villagers at the paddy field with rice beer to *Apou ragwang*. It is done by *Mu*, medicine man in front of the *Bamkai* for good crop in the year. Then sowing of seeds starts. The offerings are carried back at home, cooked and offered again at the fire place of the living house in such a way that the cooked curry may smear on the three fire stands, pot of rice beer and rice storing pot, known as *Napchan-mei.*

The ritual of first seed-sowing (*Naphun–kei–mei*), is performed individually at Khonglong on the day of sowing, fixed by *Thoubei*. An able person of the family goes to field earlier than their neighbours with seeds, *jouyu*, chilli and salt. No cooked food is allowed to carry to the field. At the village gate, a small hole is made and into it a few seeds along with a few green leaves are put. Anybody who passes by spitting on it says that pest and insects, and all the taboos committed in the last year should not follow him/ her.

On reaching the field, he makes a small area very quickly and sow the seeds. It is covered thinly with earth saying that I should finish it now. As a mark of completion he gives a blow on this area with a *Phu*.

In the bygone days, four members two each from *Khangchu* and *Luchu* used to visit every body's fields by singing. Now-a-days it is completely abandoned. In the field, one should not talk to anybody otherwise birds and insects will attack his field. While coming back home the villagers taste each other's rice beer brought back from the field. In the evening boys and girls go from house to house to taste the special dish prepared on this day.

The selected good seeds are put in different containers or small baskets (*Kampho*) used at the time of sowing by hanging around the waist.

They practise two types of sowing – broadcasting and the other sowing by making hole with hoe. They practise multiple cropping. The crops cultivated in their field are paddy, chilli, cotton, till, mustard, maize, arum, red gourd, cucumber, bimli jute, ginger, etc. There are different varieties of paddy and the time and place of sowing differ slightly according to the variety. Plants like bimli jute, maize, cucumber and red gourd are shown on either side of the patches. In the case of arum, the upper portion of taro is cut and planted in hole. For this purpose, the earth is dug about 15cms. or more deep. The planting is done mainly by the women. However gingers, used specially for ritual purposes, are planted by males.

Sowing of seed is completed by the month of April before the beginning of monsoon. As a sign of completion of sowing they perform one ceremony of throwing out of *Phu* out of the village gate on the evening of the first day (*Phuton-ngai*). On the morning of the first day village elders announce the name of the first man who cultivate the largest area of shifting field in that year. From the second day *Gudui-ngai* the festival of drinking the ginger soup, made with chicken or pork, spices and salt commences. *Taku,* the village priest worships *Apou-ragawang* offering a pig or bull at the village gate for more production and for returning the paddy grains lost during the sowing. On the next day *Taku* symbolically offers his body to the evil spirits for more production of crops in that year. After this ceremony they perform a number of rites to ward off insects, birds, rats, etc. namely *Balao-raina* or *Katu-kanoi-mei, Roi chepna, Dui luang pok lanna.*

Weeding and Harvesting

During the period from May to July, they carry out weeding three times – once to weed the unwanted bamboo shoot and twice to weed the unwanted grasses.

A ritual, *Puk-pha-ngai*, for more production and to herald the completion of weeding is performed by offering a pig or a cow to *Apou ragwang*. In the following month, harvesting of new crop, *Lao-tai-mei,* starts with a ritual called *Lao-thak-mei.* The grains are temporarily stored at *Bang kai*, situated at the middle of the field and then transported to home during the month of October. When the grains are stored in their granary at home, they will celebrate *Dong Jaomei*, a ceremony for selection of a person who can produce the largest stock of grains in the year. Prior to *Dong jaomei*, *Gan-ngai* is performed. It is followed by *Katoi ngai-* a festival of testing curry prepared from the sesame which is harvested a few months latter than paddy.

The Kabuis do not classify plots for different crops in the sifting (slash and burn) cultivation. Rather they practise mixed cropping. Arum, maize and cucumber are planted on either side of the patches to protect the paddy plants grown in the middle of the compartment. Plantation of such a variety of crops not only helps in retention of water but also help in conserving the soil.

Further they also cultivate arum, pumpkin, etc. that serve as the food supplements during the lean season when the stock of rice in the granary is exhausted. The spirit of co-operation among the villagers in the farming activities is unique among the Kabuis. Right from the preparation of plot to the harvesting, they help each other in turn.

Tools and Implements

Tools and implements used in connection with shifting cultivation are dao, sickle, axe, hoe, digging stick, threshing implement, winnowing fan, and baskets.

Bang (Dao) : It is a large knife. It has an iron blade and a handle made of bamboo and cane. The iron blade which is about 25cm in length tappers more or less towards the posterior end, that forms a tang inserted into bamboo handle, which is about 20cm to 30cm in length and has a diameter of 3.5cm (Plate 43).

Bangkhoi (Sickle) : It is an agricultural implement used in the harvesting purpose. It consists of an iron blade and a wooden handle. The blade is about in 22cm in length and 4cm in breadth and has a slightly curved serrated cutting edge. The wooden handle is short and cylindrical though slightly larger in the middle. The length of the wooden handle is about 12cm.

The serrated edge of the implement makes it convenient for cutting grasses, paddy stalks, etc (Plate 44).

Phu (Spade): It is used for digging the soil specially in the plain region. It consists of a broad iron blade and a bamboo handle of about 130 cm long. The iron blade has a breadth of about 18cm. The working end is very sharp which is placed at an angle of about 80^0 to the handle (Plate 45).

Dri (Axe) : It has an iron blade with a sharp, slightly convex cutting or working edge. The posterior end tapers and is fitted to a wooden handle. It is used for felling the trees. In another type of axe instead of inserting the butt end of the blade into the hole of the wooden handle the wooden shaft is inserted into the socket of the blade. The measurements of the blades varies, but it commonly measures about 22cm in length, 9cm breadth and about 1.5cm a thickness. The length and the diameter of the handle is about 110cm and 5.5cm respectively (Plate 46).

Phu (Hoe) : It consists of an iron blade with a straight or slightly convex working edge fitted to a wooden or bamboo handle at an angle of about 60^0. The angle of inclination of the blade to the handle varies depending on the nature of the slope where the hoe is to be used. The hoe blade is fitted to the handle with can strip. It facilitates the manipulator in changing the handle to get the hoe to the slope of the field site. It might be the method of fitting the handle during the Neolithic period. Besides this hafting technique, insertion of the iron blade into the wooden or bamboo handle is also commonly found. On the basis of size, the hoes may broadly be classified into three groups - the large one known as *Lougai* or *Keiphun phakphu* and used in scraping and tilling the soil and the medium one –*Loupun phu* used for covering the seeds or grains with the loose soil at the time of broadcasting the seeds and the smaller hoes- *Nuchou* or *phu* used at the time of sowing the seed in the field and mainly for weeding (Plate 47). Their corresponding measurements are given below (Table 10).

Table 10 Types of Hoe

Type of hoe	*Length of handle (cm)*	*Diameter of the handle (cm)*	*Length of iron blade (cm)*	*Breadth of iron blade (cm)*	*Thick-ness of iron blade (cm)*	*Angle of iron blade with the handle*
Large hoe (*Lougai*)	65	3	35	13	1	40^0
Middle hoe (*Louphun phu*)	42	2.7	28	9	1	60^0
Small hoe (*Phu / Nuchou*)	40	2.3	6	4	0.5	65^0

(Buffalo yoke and plough) : The plough having an iron blade is used for agriculture specially for tilling the soil in the terrace field. The yoke is made of bamboo and wood (Plate 48).

Jhap (Winnowing Fan): It is made of splits of a particular bamboo, *Pai*. It is rectangular in shape and measures about 55cm in length and 45cm in breadth. It is used for winnowing the unwanted grains (Plate 49: A).

Malek (Threshing Implement) : Two types of threshers are found among the Kabuis. One of the threshers preferably used in the hilly region is made of bamboo measuring about 50cm in length and has about five forks. It is used for threshing the grains. While in the valley threshers are made from the forked branches of trees. Usually it measures about 160cm in length (Plate. 49: B).

Indhi (Umbrella) : It is an umbrella made of bamboo and cane and leaves of wild plant, such as *Luikham*, wild fig and palm tree. It is parabolic in shape from the ventral view and provided with a notch forming a conical shape for head rest on the upper part and it gradually flattens towards the base. It measures about 96cm in length and 63 cm in breadth (Plate 49: C).

Thing/Tha (Threshing mat) : It is made of bamboo splits of *Duijagpai* – a type of bamboo. It is also rectangular in shape and measures about 3m in length and about 150cm in breadth. Sometimes skin of the cow or buffalo is used as threshing mat (Plate 49: D).

Shep (Digging stick) : It has an iron blade with a sharp broad working edge, the narrow posterior portion of the blade is fitted to a bamboo shaft longitudinally, which serves as the handle. The total length of the implement is 107cm whereas the length and the breadth of the iron blade is 15cm and 7.5cm respectively. It is used for digging purposes.

Laogek (Harrow) : It has a wooden frame provided with a row of thin bamboo teeth. The handle is made of bamboo pole. The length of the handle measures about 110cm while the horizontal cross bar measures about 130cm. The comb below the horizontal cross bar measures about 10cm.

Ka and Kaluang (Bamboo baskets) : A number of carrying baskets, such as *Napphungka*, (male basket for carrying paddy) *Kaluang* (female basket for carrying paddy), *Nappuarak* (carrying basket for paddy in stalk), *Kampho* (small baskets used by the female while sowing seeds) are used by the Kabuis of both the plain and hills (Plate 65).

(Buffalo sledge) : Its function is multipurpose, though, mainly used in transporting agricultural product. Bamboo and wood are the material used for this implement

Agriculture / Wet Cultivation

Agriculture is an intensive as well as a permanent way of cultivation. Though the Neolithic people were able to produce useful crops like barley, wheat and maize, full fledged agriculture started later with the production of various kinds of seeds, roots which could be deliberately planted and stored for the next season.

The Kabuis who are living in the hill hardly practise wet cultivation as the topography of their habitat does not favour agriculture. However, the Kabuis living at the foot hills do earn their livelihood by engaging themselves in terrace cultivation as the habitat permits them to do the same. Those living in the plain area again practise wet cultivation as their habitat provide them with all the necessary conditions favourable for wet cultivation. It may be inferred from these facts that the Kabuis living in different habitats successfully adapt to their environment so that they can lead a successful life wherever they live. It is also a fact that a common denominator present in the economic life of the Kabuis living in different habitats is the functional similarities of the implements, though different in form and shape in different habitats, that bear evidences of their evolutionary change with corresponding change in their material way of life.

Stages of Wet Cultivation :

a. Preparation of seed bed and sowing : A piece of land is selected and thoroughly ploughed and puddled with about 4cm deep standing water. The primary objective is to prepare a soft seed bed for the seedlings. Pudding is done with plough. The land is levelled by means of a leveler, namely, *Ukai* after pudding to facilitate a uniform distribution of water and fertilizers. Compost application helps in quick growing of the seedlings. The amount of paddy for sowing is 60-70 kg per hectare. Lighter seeds that float on water are rejected. To ensure rapid and uniform germination the selected seeds are soaked for 24 hours in water which is drained away thereafter and seeds are exposed to warm moist place for 48 hours to let them sprout for sowing in the nursery bed.

b. ***Transplantation:*** The seedlings are ready for transplantation within 20 to 25 days (1-5 leaf stage) The field for transplantation is ploughed during the summer. About a week before transplantation, water is let in and the field is ploughed and puddled by tractor or bullocks. The whole area after being levelled by means of *Ukai* is ready for transplantation and the young seedlings are transplanted. Generally, two to three seedlings are planted at 20cm to 15cm spacing in levelled fields. Womenfolks are engaged in this purpose. This operation is usually done in groups so that it takes less time. The work of transplantation is completed by July or first week of August.

c. Application of fertilizers and pesticides : Application of fertilizer is done in two stages that is before and after transplantation. Urea, DI-AMONIUM PHOSPHATE (DAP) are applied in varying doses before transplantation. These fertilizers are again applied before the inhabitation of peduncle. Different types of pesticides are applied depending on the types of pest.

d. Weeding : After about 20-25 days of transplantation, the seedlings grow into young plants. Various kinds of unwanted small plants which hinder the growth of paddy plants are to be removed from the paddy field. Weeding is generally done by manual labour. It is time consuming and expensive, and the best time for wedding is three weeks after plantation. Nowadays, alternate methods of weed control with the use of herbicide have come into vogue and have a great scope under conditions of labour shortage.

e. Harvesting : Timely harvest prevents loss in yield. When paddy plants reach maturity they require less amount of water in the paddy field. Timely draining away of water makes the field dry. Harvesting is done 25-30 days after flowering in case of late variety. Reaping is done by means of sickle. The reaped paddy plants are sparsely let down in the field so as to make them dry in the sun. When the paddy plants are dried in the sun, a piece of land within the field is selected as beating site. Usually, a threshing mat is placed at the beating site and the paddy plants are beaten on the mat and the seeds are separated from the straw. Threshing implement called *Naplak* made of a branch of a tree is also employed. Men and women work together in this activity and the work is generally completed in a day.

Transportation :

Transportation of paddy is done by means of bullock carts or trucks or tractors. The paddy is thus stored in the granary. The crops thus produced are for their self consumption.

Division of labour :

Both male and female take important role in agriculture. The duty of male includes ploughing, levelling, burrowing, harvesting, threshing and transportation. The women are engaged in transplantation, weeding, harvesting and even in threshing and transportation.

Table 11 Agricultural cycle

Month	*Local name*	*Kind of activity*	
		Hill	*Valley*
January	Chaga-Ngai-bu (Loudou-bu)	Cutting and felling of forest	Off season
February	Pamphao-bu (Louphun saut-bu)	Drying of trees and shrubs.	Symbolic preparation of paddy field commences
March	Louphun-bu	Burning and sowing of seeds	Occasional ploughing of paddy field
April	Gudui-bu	Sowing of seed completed	Preparation continues

May	Pupikhoi-bu	Weeding	Preparation continues in full swing and seedling of paddy plant
June	Duilong-bu	Harvesting of early crops	Preparation continues and transplantation of early variety of paddy
July	Pukpha-Ngai-bu	Harvesting	Late varieties are transplanted
August	Lousai-Tai-bu	Harvesting	Weeding of unwanted grasses grown along with paddy for two to three times
September	Lou-Tai-bu	Harvesting completed	Weeding continues
October	Gan-Ngai-bu	Storing of crops in the granary	Harvesting of early varieties
November	Katoi-Ngai-bu (Matui-bu)	Late harvesting of sesame seeds	Peak period for harvesting of late varieties
December	Chakak-Ngai-bu (Dong-jao-bu)	Off season	Harvesting continues till the last week

Food Habit

In many traditional societies, people greatly depend on the natural resources of the habitat for their food. Moreover, the methods of food preparation and preservation have revealed the continuum of the protohistoric and prehistoric periods. The Kabuis of interior region have the knowledge of the life cycle of various indigenous wild plants and animals, and they with that time tested indigenous knowledge, have exploited the plant and animal resources of their habitat in order to lead a successful living by way of establishing a harmonious relationship with the habitat.

The main staple food is rice. They cultivate it on the hill slopes following jhum method as well as wet cultivation in the plain areas. Besides, they also grow some vegetables although in a very limited way. A number of wild and domesticated plants and animals, as evidenced from the field study, are also consumed by people as their food. Varieties of fruits, both wild and domesticated, are also consumed by them. Numerous wild vegetables, which are locally available in the hilly regions, are still their main source of food. They have the intensive knowledge of differentiating poisonous plants from the nonpoisonous ones.

They generally take two principal meals a day, one in the morning around 8 a.m. and the other at the evening. Womenfolks usually get up early in the morning at about second cock's crow i.e. about 4a.m. Pounding of rice and cooking of food are the customary morning duties for a woman. They drink boiled water mixed with a few grains of sweet smelled rice locally known as *napheng*. Usually they take lunch together along with their children. Those who can help working in the field accompany their parents while the latter are going to field. They carry a packet of rice and curry for tiffin. Besides these, they also carry rice beer to consume during recreation. They work till evening but come back home before dark.

The locally available seasonal and perennial varieties of plants and animals, both wild and domesticated, consumed by in different seasons of a year have merits of further discussion as they play an important role in the food habit of the people. They, on the basis of their indigenous knowledge of plants, broadly divide the edible wild and domesticated varieties of plants into three groups, namely, summer plants, that is, the plants available during the period from April to September,

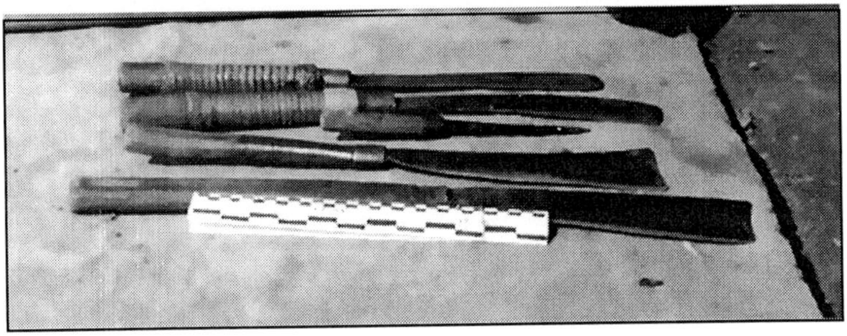

Plate 43 : Bang (Dao, iron blades of different shapes)

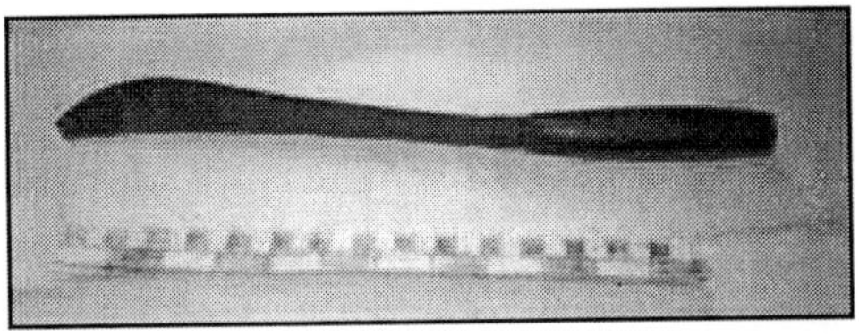

Plate 44 : Bangkhoi Sickle, a plain iron blade

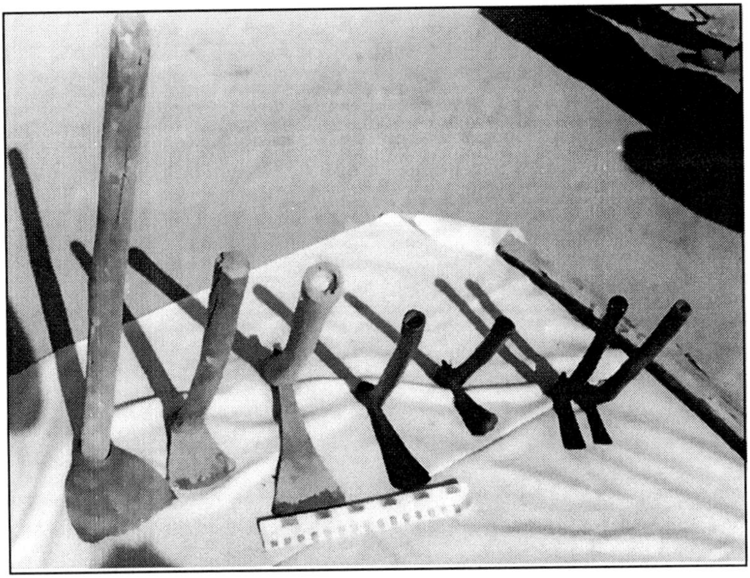

Plate : 45 Phu- Spade, of different sizes

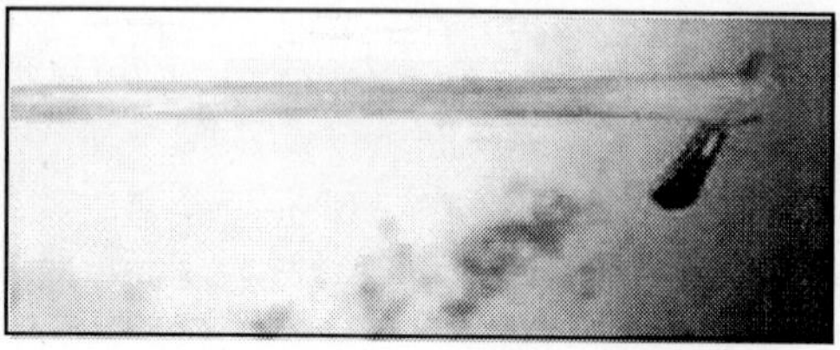

Plate 46 : Dri- axe

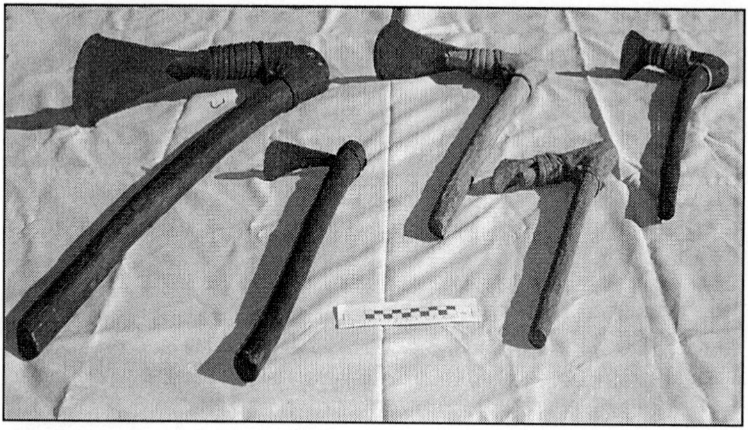

Plate 47 : Phu-Hoe, different sizes of hoes (*A. Lougai, B. Loupun phu, C. Nuchou/phu*)

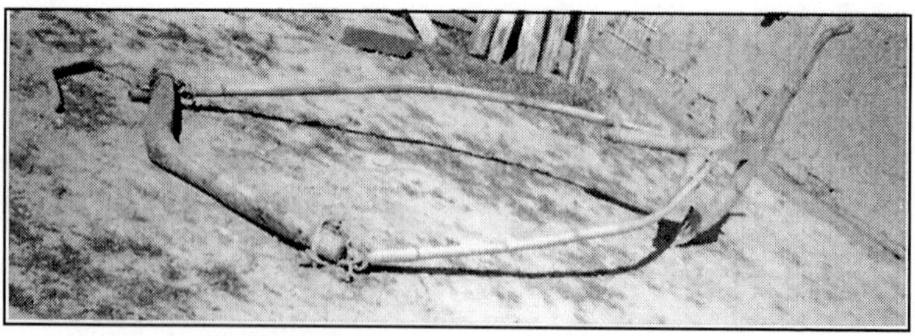

Plate 48 : Buffalo yoke and plough

Plate : 49 *Jhap*-Winowing fan; B.Malek - Threshing implement; C. Indhi –UmbrellaD. Thing/tha -threshing mat

Plate 50 : Indhi-an umbrella used by the plain Kabuis and the researcher

winter plants, that is, the plants that grow luxuriantly during winter season, that is, the period from October to March and perennial plants, that is, plants available throughout the year. The names of the plants with their scientific names are given below (Table 12-19).

Table 12 Wild Summer Plants

Local name	*English*	*Scientific name*
Gapong	East Indian arrow root	*Curcuma angustifolia*
Yentang	Palmfern (Cycad)	*Cycas pectinata*
Uthumnong	Needle wood	*Schima wallichii*
Tamtanong	Antedesma	*Antidesma diandrum*
Loklai	Common ginger lily	*Hedychium spicatum*
Gahong	White ginger lily	*Amomum aromaticum*
Thun	Bamboo shoot	*Bambusa tulda*
Phakchetnong ·	Alligator weed	*Alternanthera sessilis*
Pulai	Alpinia	*Alpinia allughas*
Takhelai	Comon ginger lily	*Hedychium coronarium*
Sinu Kompan	Jew's ear	*Auricularia auricula*
Guibaganong	Prickly amaranth	*Amaranthus spinosus*
Panei / Thingpan	Edible basidiomycetes	*Lentinus edodes*
Pantam	Split gill fungus	*Schizophyllum commune*
Kandidoi	Mushroom	*Lycoperdon pyriforme*
Pungpan	a. Mushroom	*Termitomyces clypeatus*
	b. Mushroom	*Termitomyces robust*
Guipan	Prickly	*Volvariella volvaceae*

Table 13 Wild Winter Plants

Local name	*English*	*Scientific name*
Lu	Yam	*Discorea alata*
Lamlu	Yam	*Dioscorea glabra*
Oomangkra	Cassava / tapioca	*Manihot esculenta*
Palei	Palak	*Spinacea oleracea*
Ngamlou	Wendlandia	*Wendlandia paniculata*
Kam	Parkia (Giant bean)	*Parkia roxburghii*
Yenakhat	Seutellaria	*Scuttelaria discolar*
Kokphai	Polysonum	*Polygonum posumbu*
Nungsitpu	Garden mint	*Mentha arvensis*
Kangkru	Bengal sage	*Merinda bengalensis*
Lingtu	Posostenum	*Pogostemon pubescens*
Kanghru	Greater galangal	*Alpinia galanga*
Bangmaroi	Alata Seaholy	*Eryngium foetidum*
Koukha	Arrowhead	*Sagittaria sagittifolia*
Kouthum	Sweet cyperus	*Cyperus kyllingia*

Table 14 Wild Perennial Plants

Local name	*English*	*Scientific name*
Heibanong	Ficus	*Ficus palmata*
Pantan	Cissus	*Cissus adnata*
Ngank	Plantain	*Musa paradisiaca*
Salikcat	Clerodendron	*Clerodendron serratum*
Khimpui	Adhatoda	*Phlogacanthus thrysiflorus*

Koklei	Indian pennywort	*Centela asiatica*
Gankarak	Yembum (M)	*Plantago erosa/ Plantago major*
Keipat	Plantago	*Plantago erosa / Plantago major*
Tupit	Indian sorrel	*Oxalis corniculata*
Tanangnong	Prickly ash	*Zanthoxylum acanthopodium*
Ashi heibong	Wild fig	*Ficus hispida*

Table 15 Domesticated Summer Plants

<table>
<tr><th>Local name</th><th>English</th><th>Scientific name</th></tr>
<tr><td>Tun-ngan-nap neng</td><td rowspan="18">Different varieties of Paddy</td><td rowspan="18">Oryza sativa (sp.)</td></tr>
<tr><td>Zou napneng</td></tr>
<tr><td>Nap-him</td></tr>
<tr><td>Heingmei Asantan</td></tr>
<tr><td>Pwanmei Asantan</td></tr>
<tr><td>Nap dai</td></tr>
<tr><td>Nap hui</td></tr>
<tr><td>Nap-gi-heng-mei</td></tr>
<tr><td>Bang-lai-nap</td></tr>
<tr><td>Mazin nap</td></tr>
<tr><td>Tourei-liu-nap</td></tr>
<tr><td>Pok-dun-nap</td></tr>
<tr><td>Kalu-liu-nap</td></tr>
<tr><td>Apeang-ban-nap</td></tr>
<tr><td>Phei-phan-nap</td></tr>
<tr><td>Ripiang-nap</td></tr>
<tr><td>Bung-bou-nap</td></tr>
<tr><td>Akiou nap</td></tr>
</table>

Napsu	millet	*Pinnisetum typhoides*
gita	Maize	*Zea mays*
Khongdrum	Sweet gourd	*Lagenaria siceraria*
Pongma	Pumkin	*Cucurbita maxima*
Tingsaisu	Chilli	*Capsium frustescens*
Sebot	Spongegourd	*Luffa cylindrica*
Gankheng	Bimli jute (Deccan lump)	*Hibiscus cannabinus*
Joubongma	Ashgourd	*Benincasa hispida*
Kalandri	Varieties of bean	*Phaseolus (sp.)*
Karu		
Biloi		

Table 16 Domesticated Winter Plants

Local name	*English*	*Scientific name*
Alu	Potato	*Solanum tuberosum*
Ganum	Garlic	*Allium sativum*
Maroi napakpi	Leek	*Allium hookerii*
Ganang	Mustard	*Brassica campestris*
Makhounong	Tobacco	*Nicotiana tabacum*
Ludeipui	Sweet potato	*Ipomoea batatas*
Khuithu	Soyabean	*Glycine max*
Katoi	Sesame	*Sesamum indicum*
Tilhou	Onion	*Allium cepa*
Chakhawai	French bean	*Phaseolus vulgaris*

Hawai uri	Lablab bean	*Dolichos lablab*
Hawai mubi	Broad bean	*Vicia faba*
Sagol hawai	Black gram	*Phaseolus mungo*
Heiribob	Citrus	*Citrus hystrix*

Table 17 Domesticated Perennial Plants

Local name	*English*	*Scientific name*
Thao	Brinjal	*Solanum melongena*
Bi	Arum	*Colocasia esculenta*
Phadigom	Coriander	*Coriandrum sativum*
Gu	Ginger	*Zingiber officinale*
Tezpat	Bayleaf	*Cinnamomum tamala*
Gachanglim	Turmeric	*Curcuma domestica*
Bizi	But	*Alocasia indica*

Table 18 Wild Fruits

Local name	*English*	*Scientific name*
Paroinathai	Indian plum	*Ziziphus jujuba*
Tanunathai	Meyna	*Meyna laxiflora*
Heibungthai	Mangosteen	*Garcinia peduculata*
Ruithai	Raspberry	*Rubus niveus*
Tekunathai	Walnut	*Juglans regia*
Tarouthai	Gooseberry	*Emblica officinalis*
Tamuthai	Rhus	*Rhus semialata*
Tamjinthai	Wild mango (Hog plum)	*Spondias pinnata*
Luithai	Cane	*Calamus tenuis*
Heirithai	Wild fig	*Ficus cunia*
Pukhai	Wild apple	*Microcosm paniculata*

Rambongthai	Ficus	*Ficus ben jamina*
Malhei	Apricot	*Prunus armeniaca*
Tadamthai	Dwarf date palm	*Phoenix humilis*
Dingthai / Thingthai	Chestnut	*Castanopsis tribuloides*
Heibung thai	Mangosteen	*Garcinia peduculata*
Motok thai	Loquat	*Baccaurea ramiflora*
Hari khagok thai	Stone apple	*Aegle marmelos*
Heirangkhoi thai	Amoora	*Aphanamixix polystachya*

Table 19 Domesticated Fruits

Local name	*English*	*Scientific name*
Komla	Orange	*Citrus reticulata*
Champra	Lemon	*Citrus limon*
Nobab	Shaddock	*Citrus maxima*
Pungton thai	Guava	*Psidium guava*
Thapi	cucumber	*Cucumis sativa*
Bathai	Mango	*Mangiifera indica*
Harikokthong thai	Monkey jack	*Antocarpus lakoocha*
Laphoi	Banana	*Musa paradisiaca*

Wild animals are hunted by means of traps, snares and weapons. Moreover, they also domesticate animals for their flesh. The Kabuis, living in the hilly regions of Phungong and Marangching are found to be very much aware of the proteinous value and taste of some insects. However, it is also a fact that there are slight variations in the dietary habit of the Kabuis inhabiting different ecological zones.

Table 20 Wild Animals

Local name	*English*	*Scientific name*
Angu	Indian wild dog	*Cuon alpinus*
Kamang	a. Tiger	*Felis tigris*
	b. Leopard	*Panthera pardes*
	c. Tiger (small variety)	*Panthera tigris*
Joukong	Porcupine	*Hystris sp*
Jouki	Golden cat (wild cat)	*Felis temmincki*
Alai	Indian wolf	*Canislupus pallipes*
Sasi	Fox	*Canis vulpes*
Chabom	Wild pig	*Sus scrofa*
Chalung	serrow	*Capricornis sumatraensis*
Chakhang	Sambar	*Cervus unicolor*
San/Asan	Deer	*Cervus*
Chagem	Himalayan black beer	*Melursus ursinus*
Jou	Monkey	*Macaque macaca*
Joumumei	Black monkey	*Hylobates hoolock*
Lamtoi / lambak	Bat	*Pteropus sp*
Apou/pou	Rat	*Rattus rattus*
Arou	Guinea-pig	*Cavia porcellus*

Gou	Frog	*Rana trigrina*
Guiphop	Tortoise	*Trionyx sp.*
Goichang	Mithun	*Gavaeus frontalis*

Table 21 Wild Birds

Local name	*English*	*Scientific name*
Namlou	Drongo	*Dicrurus sp.*
Chonga	Myna	*Acridotheres sp. /Sturnus sp.*
Taroidambu	Hoopoe	*Hoopoe upupaepops*
Pitna	Wagtail	*Motacilla sp.*
Dou/ dao	Nightingale	*bulbul*
Agak	Crow	*Corvus macrorhun*
Hoina/khoukna	Spotted dove	*Streptopelia chinensis*
Drick/Tidui	Pheasant	*Gallus sp.*
Langcheya	vulture	*Gyps sp.*
Rangdai	Hornbill	*Buceros / Aceros sp.*
Pomang	Owl	*Athene sp*
Jaipui	Kingfisher	*Halcyon sp. / Alcedo sp.*
Leirumpui	Coucal	*Centropus sp.*
Pangrangna	Swallow	*Hirundo sp.*
Tingkana	Sparrow	*Passer montanus*
Gathuna	Parrot	*Psittacula sp.*
Roirangna	Magpie robin	*Copsychus saularis*
Maou/Mou	Kite	*Elanus clanga*
Urou-rian	White breasted water hen	*Amallrornis phoenicurus*

Lok	Adjutant	*Leptoptilos sp.*
Thingchoupui	Wood picker	*Dendrocopus auriceps*

Table 22 Insects

Local name	*English*	*Scientific name*
Pijengpui	Varieties of Grasshopper	*Locusta (sp.)*
Routhakpui		
Pangjougaina		
Pikokpui		
Bamzongka		
Gulemka		
Thatapoi		
Pisumpui		
Pirumpui		
Luika		
Tinokompui		
Khangboi		
Thee		
Kaokaopoi		
kit	Cricket	*Gryllus sp.*
Pang	Praying mantids	*Mantis religes*
Khoidai	Wasp	*Vespa sp.*
khoi	Apis mellifera	*Apis indica*
Bu-bungpui	White ant / termite	
Droygam	Varieties of Snake	*Xenochorphis Sp.*
Droy gu		
Droythinglu		
Tan droy		
Grorui		

Table 23 Aquatic Animals and Fishes

Local name	*English*	*Scientific name*
Taneng	Pila	*Pila globosa*
Thongkoina	Unio	*Pinnotheres maculatus*
Ga	Crab	*Carcinus sp.*
Ngarin	Masta cembalus	*Macrognathus*
Kharui	Eel	*Monopterus albus*
Khakong	Prawn	*Palaemoiu mulcomsonii*
khagak	Lata fish	*C. orientalis*
Ngamu sengum	Lata fish (sp.)	*Garra gotyla*
Ukapi		*Anabas testusdineus*
Ngakijou		*L. guntea*
Kora / khabei		*Clarias batrachus*
Khameigi		*Colisa fasciatus*
Khawa		*Barilius dogarsinghi*
Erang kha		*Esomus manipurensis*
Phaboukha		Puntis chola

Table 24 Domesticated Animals

Local name	*English*	*Scientific name*
Gak	Pig	*Sus sp.*
Mewna	Cat	*Felis sp.*
Shee	Dog	*Canis familiaris*
Gai	Caw	*Bos indicus*
Goiloi	Buffalo	*Bos bubalus*

Table 25 Domesticated fowls

Local name	*English*	*Scientific name*
Loi	Hen	*Gallus gallus*
Phum	Duck	*Anas creca*

The people still depend on a variety of wild plants for their food. It bears enough evidence of the importance of gathering in the livelihood of the people. The fact that wild animals, birds and insects are the important source of animal protein of the people also shows that hunting and fishing still plays an important role in the subsistence economy of people.

They have their own method of food preparation and preservation. To make themselves free, to some extent, from the fear of scarcity of food, they also practise different methods of food preservation. It shows the hard life that they suffer in the struggle of existence.

Food Preparation

Cooking, with and without vessel, is the most important methods of food preparation prevelent among the Kabuis. The most common practice of cooking food without vessel is roasting or baking or steaming. Roots, tubers, stems, vegetables, fish, birds, and meats are generally cooked by roasting. Sometimes, vegetables, fish, insects like larva of bee are cooked by wrapping in plantain leaves and putting the same inside the burning paddy husk.

They cook either in earthen pots or metal vessels. However, they have the knowledge of cooking rice in green bamboo tubes. Most of the kitchen utensils like tongs, spoon, and drinking bowls are prepared from bamboo whereas items like dish and bowls are prepared from wood. Method of cooking rice is simple boiling and baking. The most common method of cooking for vegetables and meat is boiling with chilli, salt and indigenous spices. Vegetables are also cooked either with dry or fermented meat. Oil is rarely used in the food preparation. Vegetables or meat cooked with coarse powdered rice is known as *Gan hoi* and it is the common delicious food item of the people.

A special dish, called, *tam* is prepared by boiling vegetables or meat with fermented vegetables and meat, chilli, salt and indigenous spices. It is not only an item of daily dish but also an item of refreshment generally served in social functions.

***Tam* prepared from bamboo shoot :** Bamboo shoots which are grown wild are collected in the rainy season mainly in May, June, and July from the surrounding hills. The bamboo shoots are then cut into thin slices and boiled in plain water for about 20 to 30 minutes till the colour changes into yellow. Then, the boiled bamboo shoot is separated from the liquid and mixed with *Lumpui* (fermented beef), chilli, salt, wild coriander and wild spices. Dry pork (*Gagjam-Kangmei*) and liquid of the fermented mustard leaves (*ganang tam doi)* can also be used instead of *Lumpui* in this preparation. The remaining liquid is also used as curry. It may also be mentioned that bamboo shoot is an important item of food as boiled bamboo shoot is a compulsory item of curry in the season when it is abundantly found in the surrounding hills.

Duigan : *Duigan,* an alkali based curry, is one of the most common type of food item. The preparation is simple and made by boiling rice, chilli, salt, bamboo shoot, leaves of arum and mustard with an adequate quantity of alkali.

It is a type of curry prepared by boiling powdered rice or grain of rice with ginger leaves, *bamaroi, tanangnong*, turmeric, chilli and salt. Such a type of preparation can be made with dry or fresh meat or dry fish or *taneng* (snail). It has a special kind of flavour because of the addition of rice grains.

Preparation of Liquor

The people in general, drink four type of alcoholic beverages which are locally prepared from rice. They are locally known as *1) Timpui, 2) Pheijoubung 3) Jou-ngou 4) Jou-ju. Timpui* is prepared by fermentation of cooked rice without distillation whereas *pheijoubung* is prepared by fermentation of the boiled rice. But the main difference is that in the preparation of *pheijoubung* paddy husk is mixed with the boiled rice before fermentation. Earthen pots are used for the fermentation of timpui and *pheijoubung. Joungou* is another type of rice beer prepared by fermentation of powder rice of germinated paddy and soaked rice. It is prepared mainly in a wooden drum. *Jouju,* mainly prepared in the plain areas of Kabui settlement, is the liquor prepared by distillation.

However, among the christianised people this tradition is not in good taste.

Timpui : It is the beverage prepared by fermenting cooked rice. The preparation of *timpui* involves the following steps. First, usually, unrefined first generation husked rice is boiled and allowed to cool by spreading on *ghou* (round basket made of bamboo split having one and a half metre in diameter). In summer, the cooked rice has to be completely cooled down at room temperature before the process of fermentation but in winter it is not necessary. The boiled rice is then mixed with *Khai* (medicinal cake) at the rate of four or five *khai* (120gm) per three kg of the boiled rice. Then the mixture is put inside an earthen pot already cleaned and dried in the sunlight. The mixture is pressed slightly after putting in an earthen pot and the pot is covered with a piece of cloth or leaf of the *konghoo for* fermentation without putting water. The pot filled with the mixture is placed for about 4 days. On the fourth day when a pungent smell comes out, water is added to it in an approximate ratio of 4:3 (i.e. four liters of water to three kgs of boiled rice). The liquid, known as *timpui,* is now ready for consumption. The liquid is extracted by filtration. The residue after filtration is used as food for domestic animals like pig. Sometimes the fermented products as a whole have been consumed without filtration. In hilly areas, during the course of jhum cultivation this is the main item of refreshment of the people working in the field. Moreover it is also a favourite drink of the old people. People generally drink it before lunch and dinner.

Pheijuoubung. It is also a rice beer prepared by fermentation of the boiled rice. In the preparation of *pheijoubung* paddy husk is mixed with the boiled rice before fermentation. It differs from *timpui* in taste because of the addition of paddy husk to the cooked rice, while hot, before putting inside the pot for fermentation. Earthen pot is used for the fermentation of *pheijoubung*. Boiled rice is spread on a mat of bamboo split, *ghou* and thoroughly mixed with paddy husk while hot and then allowed to cool down. To this mixture a type of powdered yeast which was prepared earlier in the form of a cake is again added. The mixture is then ready for fermentation. Then it is put into an earthen vessel. In some cases, they do not use medicinal cake for fermentation. However, the mixture is well fermented. It is, however, said that the husk has certain properties that help fermentation and mixture the earthen pot which is primarily used for the preparation of beverage may perhaps contain some amount of yeast. These two factors may be responsible for the successful fermentation of the boiled rice without medicinal cake. The liquid may be used for the consumption after four or five days of fermentation. However, water must be added before drinking in the proportion of 4:3 i.e. four liters of water in 3 kgs of rice. In fact, this beverage cannot be preserved for more than 3 to 4 months. Sometimes, more than one person can drink together from the same pot by using separate drinking pipes at a time. As soon as the quantity of wine decreases they add more water, churn it properly and then start drinking again. It is interesting to note that even the womenfolks also enjoy this type of beverage.

Jou-ngou : It is a type of rice beer prepared out of powdered germinated paddy. In the preparation of this kind, paddy is soaked in water for about one day in an earthen pot or in a basket. The soaked paddy is then transferred to a dry basket and covered with the leaves of wild fig, and kept for three days in a shade to start germination. If the germination is not to that of the desired extent, warm water is poured over the partially germinated paddy to increase the rate of germination. The germinated paddy locally known as *napok* is spread on a mat *(ghou)* to make it dry in the sunlight. It is again mixed with soaked and dried rice grains. Then the mixture is made into powdered with the help of mortar and pestle. It is carefully pressed in a wooden barrel (*bu*) or earthen pot (*lai*). Another liquid known as *joukhai* is added to it. The *joukhai* is prepared out of a paste of powdered rice and *napok* which is finally liquidized by mixing with warm water. Then the mixture is well churned with a *bamboo* or wooden stirrer (*ballatai*). Churning repeats after half an hour. When the contents become cooled down, water is added again to the desired extent and covered with plantain leaf or *Kanghoo.* It is then, kept in a cold place for about five days. It becomes warm again within that period then it is ready for consumption. The entire members of the family, irrespective of sex and age, consume it in lieu of tea. It is mandatory for a woman to drink it after delivery. By far, girls usually use this type of drink for fair complexion. It is also offered to god at the time of rituals as well as to the visitors.

Jou-ju : It is a strong alcoholic beverage prepared by distillation of fermented rice. Preparation of *jou ju* is quite similar with that of *timpui* upto the stage of the fermentation. Fermented rice is boiled in a suitable pot which is covered with another pot having holes at the bottom. It is covered again with a pot containing cold water just to restrict the evaporation outside and to condense the vapour into liquid. Inside the middle pot, a piece of tin is placed to collect the condensed liquid in such a way that one end of the tin is kept hanging from the rim of the pot while the other end having a tube is made passing out through the pot that collects the distilled liquid.

Preparation of *Khai* (medicinal cake / rice cake) :

Rice is soaked in water for about 30 to 40 minutes and collected in a basket. Then it is powdered with the help of mortar and pestle. A bark of a tree locally known as *Yangli,* which is made into powder, is added to the powdered rice to make a paste which is finally prepared into cakes. If necessary, more water may be added. Small rounded cakes are prepared from these paste and they are placed above the paddy husk kept spread in a warm room. It is again covered by a thick cloth or jute sack to hasten the process of fermentation. In the fourth day when a pungent smell comes out, the cloth is removed and the cake is ready for use as well as for preservation.

It has been reported that the four types of alcoholic beverages are prepared by the majority of the families of Kabui villages located in the valley. In the interior Kabui villages, the people generally drink the fermented alcoholic beverages in their day to day life and on ritual occasions. They seldom drink distilled liquor.

Preservation of Food :

It is a common practice among the Kabuis to store the food items, such as dry meat, vegetables, beans and maize on the different tiers of a hanging rack constructed atop the fireplace. Bamboo tubes and earthen pots containing fermented liquid of mustard leaves, fermented meat and oil products of meat are also stored on this rack. All kinds of crops including paddy are also kept dried on the tiers before pounding. The smoke that emits from the fireplace is believed to have prevented the materials from the attack of the fungus and insects. Such types of storages are meant for lean season. The ways how the Kabuis preserve their food stuff for future use are briefly described as follows :

Ganang tamdoi : The mustard leaves collected from their jhum fields normally in the winter season are placed in the spreading baskets for nearly four to five days or till the green leaves turn into yellow. These are exposed in the sun to make them warm. The weathered leaves are kept pressed inside a Ka (carrying basket) placed on a wooden dish meant for collection of the fermented liquid. After four or five days, when a pungent smell comes out of the leaves, these are pressed with both the hands so as to squeeze out the liquid from the leaves. Afterwards, it is boiled in a vessel to form a condensed liquid known as *Ganang Tamdoi.* It can be preserved for about two years. In another method, the leaves that are collected from the field are either boiled in a pot or crushed in a mortar and spread the leaves in the sunlight for a few minute. Then, these boiled or crushed leaves are put in an earthen pot covered with *Loikhum* for successful fermentation.

Gangang kang (Dry mustard leave): The dried leaves are called *ganang kang*. They are preserved placing on the *Keikang* (atop the fire rack) to avoid the attack from bacteria and other insects.

Thunkheng (Bamboo shoot) : Bamboo shoot can be preserved for about one year after fermentation. For large scale preservation, they preserve it inside a dug out pit on the hill slope. However, for small scale preservation, they preserve it in baskets or in earthen pots. Before putting the bamboo shoots either in the basket or the pit they are wrapped in the leaves of *Luikhom* to avoid from the direct contact with air. Before fermentation, the bamboo shoots are cut into small pieces/ slices after removing the scales.

Khuithu (Fermented soya bean) : It is also an important item of fermented food prepared from soyabean. In the process of preparation, the soyabean is properly boiled with water for about 8 hours continuously. The boiled soya bean is then separated from the liquid and washed with cold water twice. It is then wrapped in a local leaf known as *Loikhom* and put on *Keikang* for five days. Generally after five days when the soyabean is fermented it is again backed in the sun to make it dried so as to preserve for a longer period.

Gankheng Khui (Fermented seed of Rossella) : The fermentation process of the seed of rossella is similar to that of the soya bean. Even the dry leaves of this plant is also preserved by making dry them in the sun.

***Gakjan-Kangme*i** (Dry pork) : The prepared pork pieces are fried in a vessel. When fried, automatically oil comes out of the flesh. The oil collected in a bottle or in a vessel of bamboo. It can be used as oil in the preparation of curry as well as hair oil. It is locally called *gak-thao*. The fried pork is collected in a basket and stored on the rack atop the fire place. It can not be preserved not more than 3 months since it is oily.

Jantha ningmei (Fermented pork) : The inner fat portion of the pig is preserved in a bamboo tube covered tightly with plantain leaf. It is placed on the rack atop the fire place. The fermented meat can be used after one month and can also be preserved for about one year. It is used in curry preparation.

Gak thao (Oil prepared from pork) : It is type of oil extracted from the pork by simply frying it in a vessel. When it cools it looks like the ghee. Sometimes it is also used as hair oil.

Lumpui (Cooked and fermented meat) : Either pork or beef along intestine is boiled with salt, chilli, indigenous spices like *ba-maroi* and *ganangnong* and preserved in an earthen pot covered with plantain leaf or a bowl. It can be preserved for a long time even more than 2 years. However, if needed it can be used after one week of its preparation. It is the most common ingredient for the preparation of curry.

Goigi-kang (Dry beef) : For the preparation of dried beef, it is simply roasted or grilled and kept on the rack above the fire place. It can be used in the preparation of *Tam* as well as curry. The most suitable herb used in the preparation of *goigi-tam* is *kangkru* (a variety of underground stem with pungent smell).

Besides, there is a practice of preserving bones of cattles for future use.

A number of bones including charred pieces and bone tools are found from Khangkhui cave in Ukhrul District of Manipur. Moreover, snails are also reported from the Neolithic site at Napachik in Manipur (Singh, 1997). As the Kabuis also consume and preserve meat and snail, the food habit of the Kabuis seems to have some similarities with that of the prehistoric man in Manipur. On the basis of the understanding inferred from the observed ethnographic facts about the Kabui mode of consumption and preservation of food we may reconstruct the mode of consumption and preservation of food which might be prevalent among the prehistoric man who are supposed to have settled Manipur in the prehistoric past by drawing a parallelism between the two - one established through observation and the other established through the study of prehistoric artifacts.

Household implements

Gu-panthon, Gu-mei (Mortar and pestle) : It is a cup shaped wooden kitchenware usually made out of a log, and used for grinding and pounding purposes. A handle is provided on the side of the body by carving out from the wood itself. It measures about 12cm in height and 20cm in diameter. The rim is thick and measures about 3cm (Plate 51:C). *Gu-mei* is a piece of a log, used as pestle for grinding purposes. Usually the working end is broader than the butt end. It measures about 20cm in length.

Panthon, Mei (Mortar and pestle): This is a husking and pounding implement. A block of a wood or a portion of a trunk of a tree is scooped out and used as mortar. Sometimes three or four scooped out portions are present in a long mortar. It is about 2m length, 60cm in breadth and 60cm in thickness (Plate 4).

The pestle is a polished wooden piece, about 2m in length and 6 to 7cm in diameter. Working end is provided with a ferrule or a ring of iron.

The mortar and pestle is customarily kept in the first room or the verandah of a house so that it may be conveniently used by women before day break. A circular winnowing basket is used winnow the pounded paddy grains by way of taking some food grains in the winnowing fan and tossing off the husks.

Hanthai (Bamboo tube) : It is a vessel made out of a bamboo of one internode in such a way that one node is used as the base of the vessel. It is used for the collection of water. Females generally carry about 5 to 6 *Hanthais* at a time keeping in a carrying basket. It measures about 36cm in length and 10cm in diameter.

Goi-chei jou-bung (Mithun horn) : Mithun horn of reasonable size is used for drinking purpose, specially for rice beer or liquor. Such a horn used as drinking vessel has decorative horn guard and made by weaving cane strips. The Kabuis consider such a horn as an important cultural artefact that deserves careful preservation (Plate 51: A and 64).

Humsaf jou bong (Bamboo cup) : Bamboo cup of reasonable sizes are also used for drinking purposes preferably for rice beer or liquor. It measures about 13cm in height and 9.5cm in diameter (Plate 51: B).

Bu (Wooden barrel) : It is a barrel made out of a log of wood by hollowing the inner portion of the log out with a simple tool and technique. The butt end is also provided with a stand having 3 to 4 legs formed by carving out some portion of the log itself. This particular implement is used mainly for the preparation of rice beer (*Joungou*). It measures about 56cm in length and 30cm in diameter (Plate 52).

Ta dop (Gourd mug) : It is made out of a small sized dried bitter gourd by making a rounded hole on the side of the body (Plate 53).

Zou-mu (Gourd wine pot) : It is a large and dried bitter gourd receptacle for keeping and carrying rice beer while going to the jhum field. It measures about 45cm in height, and 25cm in diameter at the body (Plate 54).

Jou-lai (Earthen wine pot) : It is an earthen pot usually meant for the preparation and also for keeping rice beer while drinking. Cane strips are nicely woven around the body of the pot not only for decoration but also for protection (Plate 55, 56). The wine pots found in the valley are larger in size and not decorated with can strips (Plate 56). It measures about 25cm in height at the body and 30cm and 15cm are the diameters at the middle and at the mouth of the body of the pot

Dui-lai (Earthen water pot) : A few types of ceramic pots that they purchase from the valley people are used by the Kabuis. (Plate 57).

Maigang, Mailu (Fire making wood and bamboo strip) : It is a wooden implement used for making fire by friction. It consists of a long cylindrical wooden log of about 56 cm long and 6 cm in diameter (*Meigang*), a bamboo strip of about 64 cm long called *Mailu* and some bamboo fibres called *Thut*. At one end of the *Meigang* five to six grooves are provided for placing the *Mailu* while rubbing. It is again splitted into two equal halves for a length of about 20 cm keeping a small gap by inserting either a piece of wood or bamboo in between the two halves to facilitate in producing fire. This end is used for producing fire whereas the opposite end of the *Maigang* is used for holding during manipulation.

In practice, the manipulator tightly presses the surface of the butt end of *Maigang* by his right foot and also held the two ends of *Mailu that* pass through the groove provided at the working ends of *Maigang* by his hands. Keeping the *Thut* in contact with *Maigang* he pulls the *Mailu* up and down continuously for about three to five minutes by slightly kneeling down the body to make fire. During this process females are strictly prohibited believing that in their presence fire will not come out. It is also

Plate 51 : A and B. Village elders drinking rice beer using A. Goicheibung (mithun horn) and B. Humsaf jou-bong (bamboo cup) C. Gu-panthon -wooden mortar

Plate 52 : Bu-wooden barrel with three legs

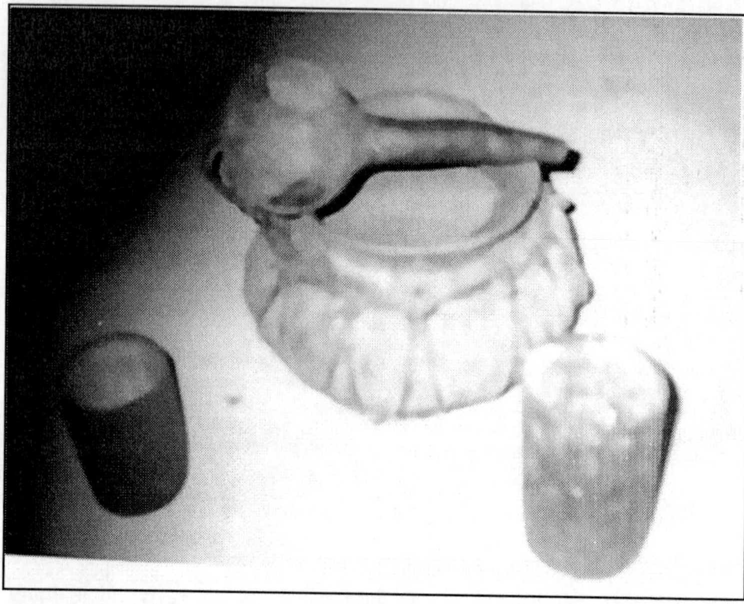

Plate 53 : Ta-dop (small gourd mug)

Plate 54 : Jou-mu (large gourd wine vessel)

Plate 55 : Earthen wine pot protected with cane strip

Plate 56 : Earthen wine pot of smooth surface

Plate 57 : Dui-lai- Earthen water pot

informed that in early days each household used to posses two *Maigang* one for jhum field and other for the household use. Nowadays such a method of fire making is still used, as an unavoidable cultural practice in *Gan ngai* and *Chagangai* festivals as well as in the ritual practices performed on the eve of new settlement or resettlement of villages (Plate 58).

La-tai-kwak (Bamboo stirrer) : It is a paddle or stirrer made of a bamboo having two nodes. One of the nodes is made into a spoon shaped structure whereas the other node that tapers towards the end forms the handle. It measures about 36 cm in length (Plate 59).

Kwak dung (Wooden plate) : It is a more or less rectangular wooden plate meant for keeping meat. Usually two types of plate – a larger one and a smaller one are found among the Kabuis. The larger plate is more elongated in shape and measures about 140cm in length with a breadth of about 45cm and a height of about 10cm, while the smaller plate measures about 110cm in length with a breadth of about 80cm and height of 5cm (Plate 60: A and B).

Thing-nap-kwak (Wooden dish) : It is a traditional circular wooden dish carved out from a flat wood. It measures about 26cm in diameter and about 5cm in height (Plate 61).

Thing-nap-kwak-phai (Wooden dish with stand) : It is a wooden dish made from large log of wood. It has four legs attached to a circular rim which serves as stand of the dish. Such a dish having different sizes is found to be used by the Kabuis. Normally it measures about 55cm in diameter and about 17cm in height (Plate 62).

Thing-tam-kwak-phai (Wooden bowl with stand) : Wooden bowl of three legs attached to a circular rim is also found among the Kabuis. The upper rim of the bowl is decorated with smaller longitudinal groves. The depth of the bowl is prominent. Normally the diameter of the bowl measures about 23cm and the height about 17cm (Plate 63).

Kampho (Small basket) : It is a small receptacle made of bamboo and cane strips and used by the womenfolks at the time of sowing seed. It measures about 20cm in height and about 12cm in diameter at the mouth (Plate 65: A and B).

Nappurak (Paddy with stalk carrying basket) : It is made of bamboo, cane and wood. It is generally used by the menfolks at the jhum field during harvesting to carry the bunch of paddy stalk. The shape of the basket is more or less cylindrical and tapers slightly towards the bottom where it rests on a rectangular base frame. One side of it is opened longitudinally to facilitate its volume size. It is usually carried by placing the strap that is attached to the basket upon the head with the basket resting on the back. The normal posture of the person carrying such baskets is inclined at an angle of about 30° to 45°. To ease the

Plate 58 : Fire making with a log-Meigang (A) and a string-Meilu (B)

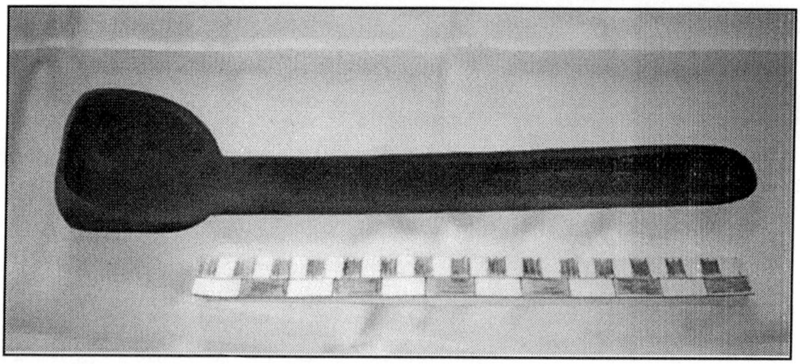

Plate 59 : La-tai-kwak -Bamboo stirrer

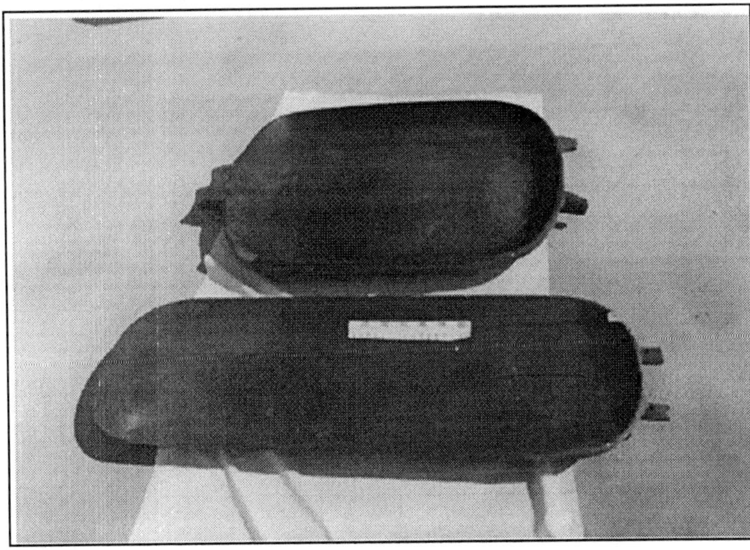

Plate 60 : Large wooden dishes for keeping dressed meat

Plate 61 : Thing nap-kwak - Wooden dish

Plate 62 : Thing tam-kwak phai- Bowl with stand (L)

Plate : 63 Thing nap-kwak phai- Dish with stand (R)

Plate 64 : Goi-chei-jou-bung-A mithun horn-used as a drinking vessel

task of carrying heavily laden baskets, they use a shoulder-length wooden appliance fixed to the strap. This appliance is placed horizontally on to the nape of the neck, but mainly borne by the shoulder. Normally such a basket measures 79cm in height, with a diameter of about 38cm (Plate 65: D).

Kaluang (Carrying basket) : It is a carrying basket made of bamboo cane and fibre of bimli jute (*Gankheng*). It is somewhat conical in shape and measures about 48cm in height and 38cm in diameter at the mouth. It is used by both males and females for carrying paddy and rice. While carrying the basket, the strap made of *Gankheng riang* and cane which is attached to the basket is placed upon the head. The weaving pattern of the basket is twilling type. Its capacity is about 25 kg.

Rangtang-ka / ka (carrying basket) : It is also a carrying basket made of bamboo cane and fibre of bimli jute (*Gankheng*). It is somewhat conical in shape and measures about 36cm in height and 36cm in diameter at the mouth. It is used by both males and females for carrying firewood. Females use this basket mainly for the collection of vegetables and for fetching water keeping the bamboo tubes or containers in the basket. While carrying the basket, the strap made of *Gankheng riang* and cane which is attached to the basket is placed upon the head. The weaving pattern of the basket is open hexagonal type. This basket is an important item of dowry among the Kabuis (Plate 65: E).

Khok (Storing basket) : It is a storing basket made of bamboo and cane. It is somewhat conical in shape and measures about 82cm in height and 46cm in diameter at the mouth. It consists of two parts- larger body having conical shape and a pointed lid. Two types of such baskets are found - one for storing clothes and the other for storing ornaments. The former is an essential item of dowry (Plate 66 and 67).

Nangmoi (Spindle whorl) : It is an implement made of bamboo split and a piece of a flat rounded pebble having a hole at the middle. The rod is inserted into the pebble in such a way that the latter divides the former into a longer, pointed working end and a shorter handle. The use of pebble is meant for adding weight which facilitates the rotation of the rod of the thread while spinning. Sometimes, *Garing* (seed of a creeper) or piece of hard cover of bitter gourd is also used as thread guard (Plate 68).

Langpai (Threshing bow) : It is a bow made of bamboo strips and cane strings. It is used for tanning cotton. It measures about 100cm in length.

Ku-wak (Adze) : It is a carpentry tool of adze type. The implement is made of two parts – a wooden shaft as handle and an iron blade of conical shape. The iron blade is attached forming an angle of about 80^0 to the shaft. The blade measures about 20cm in length and 8cm in breadth while the shaft measures about 60cm in length and 3cm in diameter (Plate 69).

Guliang (Sacks) : Grain sacs are usually made of course cotton yarn. According to the mode of use different sizes of sacs are made. The larger ones can store a volume of about 120 kg.

Langpa/Langom (wooden bed) : It is a wooden bed having a length of about 3m and a breadth of about 1m. The leg of the bed is rudimentary and supported by the logs under the planks (Plate 70: A and B).

Thing-piban (Wooden pillow) : A longitudinal half of a log having a diameter of about 30cm and a length of about 60cm is used as pillow.

Plate 65 : A & B. Kampho; C. Simpai; D. Napurrak; E. Ka; F. Kaluang

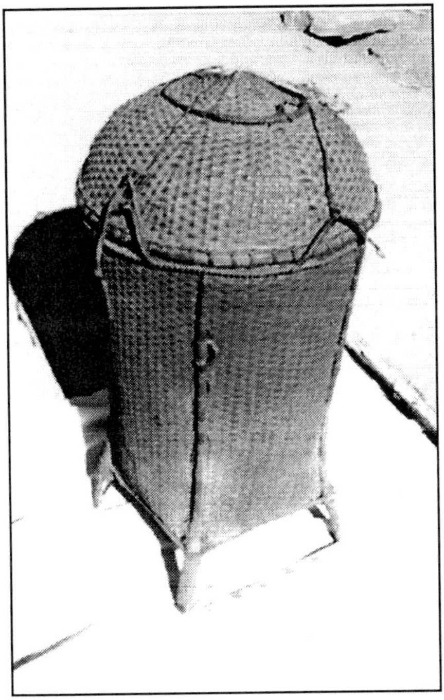

Plate 66 : Khok (Basket for storing clothes)

Plate 67 : *Khok* - Basket for keeping ornaments

Plate 68 : *Nangmoi* -Spindle whorl

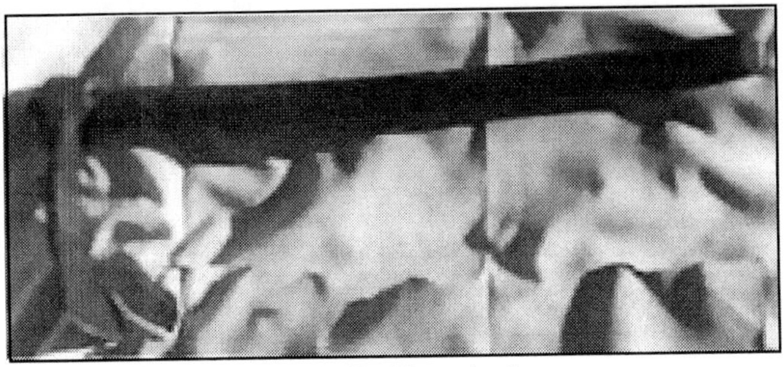

Plate 69 : *Ku-wak* adze

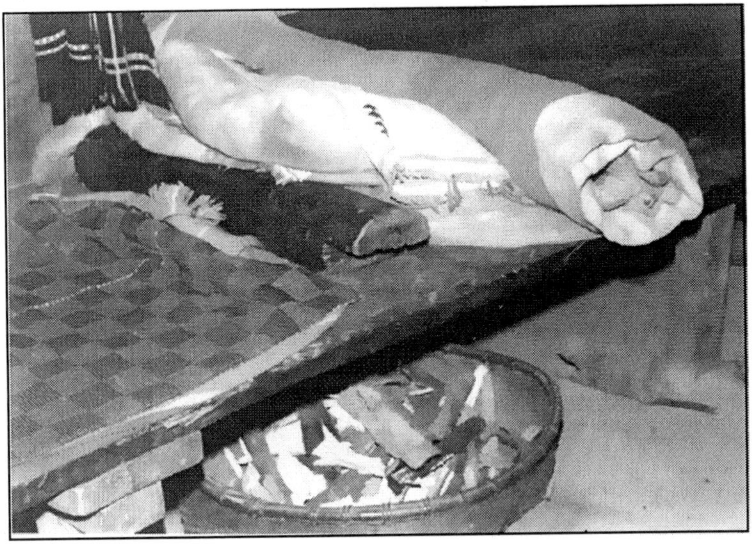

Plate 70 : *A. Langpa* / Langom Wooden bed *B. Thing-piban* Wooden pillow

4

Prehistoric Evidences

Prehistoric Cultures of Manipur

The history of archaeological research in Manipur may trace back as early as 1935, when late W. Yumjao Singh started his spade work on historical archaeology. Systematic archaeological investigation, however, was started only in 1967 when O.K. Singh started archaeological excavations in different parts of the State. The earlier reports of the British administrators also throw light on the archaeological relics of Manipur, specially about the distribution of megaliths in tribal inhabited hilly areas of Manipur. The State Archaeology Department was established by the State Government in 1978, with a view to exploring and preserving the past cultures of Manipur.

A random survey among the Meiteis in the valley and the tribals in the hills had been conducted during 1967-68, thereby collecting as many as 43 neoliths (Singh *et al*, 1969).

Another exploration of the Phunan site at Thoubal District during March, 1968 resulted in the discovery of two very large grinding stones, ground and polished neoliths of quadrangular shape and potsherds of incised, cord-marked and impressed circles.

Again, in 1969 an exploration was made at Khangkhui cave and palaeolithic remains consisting of both stone and bone tools along with faunal remains were discovered (I.A.R.

1968-69). A pebble chopper that is presently housed in the State Museum, Government of Manipur had been discovered in an open air site exploration made in 1974 at Machi, a village located on the top of a hill range bordering the south eastern corner of Manipur valley (Singh, 1980). In 1979 a cave site exploration was carried out at Tharon and a number of edge ground pebble tools were discovered (I.A.R, 1980-81). An important archaeological site called, Napachik at Wangoo in the Bishnunpur District of Manipur Valley was excavated in 1981 and 1985 and many artifacts consisting of triangular neoliths with rounded sides, tripod wares decorated with cordmarks, pottery spindle whorls, microliths, edge ground knife and grinding stone were discovered from the site. All the finds are presently housed in the State Archaeology, Government of Manipur.

In 1983 the Songbu cave site located at Chandel District near Myanmar border was explored and stone artifacts comprising scraper, flake, split pebble and core tool were collected (I.A.R. 1983-84). Many Stone Age relics, such as scrapers, blades, choppers, pebble-pick and a good number of cord marked potsherds were also collected from Nongpok Keithelmanbi in Thoubal river Valley in excavations carried out during the period of 1982-84 (Singh, 1986). In 1989 the reexploration of Tharon cave was done resulting in the discovery of more edge ground pebble artifacts that are comparable with those of the South-East Asian Hoabinhian artifacts. In 1989 another open air site at Singtom in Chandel District was explored and Palaeolithic tools consisting of ovate type of hand axe and flakes were discovered (Singh and Singh, 1991). In 1990 an excavation, carried out at Laimanai site at Kakching, results in the discovery of cord marked tripod wares, stone tools consisting of small chisel, quadrangular adze, quadrangular hoe blade, grinding stone, waste flakes and a flat pebble hammer stone. The tripod ware and the triangular hoe blade, comparable with those from the Napachick site, suggest the existence of a Neolithic tripod ware culture in Manipur valley.

The discovery of the artifacts and tools used by man bears the evidences of human habitation in different parts of Manipur during stone age period. The culture of those people, on the basis of typology of the tools so far discovered from different parts of Manipur, may be classified into Old Stone Age (Palaeolithic), Middle Stone Age (Hoabinhian) and New Stone Age (Neolithic) Cultures.

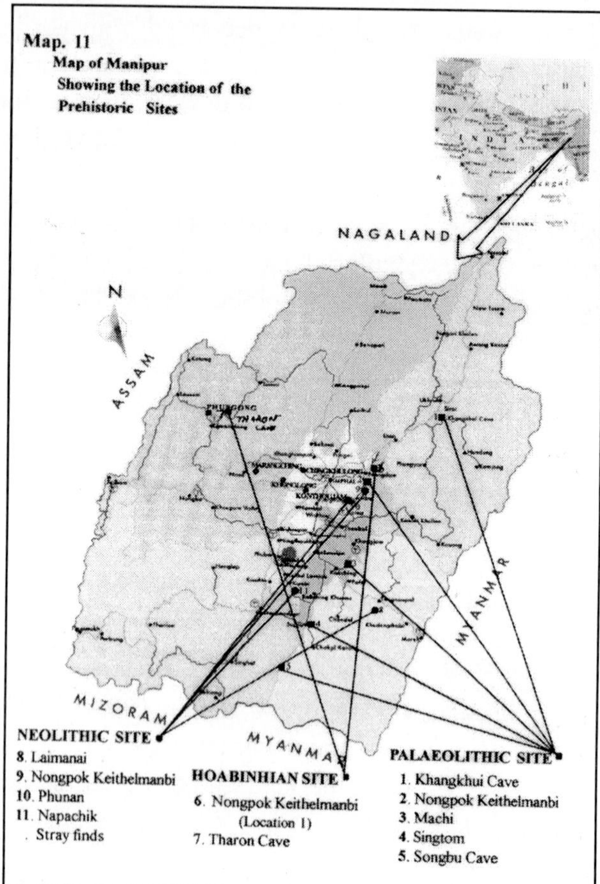

Map. 11
Map of Manipur Showing the Location of the Prehistoric Sites

Palaeolithic Culture

About the prehistoric sites from where artifacts of Old Stone Age culture have been discovered, mention may be made of the Songbu caves of Chandel District and Khangkhui cave of Ukhrul District. Besides these three other important open air sites are –Nongpok Keithelmanbi in Senapati District, Singtom and Machi in Chandel District (O.K. Singh, 1997).

Songbu cave site

The Songbu cave site is located in the midst of thickly forested hill ranges in Chandel District of Manipur very near to Myanmar. The cave looks like an arc with an opening towards south-east. The roof of the cave that slopes towards the back measures about 0.8m in height at the posterior end and 1.8m at the mouth. The broadest width of the cave measures 6.6m. There is a deep gorge just in front of the cave which is a perennial source of water. The rock type is of fine quartzitic sandstone. Almost all the cave deposits have been disturbed by the habitation of the Zou tribe during the Second World War.

The stone tools of the Songbu cave consist of split pebble, hand axe, borer-cum-scraper, points, blade flake, knife, and flake.

Split pebble – The tool is a transversely split pebble of black metamorphic rock with a narrow pointed end and a number of shallow and slender flake scars. It can be used in scooping and scraping purposes. It measures about 9.5 x 4 x 4cm, (Fig. 17.3).

Hand axe : The tool is triangular in shape, only dorsal surface is thoroughly worked with large but shallow primary flakings while the ventral surface is formed by the cortex except some primary flakings at the flat thick butt end. It is biconvex in cross section. It measures 10.8 x 9.1 x 6.7cm, (Fig. 17.6).

Borer- scraper : It is made on a lump of fine sandstone by striking off two primary flakes from both the surfaces. The edge of the borer is prepared by striking off one flake from each side on the ventral surface with step and free flaking techniques and by further retouching to produce a sharp notch at one side. It measures 12 x 9.8 x 4.3cm (Fig. 18.1).

Blade flake **:** In this type of tool either one or both the sides are sharp where the length is more than the breadth. Cross section is triangular. The number of such type of artifacts found in the site are three in number, (Fig. 17 :1,2).

Points **:** It is a flake tool made on a triangular flake of sandstone. It has a short ridge on the dorsal side and a slightly concave main flake surface with plain striking platform. The flakes that have produced two primary flake scars and step flake scars at the tip of the dorsal surface of the tool might have been stuck off prior to detachment of the flakes from the core. It measures 6.2 x 6.2 x 1.8cm, (Fig. 17: 5).

Knife **:** It is made on a sandstone flake with a plain platform and a small deep notch on the thicker side. It may be probably for pressing with finger at the time of use. The curved sharp edge is produced by removing a thin flake from the ventral surface, while the dorsal surface is of cortex except a small flake scar near the platform. It is unrolled, slightly weathered and measures 6.8 x 5.3 x 1.9cm, (Fig.18.2).

Flake **:** It is a very large and thin triangular flake of sandstone. It has a plain platform with diffused bulb of percussion on the slightly concave main flake surface. The dorsal surface is worked thoroughly with flat primary flakings. It is made by levalloisian technique. It measures 8.8x15.7x2.7cm, (Fig. 18.3).

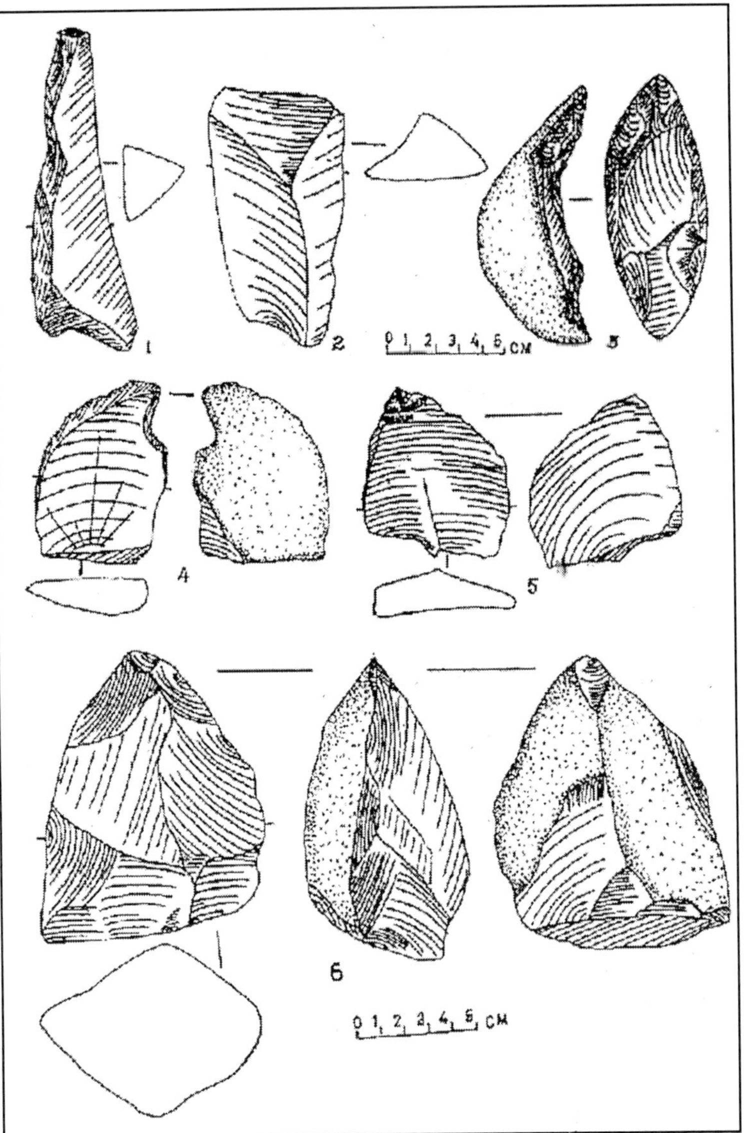

Fig. 17. Stone artifacts of Songbu cave, 1-2, Blades; 3. Split pebble; 4. Knife on flake; 5. Point on flake; 6. Hand axe (Singh, 1997: 22, Fig. 6)

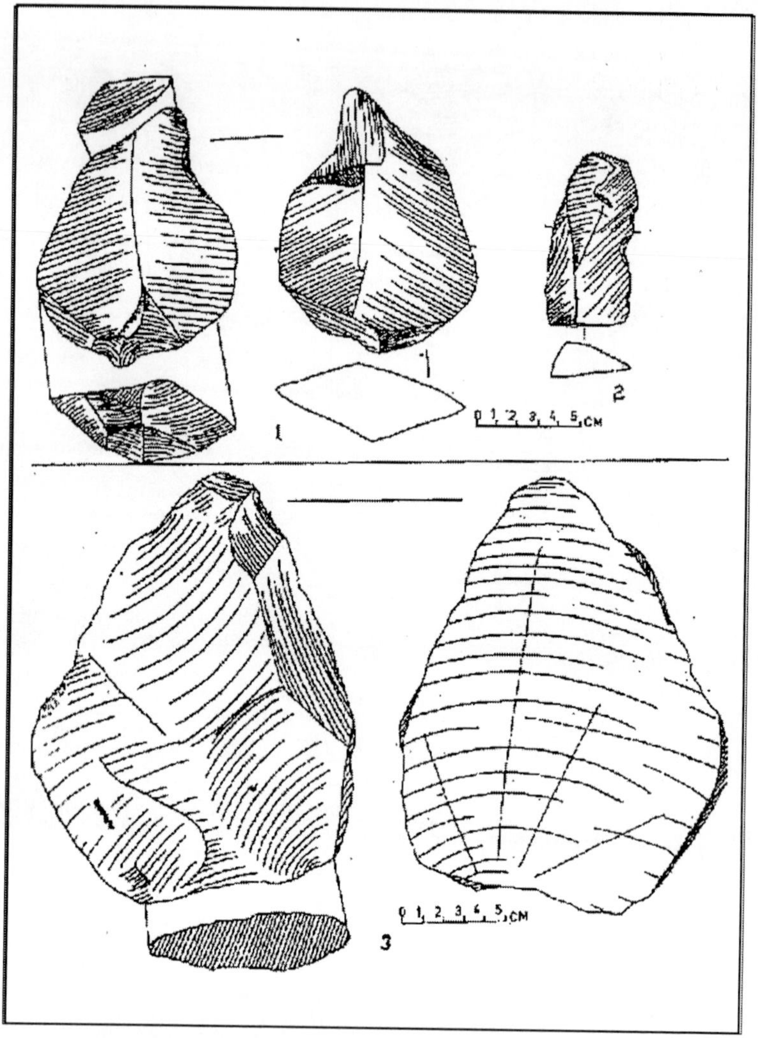

Fig. 18. Flake artifacts of Songbu Cave : 1. Borer ; 2. Knife ; 3. large flake with plain plateform and diffused bulb of percussion (Singh, 1997: 23, Fig. 7)

Khangkhui Cave Site

Another important palaeolithic site is the Khangkhui cave located near Khangkhui Khullen which is on a hill range about 11 km to the south-east of Ukhrul town, Ukhrul District, Manipur and it is at an altitude of 1767m above MSL. The rock type of the site is limestone of cretaceous origin. There are four caves at this site, of which Cave no. 1 and 2 are on the western slope and cave no. 3 and 4 are on the eastern slope of the hill.

The cave no. 1 is very long like a tunnel and has a narrow entrance. Inside is dark and damp. From the entrance of this cave a unique type of chopper and a heavily weathered hand axe have been explored. The cave no.2. is dome-shaped and is situated at a short distance to the north of cave no.1 at a little higher elevation. It is completely open and faces to the west. No artifact has been discovered from this cave.

Cave no. 3 is the biggest and located near the peak of the hillock, while cave no. 4 is on the northern side of the cave no.3 but at a lower altitude. The cave no.4 goes 7.16m vertically down from the roof of the cave mouth and bears no artifact. The cave no.3 has two entrances facing east and south-east respectively and the walls taper towards the back. In 1969 and 1972 O.K. Singh made an excavation in cave no.3 and unearthed stone and bone artifacts along with faunal remains.

The excavation exposes four layers in digging up to the depth of 152.3cm. The bottom layer (L_4) which is 45.7cm thick does not yield any tool except a broken piece of fine sandstone pebble and a few pieces of shale. It is brown in colour. This layer is overlaid by a dark gray brown coloured soil of 25.3cm thick. From this third layer (L_3) a bone tool (scarper), blade, end scraper, points, knife, tubular flakes and large fluted core of sandstone are unearthed. Associated remains are the teeth of herbivorous animals, probably of deer. Resting on this third layer there is a deposit of about 63.5cm thick pale brown coloured soil. This is a second layer (L_2). This layer contains points, blades, burins, flake-blades, small fluted cores and bone tools including blades, scrapers and points. The first layer (L_1) has a thickness of 17.8cm and dark brown in colour. It yields the largest number of artifacts which are mostly made on flakes and dominated by the end scrapers. Other artifacts from this layer are core scraper, side scraper, knife, tanged point, burin etc. Teeth probably of deer are also unearthed in association with the artifacts (Singh, 1980:151).

The exposed soil profile from the top downwards indicates two shorter wet phases favouring dense vegetation growth and two longer dry phases which do not favour the vegetation growth. This fact is again further supported by the presence of the teeth of herbivorous animals including deer, bos and sus in the first and third layers (Singh, 1980).

The tools of Khangkhui cave may be categorized into two, namely, stone implements and bone implements.

Stone Tool Industry

The classification of the Stone tool industry of Khangkhui cave by O.K. Singh (1997) is shown in the following Table 26.

Table 26 Artifact types from Khangkhui Cave

Artifacts	*Number of layers*				*Total*	*p.c.*
	1	*2*	*3*	*4*		
Blades	9	5	4	-	18	13.04
Points	9	11	3	-	23	16.66
Scrapers	6	8	-	-	14	10.14
Borers	2	5	-	-	7	5.07
Burins	-	5	-	-	5	3.62
Microliths	10	2	-	-	12	8.69
Chopping tool	1	2	-	-	3	2.17
Hand axe	-	1	1	-	2	1.44
Cleavers	-	2	-	-	2	1.44
Flakes	7	29	6	-	42	30.43
cores	4	6	-	-	10	7.24
Total	48	76			138	99.94

O.K. Singh, 1997, Table -2

Majority of the tools are made of limestone, while a few artifacts are of sandstone and chert. Most of the tools are made on small flakes with or without prepared platforms. However, some of the tools are struck off from the prepared discord and tortoise cores, (Fig. 20: 26, 27, 32) and a few have parts of the faceted platforms and diffused bulb of percussion. In some cases the flakes exhibit longitudinal edge, the beveled being done on the ventral surface. These could be used without purposes. Some of the flakes in this series may be made by the advanced method of flaking similar to the levalloisean technique. Retouching of the flakes is very rare and confined to the working edge of the tool, that too only on the upper surface, while the main flake surface is unretouched except in the case of a tanged point, (Fig. 21: 5). The tools made on flakes consists of various types of scrapers, points, burins, and borers. Scrapers include end scraper, side scraper, round scraper, core scraper and nose scraper, (Fig. 20: 11; 21 : 1-4) of which the end scraper and side scraper are predominant. Points form the largest frequency in the classified artifact types and include triangular point, tanged point, round-based point and transverse edge. These points could be used as tip of the missiles, except a few of the tanged points that could be used as lance head. Retouching of these points is marginally done at the side, (Fig. 20: 12) or to produce the tang, (Fig. 20: 17, 21: 5), otherwise no secondary working is evident after detaching from the core.

Blades form the second largest stone tool type in the collection. To obtain these blades first two parallel flakes have been struck off from the core and then the blades are detatched from the core by applying soft hammer technique, and bipolar technique in case of the blades with mid-ridges on both the surfaces. There is the evidence of using punch technique in detatching small and short blades as indicated by the flat core with fluted scars, (Fig. 20:6). Most of the blades are not retouched, except a few, (Fig. 20 :4) in which the backs are blunted. Some of the blades also have truncated ends (Fig. 20:3,5).

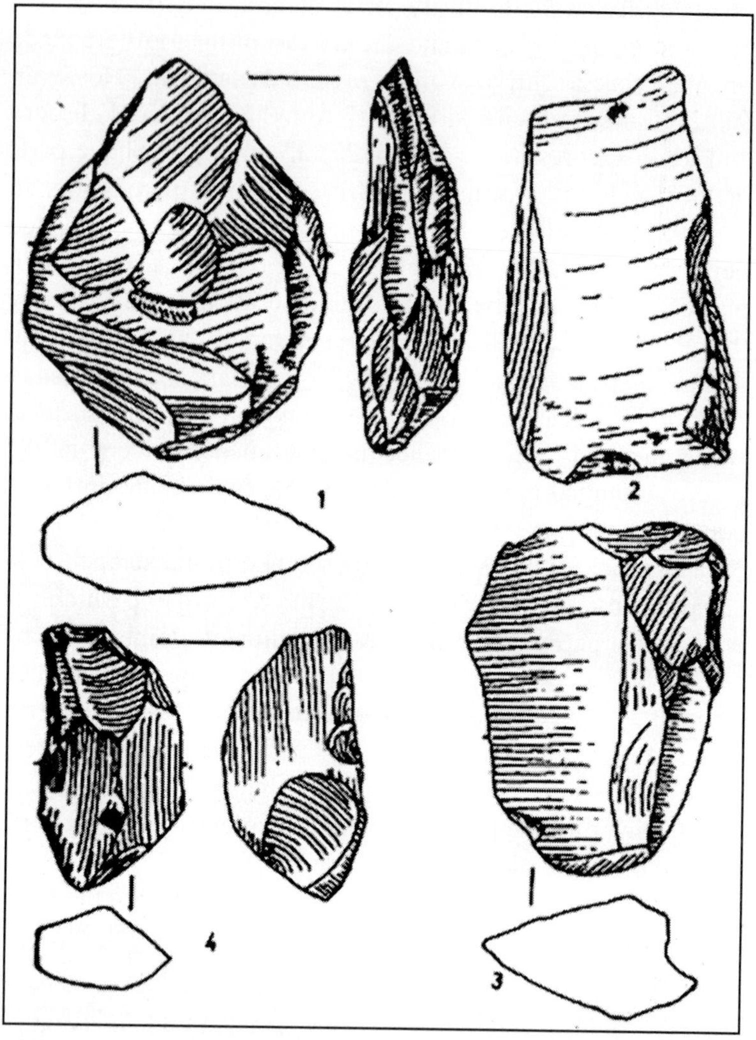

Fig. 19. Core tools of Khangkhui Cave no. 3 1. Cordiform handaxe ; 2- 3. Cleavers ; 4. Bifacial chopper

(Singh, 1997: 35, Fig. 14)

There are also a few microliths in the collection. They are of non geometric type and include blades, points and one chisel-edged microlith, (Fig.20:18-21); these range in size from 2.7 to 1.8 cm in length, 1.3 to 0.7cm in breadth and 0.8 to 0.3cm in thickness. These microliths might have been detached from prepared cores and have at least one mid ridge on the dorsal surface.

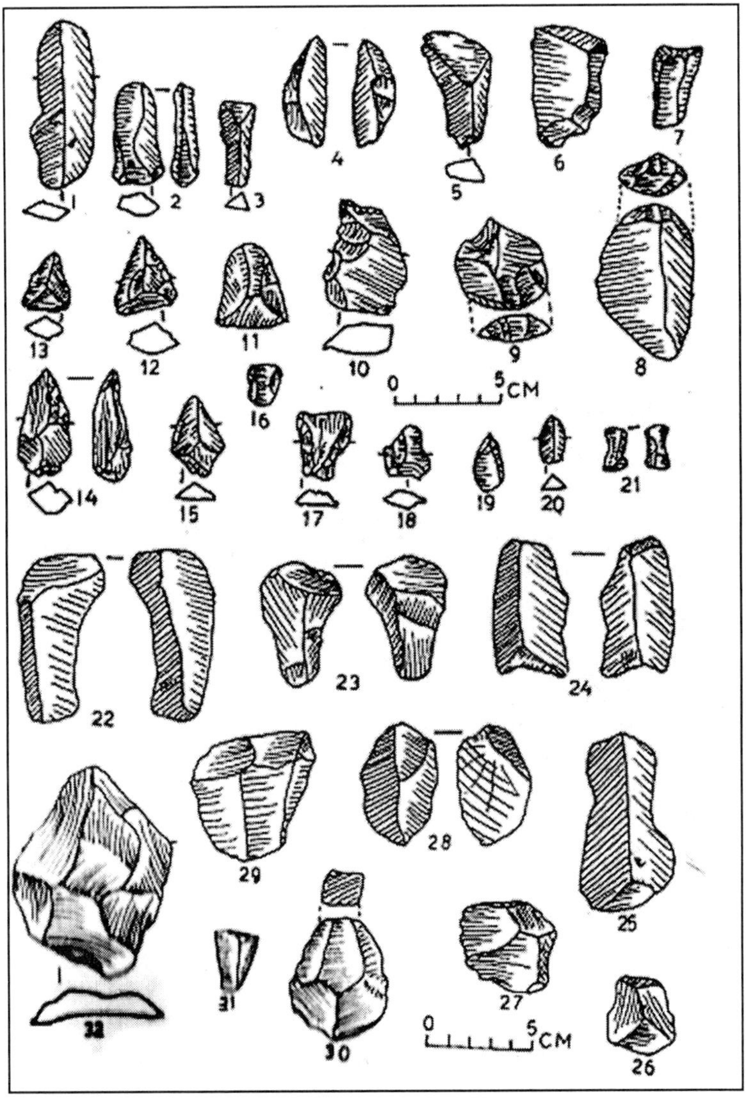

Fig. 20. Flake and Blade artifacts of Khangkhui Cave No. 3, 1-21 from Layer -1 ; 22-32 from Layer -2.

(Singh, 1997: 36, Fig. 15)

There are seven borers, of which two are made on lumps and five on flakes. Borers on flakes, which has either part of the plain or prepared platforms, have edges produced by retouching on the dorsal surface. (Fig. 20: 9). There is one borer-cum-scraper, (Fig. 20:10).

The collection consists of five burins (Fig. 20:6-8) which include three single-blow burins, one-angled burins and one polyhydric burin made on limestone flakes.

The core tools, though not large in number, include handaxe, cleaver and chopper, (Fig. 19). These core tools are made of limestone by employing both direct and controlled flaking technique resulting in both large and small flat flake scars. In case of the cleaver with thick square butt, bipolar technique might have been employed (Fig. 19:2). There are heaps of chips and waste flakes in the collection thereby indicating a factory site.

Handaxe is rather rare. Only two specimens made of limestone are included in the classification of 138 artifacts. One in the third layer is very thin in section and oval in shape with wavy profile line. The flake scars on both the surfaces are large and flat. The flakes might have been produced by direct stone hammer technique. No secondary working is evident. The second one is nearly cardiform in shape and worked with controlled flaking technique resulting in almost flat and a few step flake scars. The section is not thick and biconvex (Fig. 19:4). There are also two cleavers in the collection from the second layer. These are made of limestone with direct stone and step flaking technique. The median cross section is either square or biconvex.

The chopping tools are made of limestone blocks and the working edge is found to be produced by flaking at one end or side unifacially or bifacially (Fig. 19:4). The side or end, opposite to the working edge, is made thick or blunt by striking off small flakes with controlled flaking technique. The one collected from the floor of the cave no.1 has a long handle with a ring around for firm hand grip.

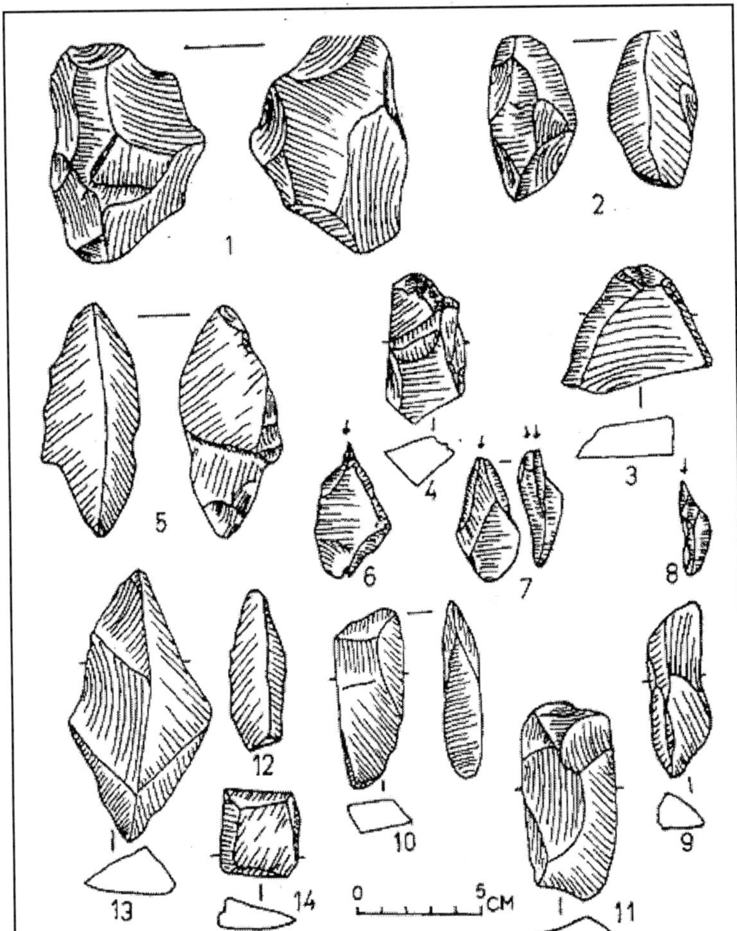

Fig. 21. Flake and Blade artifacts of Khangkhui Cave No. 3. 1- 8. from Layer 2 ; 9 - 14. from Layer 3

(Singh, 1997: 37, Fig. 16)

The numbers of cores in the artifact assemblage of the Khangkhui cave no.3 is ten and they can be divided into fluted and amorphous cores, (Fig. 20: 6,7,29,30,31). The fluted cores are six in number and found in the first and second layers. They are small; and the removal of the flakes or blades from these cores might be done with both direct and indirect percussion techniques. Some small fluted cores have either plain or concave striking platforms, and have narrow chisel like end opposite to the platform. The amorphous cores are the result of cross flakings and a few have tapered end. Almost all the amorphous cores are small and generally small flakes of length 2.3-4.0cm and breadth 1.5-2.1cm have been removed from these cores.

Bone Tool Industry :

In addition to the stone tool industry described above, a large number of bone tools are also found in the Khangkhui cave no. 3. The raw materials might be the bone remains of the hunted animals – cervus, sus, and bovine. The bone tool industry comprises points, scrapers, perforators and blunted back blade. Majority of them have been discovered from the lowest level of the second layer, but one tanged point has been unearthed from the middle level of the first layer. The presence of many bone splinters in the second layer may be regarded as the reflection of the maximum development of bone tool industry in this layer. The suitable pieces of bone might have been obtained by using groove and split methods, (Fig. 22: 14). The burins might have been used in grooving. The micro wedge, (Fig. 20:21) might be hammered into the groove for splitting the bone blank. After obtaining the desired bone blank, they might be first dressed into required shapes by flaking techniques. There is also evidence of pressure flaking technique in secondary working to obtain the effective working edge or shape of the tool. Whittling and grinding might also be used for smoothening the surface of the perforators. The classified bone artifacts are given below in a tabular form.

Table 27 Bone Artifact types of Khangkhui Cave No. 3

Artifacts	*No.*
Scraper	
Convex-side scraper	1
End scraper	2
Points	
Triangular points	1
Tanged point	2
Blunted back knife	1
Perforators	6
Grooved bone	1
Bone splinter	1
Total	15

Singh, 1997, Table-3

The scrapers are found to be made on the pieces of limb bone, the scrapping edge being present at the convex side or end. The working edge of the end scraper, (Fig. 22 :4,5) has been produced by trimming with a narrow edged implement like burin. These trimmed scars are present almost parallel to each other only on the dorsal surface. It will be convenient in scrapping the small cylindrical arrow shaft. The sharp edge of the convex-side scraper is produced by the intersection of parallel grooving scars on both the surfaces while the side opposite to the scrapping edge is made blunt by pressure flaking, (Fig. 22:6).

The bone points are made with either slicing or chipping on both the sides to produce a sharp pointed edge as well as the tang, (Fig. 22 :1-3). These are generally triangular in shape and two of them have tapering base as a tang. These points could be used as the tips of missiles.

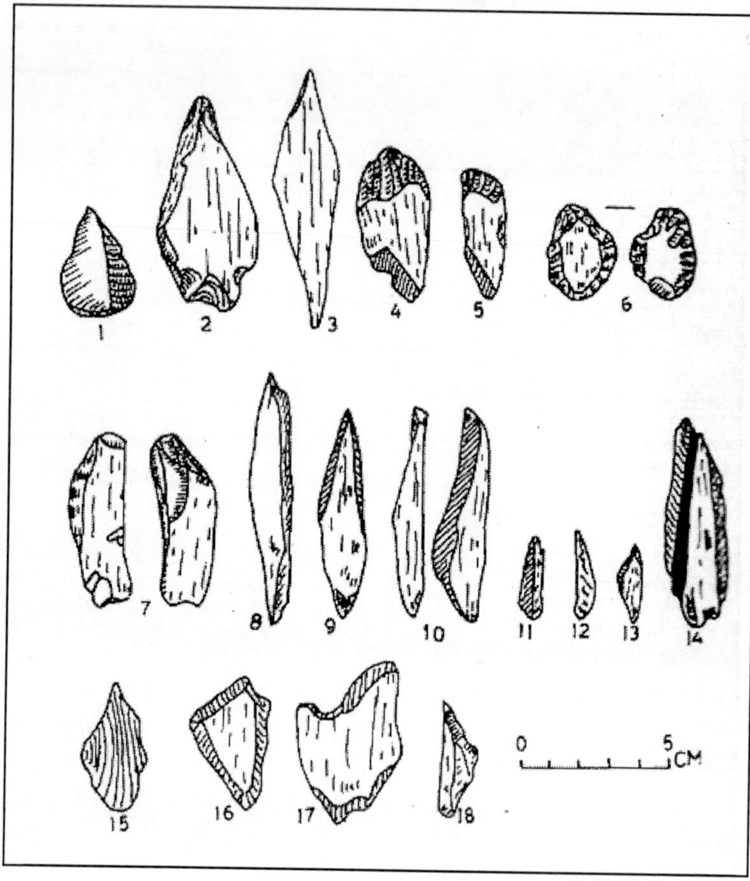

Fig. 22. Bone artifacts of Khangkhui cave No.3

1-3 points ; 4-6. scrapers; 7, blade ; 8-13 perforators ; 14, bone blank with a groove; 15-18, fragmented bones.

(Singh, 1997: 38, Fig. 17)

The blunted back blade is represented by only one tool, (Fig. 22:7). It has a slightly convex sharp edge and a thick convexly blunted back. The blunt back might have been produced by chipping with a chisel edged tool. Slightly convex thin edge has been formed by removing a long splinter. The ventral surface is also formed by chipping. There is an evidence of grinding along the cutting edge.

In the collection there are six specimens, (Fig. 22: 8-12) which could be classified as bone perforators. The narrow and pointed edge might be produced by slicing from both the sides either symmetrically or asymmetrically. Whittling and grinding methods might also have been applied to give a finishing touch to the tool. In one case there is a very small side notch near the tip probably to carry the string while sewing, (Fig. 22:11). Fig. 22:10 is a chisel, the narrow chisel edge is being produced by chipping and then smoothed by whittling technique.

Economy :

The Khangkhui cave men, as evident from the faunal remains, lived on hunting economy. Deer, cattle, boar, small reptile, small herbivorous animals and fowls are included among the hunted games. The tool types, particularly the different types of points including the missile points, suggest that they used both spear and the lance and bow and arrow in hunting. To obtain the shaft of the spear or arrow different artifact types, such as chopping tools, blade flakes, scrapers, and notches might have been used. The cleaver and the blade might also have been used in cutting the hide of the hunted animals and butchering the meat. All the limb bone remains from the Khangkhui cave are found broken. It might be inferred that they might have extracted marrow for their food or broken the bones in the process of making the tool. The presence of a few chert bone pieces may also be considered evidence of roasting the hunted games. But regarding the gathering of forest products there is no direct evidence. However, the probability of practising gathering by them may not be ruled out, for in a subsistence economy hunting, as evident from the ethnographic studies of the contemporary primitive societies, always goes hand in hand with gathering.

Nongpok Keithelmanbi :

Nongpok Keithelmanbi is a small Meitei village situated

at the foothill of the mountain ranges which border the eastern periphery of the Manipur valley. The Thoubal river, a tributary of the Imphal river also flows at the foothills where the village is situated. Exploration during 1982 to 1984 resulted in the identification of a sequence of four terraces represented by T_1, T_2, T_3 and T_4 of the Thoubal river. The terraces are on the right bank of the river and have different heights of 35m, 33m, 12m and 7m from the present river bed.

The T_1 is an agradational strath terrace and has a cone shaped profile. The filled in materials rest directly on the rock (Disang shale) which is an extension of the same rock cut section of T_2.

On the top of T_1, there is 9.15m thick alluvial deposit which is very hard and yellowish red, clayey, fine sandy silt. In this alluvium, unweathered pebbles and cobbles, mostly sub-rounded to rounded, of quartzitic sandstone are sparsely distributed. Three flaked pebbles of quartzitic sandstone and pieces of eratic conglomerate are also discovered from this alluvium. The flaked pebbles are found embedded in the alluvium at a depth of 40cm to 60cm. The alluvium deposit rests directly on the bedrock. This T_1 extends from T_2 for about 500m towards south-east.

T_2 is also a strath terrace. The rock cut section is 25.85m high. On this rock there is a clatch of gravel deposit of 3.2m thick. The lithic composition of the deposit is dominated by sandstone which is generally weathered. In the gravel, a rounded pebble of an erratic conglomerate is found. This gravel is overlained by 85cm thick reddish yellow silt affected by weathering. On this thin alluvial deposit there is another 45cm thick matrix. Its lithic composition is found to be dominated by coarse grayish sandstone which is heavily weathered and rounded to sub-rounded in character. The deposit is capped on the top by 2.65m thick alluvium of weathered clayey fine, sandy silts.

The T_3 is a filled up terrace and is capped on the top by an alluvial deposit of 1m thick which is very hard, fissured, clayey silt having light yellowish colour. The gravel deposit is not exposed upto the base. It is gravelly, sub-rounded to sub-angular in character. It is dominated by slightly weathered coarse to fine sandstone.

T_4 is the youngest field terrace. The exposed section has a deposit of 4.6m thick mottled, flood fine, sandy silt underlain by a gravel deposit of 2.4m thick. Lithologically, the gravel is dominated by fine sandstone and quartzitic sandstone with a few jasper pebbles. The gravel deposit is unweathered but a few at the base are ferroginous. T_1 alluvium is more heavily weathered than the rest. T_2 gravel is heavily weathered. Weathering becomes lesser and lesser towards the upper terrace. T_4 gravel is almost fresh. Thus chronologically T_1 is the oldest and T_4 is the youngest in the terrace sequence. The degree of weathering of the materials found in this four terraces indicates that this region has experienced climatic changes during the late Pleistocene.

The archaeological sites are represented by three Localities, namely, Locality 1, Locality 2 and Locality 3 respectively. Locality 1 locates towards south at a distance of about 2km downstream from Keithelmanbi bazar. It is on the top of a flattened hill ridge. The site is 45m high from the river bed and gradually slopes towards the river bed. The artifacts found at Locality 1 are pebble tools with a few flakes and a blade. The raw material used for making the artifacts is quartzitic sandstone except a blade and a scraper which are made of chert. The artifacts of the Locality 1 is classified as belonging to Hoabinhian culture (Singh, 1997).

Locality 2 is situated on the left bank of Thoubal river at an altitude of 50m above the river bed and is at a distance of 1km downstream towards the south of Locality 1. Seven split pebbles, one big chopper and one scraper were unearthed. A trial trench of 1m square was dug on the top and exposed 60cm thick layer of compact yellowish (breccia) that rests directly on the weathered parent rock. After the depth of 5cm from the surface, stone artifacts consisting of split pebbles, flat blades and scrapers were found along with pebbles and cobbles in breccia (rock consisting of angular fragments cemented by fine chalky materials) deposit, but below this depth no artifact was found.

Locality 3 is situated to the east of Thoubal barrage at a distance of 2km upstream from Locality 1. There is a small hillock that juts out of the main mountain range. From the western foot hill of it a fan deposit stretches sloping towards the left bank of the Thoubal river. It appears that jhum cultivation was practised on the slopes of the hillock in the recent past and consequently the soil of the hillock was almost eroded along with the archaeological relics thereby forming a fan deposit at the foot hill. At places there are accumulations of pebbles and cobbles and amidst which are also found pebble chopper and split pebbles (Singh, 1997).

The Palaeolithic stone tool industry of Nongpok Keithelmanbi comprises core and flake tools and a few blades. However, at Locality 3 only core tools have been found. The artifacts are made mostly on quartzitic sandstone pebble and a few are on chert. The core tool consists of pebble chopper, scrapper and graver. Direct stone hammering technique resulting in the removal of flat flakes has been used in making the core tools. The chopping edge is produced by striking off alternate flakes at one end from both the surfaces, whereas cortex forms the major surface of the tool. In the case of chopper, one side of the pebble is flaked off unifacially and retouched with step flaking to produce the working edge. In most cases the butt end is left unworked as cortex. Both the surfaces of the scraper have been shaped by flat primary flaking and scraping edge is produced by unifacial retouching. The graver is made from split pebble; the edge is formed by pressure flaking technique. The industry also includes a notch implement made on a quartzitic sandstone pebble by flaking bifacially, the ventral surface is completely flaked with flat flake scars. The side notch is produced by striking off a steep conchordal flake from the dorsal surface and another long flat flake is also struck off along the length.

Generally, the flakes show marked or diffused bulb of percussion on the main flake surface and have been struck off from the unprepared amorphous core by direct percussion technique.

Table 28 Stone artifact types of Nongpok Keithelmanbi Locality 2 and 3

Artifact types	*Loc.-2*	*Loc.-3*	*Total*
Chopper	1	2	3
Scraper	4	-	4
Blade	3	-	3
Notch implement	-	1	1
Flake	7	-	7
Pebble graver	1	-	1
Core	4	-	4
Split pebble	11	3	14
Waste flake	1	2	3
Total :	32	8	40

Singh, 1997, Table- 4

A suitable flat pebble surface or a flake plain surface is used as striking platform. Most of the flakes have part of such a platform, and also cortex on the dorsal surface. Some scrapers have been made by retouching at one end of the cortical surface only, while the main flake surface is left unretouched.

The lithic assemblage includes three blades that have a mid ridge on the dorsal surface. One of them has one thick side and a truncated ends and the blade edge is produced by striking off one flake from each surface respectively along and across the length. The blades do not show any retouch. There are also manuports of pebbles and cobbles probably collected by men for their use.

Singtom :

Singtom lies in Chandel District of Manipur. It is on a cone shaped fan deposit bounded by hills on the east, north and south, and by the Chakpi river valley on the west. The Chakpi river flows from south to north at a distance of about 100m to the west of the site. The Zou tribe has been occupying the site since 1946. A Palaeolithic tool was discovered from this site by Mr. Joseph, a villager of Singtom, and presented to the Department of Anthropology, D.M. College of Science. In order to ascertain its archaeological potentiality, O.K. Singh made an exploration of the site in 1989 and discovered stone age relics consisting of worked flat pebbles, broken handaxe, a few flakes, a blade and pebble disc. The artifacts do not show any rolling. The statistics of the finds are given below.

Table 29 The Stone Tool Types of the Singtom Site

Artifacts	*No.*
Handaxe (one broken)	2
Worked flat pebble with round edge	1
Flaked pebble	1
Blade	1
Flake	1
Pebble striker	1
Split pebble	3
Waste flake	6
Total	16

Singh, 1997, Table- 5

The industry consists of core tools and flake blades. All the artifacts are made on quartzitic sandstone. The handaxe is of ovate type with a slightly 'S' twisted profile and biconvex cross section. It is made with controlled flaking technique. Alternate free flaking technique is used in the case of the flat pebbles to produce the round edge. The blade is very short with a mid ridge on the dorsal surface. One margin of the dorsal surface has also been retouched (Singh, 1997).

Machi

Machi is a Maring village located on the top of a low hill range at the south-eastern corner of Manipur. It is in the Chandel District. A pebble chopper was explored by O.K. Singh in 1974. It is made on an oval sandstone pebble by unifacial flaking with direct stone hammering technique. It measures 11.5 x 13.5 x 4.1 cm and unrolled.

Hoabinhian Culture

The prehistoric sites where the Hoabinhian artifacts found are Nongpok Keithelmanbi Locality 1 and Tharon Cave.

The existence of Mesolithic culture characterized by microliths is not found in Manipur. However, as in other parts of South-East Asia, there are assemblages of a stone tool industry made on river pebbles either by flaking or edge grinding, which, in South-East Asia, is identified as Hoabinhian culture.

O.K. Singh (1997) states that "the main components of the Hoabinhian assemblages are a flaked stone industry fashioned off rolled river pebbles, edge ground tools, grinding stone and mortars, a few bone artifacts and sherds of simple earthen ware in the later stage".

The classified stone artifact type consists of strikers, points, almond-shaped tools, coup-de-poing, short axes, grinding stones, mortar and pestles, scrapers including pebble-core scrappers, small utilized flakes (Mathews 1966 : 88-90, Gorman 1971:312). Another type of Hoabinhian lithic tool is

"Sumatralith" that was found in Sumatra; this is also a pebble tool worked unifacially by centripetal flaking (H.V. Tan 1976:131). Besides the lithic assemblage, Gorman (1971:312) suggested the probability of manufacturing the wooden implements. He further postulated that food was cooked in the cut-bamboo pieces (ibid). Considering the artifact types of the Hoabinhian culture of South-East Asia, it may be presumed that the stone artifact assemblages from Nongpok Keithelmanbi locality-1 and Tharon cave represent the Hoabinhian culture of Manipur (Singh, 1997).

Nongpok Keithelmanbi locality-1.

Nongpok Keithelmanbi locality-1 is at a distance of about 2km to the south of Keithelmanbi bazar. It is located on the top, which is at a height of about 45m above the river bed, of a flattened hill ridge that gradually slopes towards the river site. The western end of this projected hill ridge has been leveled for the construction of the irrigation canal under the Thoubal river Project, and it has resulted in the exposure of a number of cord-marked potsherds. In 1983, an experimental digging was done by O.K. Singh on the ridge and 143cm thick deposit of three soil layers has been exposed. No artifact is found in the first layer. The artifacts are found only in the second layer.

Industry

The Hoabinhian industry of Nongpok Keithelmanbi locality-1 is a pebble tool industry with a few flakes and a blade. Quartzitic sandstone is the only raw material used for making the Hoabinhian artifacts, except a blade and a scrapper that are made of chert.

The classified types of the Hoabinhian artifacts are shown below.

Table 30 Hoabinhian Artifact Types of Nongpok Keithelmanbi Locality-1.

Artifacts.	*No.*
Chisel shaped pebble tool	6
Round edged pebble tool	2
Pebble pick	2
Scrapper	1
Blade	1
Split pebble	30
Pebble with batters marks	24
Pebble with ground faces	1
Flake	5
Manuport	7
Total	79

Singh, 1997, Table-6

The pebble tools are made without completely deforming the original shape of the pebbles, only one end of which has been strucked off with two or more blows either unidirectionally or bidirectionally to form the working edge without further retouching, except in the pebble scrapper which has been made from a small chert pebble by alternate and fine secondary flaking. The edge of the tool is produced by intersection of two flat flake scars struck off from either side of one end, while the rounded surface of the butt end remains unworked. Steep controlled flaking technique is used in the preparation of the round edged pebble tool.

Pebble pick has been prepared from an elongated flat pebble by striking off the two ends, and two alternate flakes have also been detached to produce the pick edge. The split pebbles form the highest number in the collection and these are the pebbles broken transversely or longitudinally with a single blow. The edge of some of these split pebbles are blunt, and a few of them have battered marks at the butt end. The tools might have been used in crushing or pounding purposes. The specimen illustrated is a split pebble that has been knocked off from a flat quartzitic sandstone with a single blow. Another flake has also been detached at one end to form a slightly concave edge which can be used in scrapping purposes. The presence of a flat, smooth, ground surface and batter marks at the periphery indicates that the Hoabinhian people knew grinding too. There are also a number of pebble strikers in the collection. The lithic assemblage also includes flakes which had been struck off from the pebble by using any suitable pebble surface as striking platform. A part of the cortex is also present on most of these flakes (26.5). A flake has a bulb of percussion on one surface and negative bulb of percussion on the other and these flake surfaces intersect at one longer side to produce a sharp edge. From the nature of flake scars present on the flake it appears that series of small flakes have been struck off from the pebble core;

The flake is a prepared flake with a narrow end and thin base. The three small and shallow flake scars on the upper surface have been detached prior to the removal of the flake from the core while the undersurface is formed by a single flat flake scar. It can be used as a tip of a projectile. One most significant feature of these flakes is that none of them has been retouched after the detachment from the core. The lithic industry of locality-1 also includes a small blade of chert. It has a mid-ridge and a side notch with slightly concave under surface.

Tharon cave site

The Tharon cave site is situated at a distance of about 2.5km to the north of Tharon village amidst the thickly forested Reyanglong hill in Tamenglong District. The cave is locally known as Kalemki (*Kalem* -bat, *ki* -house), that is the house of bat. A stream known as Kalemkimagu flows near the caves and it finally forms a waterfall on its way towards the west. The rock type of the area is sandstone of Barail series.

In 1979, O.K. Singh explored five caves at this site which he again reexplored in 1989. Cave no.1 is very long and looks like a curved tunnel having fourteen passages which are completely dark. The cave has three openings, two of which lead to the stream. Cave no.2 locates at a short distance from cave no.1 which faces towards the stream. Cave no.3 locates to the north of cave no.1 at a little higher altitude, while cave no.4 and cave no. 5 locate just opposite to the third cave across narrow plateau. The floors of these caves are filled with sandstone slabs that fall from the walls and roof, and no artifact is found inside the caves in the exploration. But edge ground pebble tools are found in the course of exploration around the cave site along the stream (Fig. 23, 24, 25).

Industry :

The Hoabinhian industry of the Tharon cave site consists pebble tools only. A suitably shaped sandstone pebble is selected from the nearby stream and only one end has been flaked to produce a working edge. Grinding is done always unifacially, step flaking and flat flaking have also been employed in making some of the tools. The classified types of Hoabinhian tools consists of chopper, handaxe, hand adze, pointed tool, scraper, edge-ground knife, pebble quern and grinder.

Table 31 Hoabinhian artifact types of Tharon Cave site

Artifacts	*No.*
Chopping tool	1
Hand axe	1
Hand adze	4
Pointed tool	1
Scrapper	3
Edge ground knife	2
Quern	1

Grinder	1
Unclassified ground pebbles	25
Total	39

Singh, 1997, Table-7

The chopping tool, (Fig. 24:1) is made of thick sandstone pebble. The edge is formed by unifacial grinding. The opposite side is thick and convex. It has a 'V' shaped cross section. The tool is weathered and patinated. The handaxe is made of an elliptical shaped sandstone pebble by flaking thin and narrow flakes from both the surfaces. The pointed working edge is produced by small bifacial flaking. Cortex is present at the thick butt end (Fig. 23:5). The edge of the pebble tool is produced by grinding at the sides of both the surfaces of the narrow end and a suitable hand grip is also made by grinding at the sides (Fig. 23:1). The handadze is made from a flattish ovaloid or trianguloid sandstone pebble by unifacial grinding on the broader end with or without flaking on the opposite side, to produce the unibevelled cutting edge.

The scrapers have concave or hollow scraping edges that are produced by either unifacial grinding or bifacial flakings with thin and narrow scars. This concave edge is further extended to a narrow end which could be used for scooping or grooving purposes. The smooth and lustrous surface might also be due to use. The specimen shown in (Fig. 24:5 (31 ok).) could be used as scraper cum-digging tool, as it also has a narrow elongated edge and the blunted butt with fine flat flakings.

The edge-ground knife is made of a flat sandstone pebble by grinding alternately on its longer side. The assemblage also includes quern and grinder. The quern is made of a rectangular sandstone slab. One end is made thicken by thin and flat flakings. It appears that it was made of a damaged chopping tool by making the damaged anterior end concave. The grinder is of an elliptical shaped sandstone pebble with grinding facets all over. It directly fits into the concave grinding facet of the quern. There are also a number of flat pebbles with slightly ground facets. These appear to be unfinished artifacts.

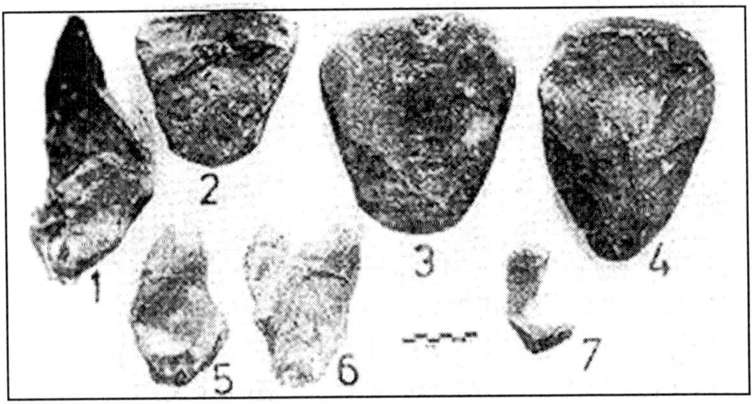

Fig. 23. Edge-ground Hoabinhian artifacts of Fig.

1, Pointed edge tool; 2-4, edge ground adze 5, hand axe; 6, edge ground hand adze; ground tool; 7, concave scraper 5, edge ground knife.

(Singh, 1997: 57, Fig. 27)

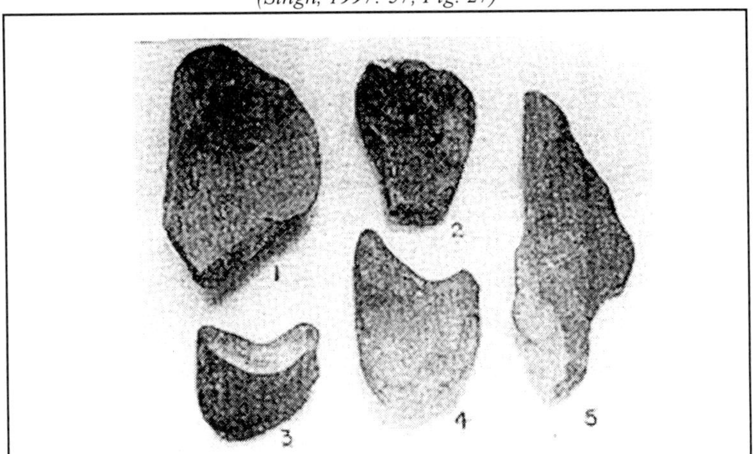

24. Edge ground Hoabinhian pebble Tharon Cave Site tools of Tharon Cave Site

1, Chopping tool; 2, incomplete edge-ground 3-4, concave scraper; 5, edge ground knife

(Singh, 1997: 59, Fig. 28)

Fig. 25. Sandstone quern and grinder of Tharon Cave Site

(Singh, 1997: 59, Fig. 28)

Neolithic Culture

Neolithic cultural objects are found both in the hills and the valley of Manipur. The Neolithic stage of the stone age cultures of Manipur is characterized by the stone tools consisting of chisels, hoe blade, triangular axe, quadrangular adze and pottery (O.K. Singh 1988b ; 63-65). The stone tools are mostly made by grinding and polishing technique. Moreover, chipping, sawing and pecking techniques are also evident in a few neoliths. These stone tools have oval, circular, square or rectilinear median cross section. Typologically, these can be compared with those found in South, East and South East Asia (O.K. Singh, 1980 : 155-56). In 1949, Worman defined Neolithic as a pre metal, Stone Age, food producing culture. According to him a full Neolithic archaeological site may be characterized by the presence of domesticated plants or animals or by pottery and smooth stone tools. However, these Neolithic traits are rarely found together at a single site but a culture associated with the ground stone axes, adzes and chisels may be designated as Neolithic (Thapar, 1965 :87, Verma, 1988: XI). A true Neolithic stage has no knowledge of metal and on this basis Sankalia (1974 : 279-80) used ground tools of stone and bone and hand made pottery as characters of the pure Neolithic culture of India.

In Manipur only four Neolithic sites viz, Nongpok Keithelmanbi in Senapati District, Napachick in Bishnupur District, Laimanai and Phunan in Thoubal District, are so far discovered, however, a good number of ground and polished stone tools have been reported from different parts of Manipur. On the basis of pottery types, the Neolithic culture of Manipur can be further subdivided into i) Corded ware culture, ii) Tripod Ware Culture and iii) Geometric Ware Culture. The corded ware culture is represented by the handmade and ill fired pottery decorated with cord marks from Nongpok Keithelmanbi Locality-1. Here, corded ware overlies the Hoabinhian culture after a short break in the stratigraphy and is dated to the first half of the third millennium B.C. (O.K. Singh, 1986). However, by the absence of any other Neolithic characters the corded ware culture may be a sub Neolithic type as in other parts of south east Asia (Chang, 1974: 277).

Napachik, a Neolithic site of Bishnupur District lies at Wangoo village. It locates on the right bank of the Manipur river which flows into the Chindwin river of Myanmar. It was discovered by O.K. Singh in 1981 and a trench (4 X 2 sq m) was dug at the south western slope and another trench 5 x 2 sq m was dug in 1985 at the eastern foot hill. The first excavation shows the character of redeposition after being washed of the upper slope. However, the latter excavation appears to be undisturbed deposits and eight soil layers have been exposed.

Table 32 Stratigraphy of the 1985 excavation and archaeological finds at Napachik

Layer	*Depth in metre*	*Soil*		*Archaeological finds*
		Texture	*colour*	
1	0-1.52	Clayey silt	Brown(10 yr-5/3)	Sterile
2	1.52 -2.36	Clayey silt	Light brownish grey (10 yr-6/2)	Sterile
3	2.36-2.54	Sandy with hill wash granules	Brown (10 yr-5/3)	Fresh water mollusk, micorlith, corded ware
4	2.54 -3.23	Clay	Light yellowish brown with grey mottle (10yr-6/4)	Neolithic celt, microliths, grinding stone tripod ware with cordmarks
5	3.23 -3.46	Clay with hill wash granules	Grayish brown 10yr-5/2)	Neolithic celt, micorliths, cores, grinding stones, quartz crystal with ware marks, spindle whorls of pottery, tripod wares with cordmarks.
6	3.46 -3.85	Clay	Pale brown with light grey mottle (10yr-6/3)	Microliths, cores, a net sinker, flakes, grinding stones, tripod and ring footed wares.
7	3.85 -4.14	Clay with hill wash granules and ash at the base	Grayish to dark grayish brown (10 yr -5/2 to 10 yr -4/2)	Microliths, flakes, tripod and ring footed wares.
8	4.14 -4.62	clay	Light yellowish brown (10yr -6/4)	Microliths, cores, perforators, quartz, crystal, tripod and ring footed wares.

Singh, 1997, Pp.69

The nature of the soil of the layers shows that there was climatic fluctuation of wet and dry at the time of deposition.

The Tripod ware culture is characterized by the cord marked pottery provided with tripod legs. At these sites the tripod wares are found in association with ground Neolithic stone tools. The tools found in the excavation are given below :

Table 33 Neolithic stone implements from Napachik

Sl. no.	*Lithic artifacts*	*Number found in*		*Total*
		1981	*1985*	
1	Pebble tool	3	-	3
2	Flake tool	1	50	51
3	Flake	3	18	21
4	Core	-	27	27
5	Ground celt			
	a . complete	1	2	3
	b. broken	2	2	4
6	Grinding stone	-		
	a. complete	-	2	2
	b. broken	1	4	5
	Total	11	105	116

Singh, 1997, Table-8

The associated finds includes ground triangular celts with oval cross section, microliths, edge ground knife and perforators, net sinker and spindle whorl of pottery. The edge of the knife has lustrous surfaces, which indicates the use of the tool in cutting purposes probably soft fibrous plants. Microliths consisting of blades, points, burins and scrapers made of quartz are also found. In the excavation of these sites a large number of charcoal pieces and ash of reeds are also found along with the cultural deposits.

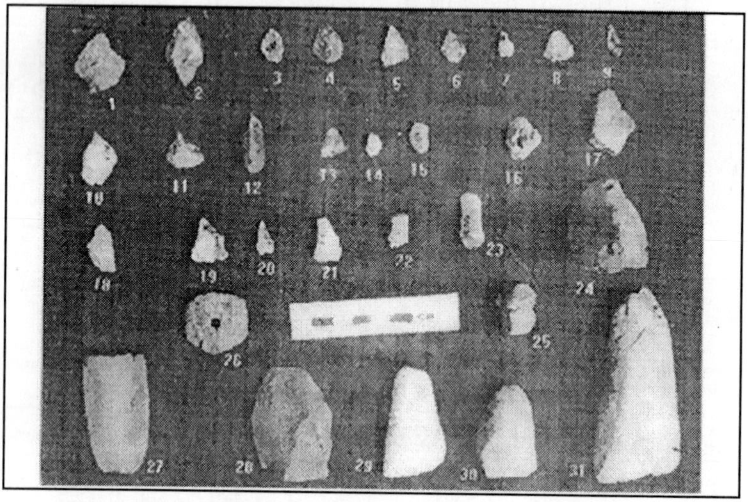

Fig. 26. Neolithic artifacts of the Napachik Site.

1-3, tanged point; 4-9, simple points, 10-12, borers; 13-15, blades; 15-17, scrapers; 18-23, burins; 24, core; 25, net sinker; 26, spindle-whorl of pottery; edge-ground knife; 28, flake; 29-31, ground celts. *(Singh, 1997: 71, Fig. 36)*

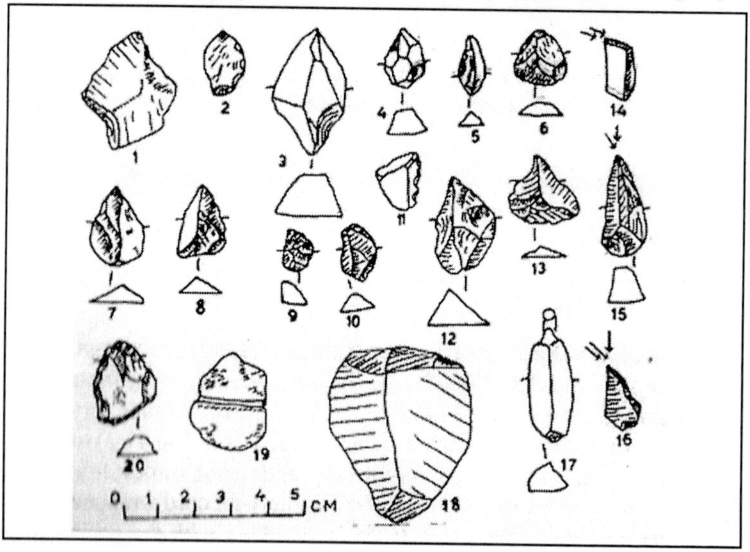

Fig. 27: Neolithic artifacts of Napachik.

1-3, Tanged points, 4-8, simple points; 9-11, blades; 9-11, blades; 12-13, borers; 17, edge-ground borer; 18, core; 19, net sinker; 20, scraper *(Singh, 1997: 73, Fig. 40)*

The stone tool assemblage as a whole has suggested that Napachik Neolithic culture is based on hunting, fishing and probably plant cultivation. It implies that the tripod ware culture was based on plant cultivation supplemented by fishing and hunting economy and people also knew the spinning of thread. The pottery might be used in cooking also. The Napachick culture is as old as 1450 B.C. (O.K., Singh, 1997).

Laimanai, a Neolithic site is located at a distance of about 5km to the south west of Kakching, Thoubal District. The artifacts from the Laimanai site are given below :

Table 34 Neolithic Stone Artifacts from Laimanai site

Sl. No.	*Artifacts*	*No.*
1	Chipped celt	1
2	Chipped and ground celt	3
3	Fully ground celt	2
4	Ring stone (broken)	1
5	Flat pebble hammer	1
6	Grinding stone	-
	a. Complete	1
	b. Broken	7
7	Waste flakes	5
8	unclassified	1
	Total	22

Singh, 1997, Table-9

The lithic artifacts are made of sandstone by employing chipping and grinding technique. These include triangular hoe, blade, small chisel, and small trapezoidal celt (Fig. 26). The cross sections of the tools have ovaloid and rectangular forms. The pottery found along with the stone tools are hand made and mostly tempered with coarse sand and quatzitic particles. The surface decoration is done with impression of cord wrapped paddle. The presence of conical type of tripod leg at Laimanai site suggests that it belongs to the same cultural tradition of Napachik site.

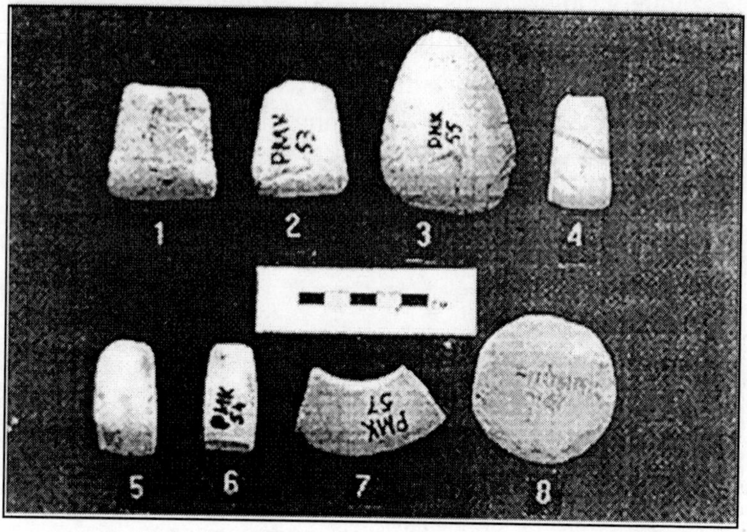

Fig.28. Neolithic stone artifacts of Laimanai Site

(Singh, 1997: 77, Fig. 44)

Phunan Site

Phunan, a prehistoric site is located to the south west of the Phunan Maring village at a distance of 22km south east of Imphal. In an exploration in 1967, O.K. Singh explored a number of potsherds and two very large grinding stones. Three ground stone tools consisting of triangular hoe, chisel and quadrangular axe are also found in Phunan hill. The tools are dominated by square cut sides with rectilinear median cross sections and are made by grinding and polishing technique.

Potteries from Phunan site are hand made and decorated in geometric pattern consisting of circles, parallel lines, wavy or straight lines either in pairs or band .

In south China also a sequence of three phase Neolithic culture was established and the late Neolithic culture dating between 1500 B.C to 700 B.C. was represented by the geometric ware horizon, Chang-1974:370-71).

A number of Neolithic celts are explored from different parts of the State. A Neolithic celt is also collected from Chingkhulong village during the field work.

Some of the stray findings discovered from different parts of Manipur other than the above mentioned excavation sites are given below

Table 35 Districtwise Neolithic stray finds from Manipur

District	*No.*
Imphal	34
Thoubal	49
Bishnupur	5
Churachandpur	12
Ukhrul	23
Chandel	37
Senapati	2
Tamenglong	1
Unknown locality	6
Total	169

Singh, 1997, Table-10

5
Discussion and Conclusion

Ethnographic Postulates about the Kabuis

Subsistence Economy

Ethnoarchaeology, though still in its prime, has created its own niche in the field of archaeological research. One of its important objectives is to throw light on the understanding of the relationship between the patterned behaviour and the elements of the material way of life that may be preserved in the archaeological record. It is, therefore, basically based on the logical assumption that the comparative study of the artifacts which are far removed from us in time and space and the items of the technical culture and associated behaviour of the contemporary non literate societies, if the two items of the technical culture bear some basic similarities in terms of their morphology and function, may hold clue to the socifacts related to the behaviour pattern of the people living in the archaeological past.

In the context of the present study the different prehistoric tools excavated from different sites of Manipur represent the relics of the archaeological past whereas the various technical items associated with the material way of life of the Kabuis of Manipur represent the artifacts of the ethnographic present. The behavioural pattern refers to that of the producers and users of the artifacts. The ethnographic study of the subsistence pattern of the Kabuis inhabiting the different ecological zones and direct search for material correlates of their behaviour (Thomson 1991 : 239) may throw light on the behavioural pattern of the people who are supposed to have used the prehistoric tools by way of bridging the gap between the archaeological past and the ethnographic present. The inferred ethnographic postulates that are found fruitful in the reconstruction of the behavioural patterns of the prehistoric hunting and gathering populations of Manipur may be enumerated as follows :

1. The subsistence economy of the Kabuis that centers around hunting, gathering, pastoralism, horticulture and cultivation has been made effective by way of organising labour on the basis of age and sex within the economic unit of family on one hand and collective economic effort at the level of the community on the other.
2. The resource mobilisation has been successfully made by organising their economic activities in line with an annual economic cycle based on the exhaustive indigenous knowledge about the life cycle of the different varieties of plants and animals available in their surroundings.
3. The food habit of the Kabuis is found to be characterised by the regular, though not daily, consumption of one of the items of preserved food of either fermented or dried kind. Not only does this food habit account for the seasonal abundance of the certain varieties of collected food items, whether they be plants or animals, but it helps account for the judicious management of the limited, natural food resources by way of making them available throughout the year in the preserved form. One ethnographic inference that can be arrived at is the maximization of the life chances by the optimum use of the available food resources.

4. Domesticate animals, no doubt, occupy an important position in the economic life of the people, for some economic activities, such as hunting of some wild games, tilling of soil particularly in the plain region become next to impossible without the service of some domestic animals like dog, bullock, etc. However, some of them are not only the cherished items of food but also important source of protein for the people. On the surface it seems that rearing of a number of pigs by every Kabui household is an economic wastage as the households have to keep some food reserved for them. A closer analysis has, however, established beyond doubt that is nothing but an economic strategy, for pigs are the walking food reserved. Moreover, it is also a socifact that whatever reserved for the pigs are the leftovers of their daily food thereby making a provision for storage of their waste food in the form of living pigs in order to make them enable to use the same whenever necessity arises. There lies the economic rationality of the indigenous knowledge of the people by means of which they can maximise their life chance by adapting to the prevailing situation demanded by their habitat.
5. Consumption and distribution patterns of food have also been channeled through the cyclic rituals celebrated in different months of a year at either the familial or the community level. Pork is customarily consumed at the time of celebrating these rituals thus enabling the people to get protein all the year round. There are ritualistic mechanism of maintaining the egalitarian social system of the Kabui society. The homeostasis of the system is maintained through a pattern of redistribution of the accumulated property made by the big and rich men of the society. When a rich man likes to build a *Tarangkai*, the traditional house of the Kabuis, he has

to perform a number of rituals associated with grand feast customarily arranged for the villagers. In such a way the surplus food accumulated at the hands of the select few is made available to the common villagers who are generally facing the problem of food shortage. Redistribution of surplus food has also been made by the chief of the village by making feast of merit. The ritual observances of the people, as revealed by the aforementioned analysis of man-environment relationship, may be interpreted as the mechanism of adaptation to the habitat by the people to maximise their life chances. Moreover, this man-environment relationship has been kept alive for generations together by preserving it in the form of belief and ritual practices.

6. The material way of life of the Kabuis inhabiting different ecological zones bears striking similarities though it contains some elements of differences which are in degree but not in kind. The similarities are in the mode of adaptation to the habitat and the technology and artifacts that are the product of the interactive process of the nature and culture whereas the differences are in the degree of the complexity of the morphological characteristics and functional effectiveness of the artifacts. It may be postulated on the basis of the comparative study of the artifacts used in different economic pursuits that the Kabui of different ecological zones have in common with one another that there is an evolutionary sequence in respect of these artifacts as the Kabuis migrate from the high altitude habitat to the plain habitat through the foothill habitat. Such an evolutionary change is again reflected in the material way of life of the people and associated non material dimensions of their lifeways. In this sense, the Kabui lifeways in different ecological zones cannot be

regarded as the dichotomies resulted from the dialogue between habitat and Kabui culture. But then again they may be considered parts occupying specific position in the continuum of Kabui cultural spectrum. A fact that merits a special mention in this connection is that some agricultural implements like different types of hoes, which are presently used by the Kabuis of the interior, high altitude regions in their shifting cultivation, are used by the plain Kabuis symbolically in the festivals performed in connection with the harvesting though they do no longer practise shifting cultivation. Such cultural objects, which are cultural survivals in one Kabui society but functional implements in another Kabui society, clearly authenticates the cultural linkage of the Kabui societies inhabiting different ecological zones on one hand and the continuity of the former from the latter particularly in respect of their subsistence pattern on the other.

7. Another worth considering fact is that the Kabuis living in the isolated, upland habitat still use neolithic celts, though not large in number, for magico-religious purposes. They, however, do not understand that the artifact was once used by their prehistoric forerunners in economic pursuits of their survival. In such a way, the tool which was very much functionally significant during the prehistoric days has become a cultural object of unknown origin among the Kabuis of the geographically isolated hilly region of Manipur. In the same way, the Kabuis of the valley of Manipur who use different types of daos symbolically are not very much aware of the functional significance and economic importance of the same. A logical postulate that may be drawn from the aforementioned empirical observation is that though there is hardly any evidence in support

of the continuity between the prehistoric culture of Manipur and the Kabui culture of the upland region it, at least, forms the basis for analogy between the ethnographic present of the Kabuis and the prehistoric pasts of Manipur.

Ethnographic Analogy

Archaeologists have used ethnographic evidences in effective ways for the explanation of the past human behaviour (Lynton, 1984). It is also an agreed fact that hypotheses and inferences must be made on the basis of some set of analogy between directly observed ethnographic evidences and the archaeological materials. (Watson 1971). In such a way, analogy, in its true sense, is the transportation of information from one object to another on the basis of some relations between them (Umeov, 1970; Wylie, 1980).

In the context of the present study, an ethnographic analogy will be made between the material way of life of the Kabuis that explicitly reflects their subsistence pattern and the associated behaviour, both economic and social, and the prehistoric materials particularly the tools discovered from different prehistoric sites of Manipur that represent the archaeologically observed data. These two sets of the ethnographic and the archaeological data are being compared taking the similarities in their physical properties particularly the morphological features and function that have been described in the light of the ethnographically observed facts in case of the former and the archaeologically observed data in case of the latter into account. In the consideration of the dimensions of time and space the present comparison comes under the theoretical purview of 'general comparative' approach of Paterson (1971), the 'discontinous model' of Gould (1974) and 'buckshot' method of Yellen (1974) as these two sets of data are desperate both in time and space.

The findings drawn from the comparative study of the archaeological materials with their ethnographic analogues which are the gathering, hunting and horticultural implements of the Kabuis are delineated in the following paragraphs.

1. The prehistoric material remains of Manipur are rich in Neolithic celts, both axe and adze, that may be compared with the different types of hoes used by the Kabuis in shifting cultivation. Here, the comparison is restricted to the typological similarities of the two in order to throw light on their functional similarities which, in turn, may lead to the near similarities of the economic activities associated with them. Two typological variation of hoes – one hafted transversely to the axis of the shaft and other hafted parallel to the axis of the shaft – are found to be used by the Kabuis in their shifting cultivation. The former is used for digging or tilling the soil whereas the latter is generally meant for cutting purposes. These agricultural implements bear typological similarities with the Neolithic celts of different types, such as rectilinear, quadrangular adzes and axe type celts. These prehistoric tools, like the different types of hoes, namely, *Lougai*- a large hoe used for tilling soil, *Louphun phu* – a medium sized hoe used for digging hole in loose soil and *Nuchou* – a small hoe used for weeding, might have been used for tilling, digging, and weeding purposes. It may also be inferred from the typological similarities of the axe used by the Kabuis and the triangular and rectilinear neolithic celts of axe type that the latter might have been used for cutting small trees and branches.

2. Chopping, scraping and cutting tools, such as chopper, concave scraper, chopper and edge ground knives have also been discovered from different prehistoric sites of Manipur namely, Tharon cave and Napachik. Though not much typological similarity is noticed between

these prehistoric tools and the cutting and chopping implement of the Kabuis known as daos, their functional similarities can not go unnoticed as the prehistoric tools particularly the Hoabinhian edge ground knife and the dao of the Kabuis share much similarities in respect of their cutting edges. From this functional similarity one may generalise, though not perfectly accurate, that the Hoabinhian chopper and edge ground knife might have been used for the same purposes that the daos are presently using.

3. The Kabuis use different types of spears ranging from the bamboo spear made of one piece of bamboo made pointed at one end by cutting on the slant to the iron spear made of iron blade of different shape and size, bamboo or wooden handle and iron butt end for hunting purposes. The iron blades of the Kabui spear bear morphological similarities with different bone and stone points including tanged points discovered from various Palaeolithic and Neolithic sites of Manipur, such as Khangkhui cave and Napachik. It is also established beyond doubt that these points might have been used as spear heads after hafting in a bamboo or wooden handle. In such a way it is very much logical to draw a parallelism between the hunting lifeways of the Kabuis and the prehistoric man of Manipur as the past lifeways of the latter may be interpreted in terms of the ethnographic present of the former.

4. Fishing is an integral part of the Kabui subsistence pattern, for they practise fishing as a part of their way of life but not as a profession. They use different types of implements like nets, traps and spears for fishing in accordance with the suitability of the implement to the place where fishing is done. One important fishing implement that has merit for making ethnographic

analogy with the prehistoric tools is cast net as ceramic sinkers have been discovered from a Neolithic site of Manipur, called, Napachik. It is worth mentioning that the Kabuis use iron sinkers in their cast nets and moreover the two sinkers, though they differ in the materials used, have typological and functional similarities. The Kabui ethnography of fishing will thus throw light on the fishing life of the prehistoric men who are supposed to have settled the Napachik prehistoric site.

5. The Kabui household utensils generally consists of three legged wooden dishes, bowls and barrels that show morphological affinity with the tripod ware legs as well as corded tripod wares that have been excavated from Napachik and Laimanai prehistoric sites. This similarity is, no doubt, a point on the basis of which a parallel may be drawn between the Kabui lifeways and the probable life style of the Neolithic man of Manipur. The Kabuis still do not possess the knowledge of making earthen pots. What is important here is the fact that why the Kabuis use three-legged wooden utensils because this point bears significance in making a discontinous relationship and consequently comparison between two lifeways representing the ethnographic present and the prehistoric past thereby casting light on the knowledge about the probable prehistoric way of life.

6. One more wooden utensil that is another center of fruitful and analytic deliberation is wooden quern and grinder used by the Kabuis that reflects the mode of preparation as well as items of food. It is worth reporting here that a sandstone quern and grinder that belongs to the Hoabinhian culture has been excavated from Tharon cave. From the point of view of the functional similarity of the two it may be said past all doubt that there will be similarity between the Kabuis and prehistoric men, who

are supposed to be the author of the sandstone quern and grinder, in respect of their mode of food preparation and certain items of food. The study of the archaeological ethnography of the Kabui food habit has, thus, become meaningful in the attempt of reconstructing the food habit of the prehistoric man.

7. The Kabuis use stone spindle whorl for spinning cotton into thread which is again weaved into different clothes used by them. Weaving is entirely at the hands of thc womenfolk as it belongs to the domain of domestic chores. This stone spindle whorl has similar features with the ceramic spindle whorl discovered from the Napachik Neolithic site of Manipur. This prehistoric artefact does not tell more than the fact that the prehistoric man of Napachik might have spun threads for weaving their cloths. Many questions related to the sex of the manipulator, social convention associated with the use of the artifact and what not remain unanswered as the ideational culture, unlike the technical one, dies with the death of its bearer. These contents of the ideational culture which have been faded into the mystery of history as time rolls on may be explained, to a great extent, in the light of the ethnographic data on the lifeways of the Kabuis who are still using the same artefact.

Conclusion

1. The present study that vigorously attempts to make a bridge between the lifeways of two different groups of people, one living at the ethnographic present and the other at the prehistoric past, by way of making analogy between the artifacts used by them is rooted theoretically in the premises that the specific ethnographic postulates formulated from the ethnography of the Kabui subsistence pattern and the functional equivalence of the implements used by the Kabuis and the tools used

by the prehistoric man established on the basis of the ethnographic parallelism will be able to throw light on the reconstruction of the probable behaviour related to the subsistence pattern of prehistoric man. It, however, does not lose sight of its limitations while making an attempt to reconstruct the fossilised lifeways of a society which is very much far removed from us in time since there is hardly any evidence of historical continuity between the two societies under study. It further admits that the number of implements selected from the domain of the ethnographic present for comparison with the tools representing the prehistoric past is not many. It may, however, be explained in the light of the fact that first, the implements and tools are the representative specimens of their typological families; second, the historical discontinuity of the two societies far removed from each other in time is self explanatory as to the availability of the less number of tools that share typological similarities and consequently functional equivalence; and third only a segment of prehistoric life, that is, subsistence pattern has been selected for reconstruction in the light of the model of ethnographic parallels.

One may further argue that the availability of the less number of implements and tools that share typological similarities is a negative evidence for drawing an ethnographic parallelism between the two societies under study. But a negative evidence is not a solid foundation for making an ethnographic analogy invalid. The fact that the Kabuis are still practising hunting, fishing and gathering as a part of their way of life and that the prehistoric man also led a life of hunting and gathering are an evidence strong enough for making an ethnographic analogy between the two.

The theoretical understanding of the ethnographic

postulates and analogy, employed in the attempt to reconstruct the fossilised behaviour and cultural pattern related to the subsistence economy of the prehistoric man once lived in the prehistoric past of Manipur against the backdrop of the culture of the Kabuis living in the ethnographic present, has led to the formulation of the following generalizations about the subsistence lifeways of the prehistoric man of Manipur.

2. The prehistoric people who share similar lifeways of hunting, fishing and gathering with thc Kabuis, as done by their living counterpart, might have organised their labour along the age and sex lines within the economic unit of family in particular and at the level of the community in general to make their economic pursuit more effective.
3. The Kabuis have mobilised the resources available in their surroundings by following strictly an annual economic cycle made operative in line with the seasonal availability of the different varieties of plants and animals. Moreover, they are also fully informed about the life cycle and habitat of those plants and animals. The prehistoric people, like their ethnographic analogue, might have successfully exploited their available plant and animal resources by scheduling their economic activities in accordance with their exhaustive knowledge about the availability of different varieties of plants and animals at different places of their habitat and in different seasons of a year.
4. Preservation of food items in the fermented or the dried form is a way adopted by the Kabuis to make certain seasonally abundant food items available throughout the year. Moreover, they also store their food in the form of domesticated animals. These are the economic strategies made by the people for the judicious management of their limited, source food resources with a view to maximising

their life chances by adapting to the demand of their habitat. The prehistoric forerunners might have adopted the practice of preserving food either in the fermented or in the dried form to make judicious management of their limited food resources in the same way as done by their contemporary counterpart. It may also be inferred that the Neolithic people, who domesticated animals for different economic purposes, might have consumed the meat of their domesticated animals.

5. Redistribution, as evident from the archaeological ethnography of the Kabuis, is an economic mechanism of keeping all members of the society free from hunger when some members of the society have surplus food in their hands. As redistribution is also a mechanism resulted from adaptation for maximisation of life chances, the prehistoric people might have also adapted to their habitat having limited, source food resources by distributing whatever they had collected equally among themselves. In such a way no one might have remained starved when some of his community mates have something to eat. In other words, the degree of redistribution might be very high among the prehistoric people.

6. The continuity in the subsistence lifeways of the Kabuis living in different geo-ecological zones is reflected in the typological evolution of the artifacts used by them in their different geo-ecological zones. It is again authenticated by the availability of artifacts which are symbolic in one community but functional in the other. Though no continuity has been established between the subsistence patterns of the Kabuis and the prehistoric man, the Neolithic celts used by the Kabuis living in upland habitat for magico-religious purposes are the supportive evidence that makes the ethnographic

analogy between the two groups of people, who are very much apart from each other both in time and space, meaningful.

The tools and implements used by the Kabuis for their livelihood which still, to a large extent, at the subsistence level bear great similarities with those of the prehistoric forerunners in respect of their morphology and function though the materials used are found to be different. For instance, the Kabuis use bamboo, wood and iron for making their hunting, gathering, fishing and agricultural implements whereas their prehistoric counterpart used stone bone and wood for making their tools. The difference is, therefore, not in kind but only in degree. It leads to the logical conclusion that both communities representing the ethnographic present and prehistoric past lead similar hunting lifeways and simple hunting methods employed by the Kabuis might have also been adopted by the prehistoric man. The same also holds true in case of the fishing methods, for there is evidence of using seine or cast net both by the Kabuis and the prehistoric man.

7. The typological similarities reflected particularly in the household utensils, such as three legged wooden dish and containers used by the Kabuis and tripod wares excavated from Laimanai and Napachik and wooden quern and grinder used by the Kabuis in the preparation of their food and its prehistoric counterpart sand stone quern and grinder discovered from Tharon cave may also lead to the logical deduction that the food habit and method of food preparation of the prehistoric people may not very much different from those of their ethnographic analogue.
8. The stone spindle whorl of the Kabuis and the ceramic spindle whorl excavated from Napachik site bear great typological similarities. It testifies that the Neolithic people of Napachik practised weaving, however, the

ideational culture associated with weaving does not leave any trace as the same fades away into the mystery of the unrecorded history. Weaving, as revealed by the ethnography of the Kabuis, is in the domain of household chores and consequently it is the monopoly of that womenfolk. The same may hold true in case of the prehistoric forerunners.

Bibliography

Allchin, Bridget. 1994 *Living traditions : Studies in ethnoarchaeology of South Asia.* New Delhi : Oxford & IBH.

Allchin, Bridget and R. 1993 *The birth of Indian Civilization.* New Delhi : Penguin books India (P) Ltd.

Allen, B.C. 2002 *Gazetteer of Naga Hills and Manipur*. Delhi : Mittal Publications (photographically reproduced).

Anderson, J.S. 1982 *The people of India*, (Reprint). Delhi : Bimla Publishing House.

Ansari, S.A. 1976 *Economic Geography of Manipur*, Imphal : Trio Book Store.

1985 *Some aspects of the Geography of Manipur*. Delhi : B.R. Publishing Corporation.

1991 *Manipur : Tribal Demography and Socio-Economic Development*. Delhi : Daya Publishing House.

Ascher, R. 1961 Analogy in archaeological interpretation. *South-western Journal of Anthropology,* **17**:317-325.

Ashraf, A. A. 1990 Prehistoric Arunachal : *A report on archaeological exploration and excavation at Kamla Valley with reference to Parsi Parlo of Lower Subansiri District, Arunachal Pradesh.* Directorate of Research. Govt. of Arunachal Pradesh-Itanagar.

Avebury, Lord. 1989 *Prehistoric times as illustrated by ancient remains*, (Reprint). New Delhi : R. Kumar for Omsons Publications.

Bahadur, M. 1994 *Cane and bamboo crafts of Manipur*. Imphal : Mutua Museum.

Banerjee, H. 1990 *Introducing social and Cultural Anthropology.* Calcutta: Kitab Mahal Agencies.

Banerjee, A. and Dayal. 1968 'Investigation of nickel and copper mineralization in the Moreh area, Manipur state' *Manipur Gazette, No. 132 –E-110, August 26*, Imphal : Government Press.

Basu, M. N. 1957 *Material existence of man*. Calcutta : Dipika Publishing, Cornwallis Street.

Beals, R. L., Harry H. and Alan R. B. 1977 *An introduction to Anthropology*, (5th edition) London : INC : Macmillan Publishing Co., New York; Collier Macmillan Publishers.

Behera, M.C. and N.C. Roy. 1997 *Trends in Agrarian structure in the hills of North East India*. Delhi : Commonwealth Publishers.

Bhattacharya, D. K. 1972 *Prehistoric archaeology, A comparative study of human succession*. Delhi : Hindusthan Publishing Corporation (India).

Bhowmick, P.K. 1976 'Shifting cultivation : a plea for new strategies'. In, Pakem, B. ; J.B. Bhattacherjee B.B. Dutta, B.Datta Ray (eds), *Shifting cultivation in North East India,* Pp. 5-10. Shillong : North East Council for Social Science Research, Meghalaya.

Binford, R. L. 1968 'Methodological considerations of the archaeological use of ethnographic data'. In, R.B. Lee and I. DeVore (eds), *Man the hunter*. Pp 268-273. Aldine : Chicago,

1977 General introduction. In, Binford, L. R. (ed), *Theory building in Archaeology,* Pp.1-10. New York : Academic Press.

1978 *Nunamiut Ethnoarchaeology*, New York : Jovanovich, Academic Press.

1983 *In pursuit of the past*. London and New York.

2001 Where do research problems come from ? *American Antiquity*, **66** :669-678.

Braithwaite, M. 1982 'Decoration as ritual symbol, A theoretical proposal and ethnographic study in Southern Sudan'. In, Hodder, I. (ed), *Symbolic and Structural Archaeology.* Cambridge : Cambridge University Press.

Bose, N.K. 1980 *Tribal life in India*. Delhi : National Book Trust.

Bower, U.G. 1950 *Naga Path*. London : John Murvey.

Bowles, T. G. 1977 *The people of Asia.* London : Weidenfield and Nicolson. St. John's Hill.

Brown, R. 1873 *Statistical account of Manipur*. Delhi : Sanskaran Prakashak,

Budhi, C. 1988 The ethnonym "Meitei". In, Naorem Sanajaoba (ed), *Manipur past and present, Vol. 1,* Pp.72-81. Delhi : K.M. Mittal Publications.

Burkitt, M.C. 1977 *The Old Stone Age*. Rupa and Co, Delhi.

Butzer, K. W. 1974 : *Environment and Archeology : an ecological approach to prehistory* Aldine : Aldine Publishing company.

Carr, C. 1995 'A unified middle-range theory of artifact design'. In, Carr, C. and J.E. Neitzel (eds), *Society and Person, Archaeological and Ethnological Perspectives.* New York : Style, Plenum Press.

Census of India. 1961 *Waromung : An Ao Naga Village. Vol. 1: Monograph Series part VI.* New Delhi : Office of the Registrar General, India, Ministry of Home Affairs.

Chakravartti, R. 1986 *People of Manipur : Anthropogenetic study of four Manipur population groups*. New Delhi : B.R. Publishing Corporation.

Chang, K.C. 1967 Major aspects of the interrelationship of archaeology and ethnology. *Current Anthropology*, **8**: 227-247.

Chang, K.C. 1974 Ancient farmers in the Asian tropics : major problems for archaeological and Palaeoenvironmental investigations of Southeast Asia at the earliest Neolithic level, In, *Perspectives of Palaeoanthropology.* A.K. Ghosh (Ed), Pp 273-286. Calcutta : Firma K.L. Mukhopadhyay.

Childe, V. G. 1957 *The dawn of European civilization*. Bungay : The Chaucer Press, Ltd. Suffolk Set in Monotype Ehrhardt.

Clarke, D. L. 1978 *Analytical archaeology,* (2nd edition). London : Methuen & Co. Ltd.

Clark, J.D. 1968 'Studies of hunter gatherers as an aid to the interpretation of Prehistoric societies'. In, Lee, R. B. and I. DeVore (eds), *Man the Hunter* Aldine : Chicago

Clark, G. 1948 Fishing in Prehistoric Europe. *Antiquity*, **28**: 45-85.

1951 'Folk culture and the study of Europe prehistory'. In, W.F. Grimes (ed), *Aspects of archaeology.* London : Edwards.

1952 *Prehistoric Europe : The economic basis*. Cambridge.

1961 *World Prehistory : in new perspective*, (3rd edition). Cambridge: Cambridge University Press.

1965 *Archaeology and society*, London : Methuen.

1967 *Stone Age Hunters* : London.

1977 *World Prehistory in new perspective,* (3rd. edition). Melbourne: Cambridge Univ. Press.

Das, A.K. 1979 *Tribal art and craft*. Delhi : Agam Kala Prakshan.

Das, R.C. 1967 *Elements of Anthropology*. Gauhati : Arya Book Stall.

Das, R. C. 1989 *An introduction to Anthropology*. Guwahati :Sangam Prakash,

Das, R. K. 1985 *Manipur tribal scene*. New Delhi : Inter India publications.

Das, T. C. 1945 *The Purums : an Old Kuki tribe of Manipur*. Calcutta: University Press, Calcutta.

Devi, K. Shantibala. 2002 The traditional costume of the Zeliangrong tribes : a case study of ethno aesthetic history. *Unpub. Ph.D. thesis*, Manipur University, Manipur.

Devi, Kh. Manglembi. 1978 Kabui Naga village : Anthropological study. *Naharol*, XXI : 37-42. Gauhati.

Devi, L. Kunjeshwori. 1988 A study of archaeology in Manipur since prehistoric times. *Unpub. Ph.D. thesis,* Manipur : *Manipur University*.

Devi, P. Binodini. 1993 Studies on the Megalithic remains of Manipur. *Unpub. Ph.D. thesis,* Guwahati : *Gauhati University*.

David, N. 1973 'On Upper Palaeolithic society, ecology and technical change : the Noaillian case'. In, Renfrew, C. (ed), *The explanation of culture change*. London : Duckworth.

Ember, Carol R. and M. Ember 1995 *Anthropology,* (7th edition). Delhi : Prentice Hall of India Private Ltd.

Engels, F. 1891 *The origin of the family, private property and the state,* (4th edition). Moscow : Foreign Languages Publishing House.

Gonmei, R. H. 1980 *Mairam (torch) a brief history of Dailong Baptist Church, 1928-1980*. Manipur : Dailong Baptist Church.

Gorman, C. 1971 The Hoabinhian and after : subsistence patterns in Southeast Asia during the Late Pleistocene and early Recent periods, *World Archaeology* 2 (3) : 300-319.

Gould, R. A. 1968 Living Archaeology, the Ngatatjara of western Australia. *South-western Journal of Anthropology*, 24 : 101-122.

Gould, R. A. 1969 Subsistence aborigines of Australia. *Oceania.* 39:253- 274

1969 Subsistence aborigines of Australia. *Oceania*. 39:253-274.

1971 The archaeologists as ethnographer : a case study from the western deserts of Australia. *World Archaeology*, 3 : 143-177.

1974 'Some current problems in Ethnoarchaeology'. In, Donnan, C.B., and C.W. Clewlow (eds). *Ethnoarchaeology.* Los Angeles : Institute of archaeology, University of California.

1977 Puntutjarpa Rockshelter and the Australian desert culture. *An Anthropological Papers of the American Museum of National History*, 54, 187.

1978 *Exploration in ethnoarchaeology*. Albuquerque : A School of American Research book, University of Mexico Press.

1979 The archaelogists as ethnographer : a case study from the western desert of Australia. *World Archaeology*, 3:143-177.

1980 *Living Archaeology*. Cambridge : Cambridge University press.

1981 *Modern material culture : the archaeology of us*. San Francisco : Academic Press.

Gosden, C. and J. Hather. 1999 *The Prehistory of food: appetites for change*. New York : Routledge , 11 New Fetter Lane, London.

Government of Manipur. 1981 *Statistical handbook of Manipur.* Imphal : Directorate of Economics and Statistics of Manipur. D.O.E.S.

Government of Manipur. 1983 *Tribal Benchmark Survey of West District*. Imphal : Directorate of Statistics, Government of Manipur.

1985a *Tribal Benchmark Survey of Zeliangrong inhabited villages of Manipur valley districts.* Manipur : Directorate of Statistics, Government of Manipur.

1985b *Statistical handbook of Manipur.* Imphal : Directorate of Economics and Statistics of Manipur.

2001 *Statistical abstract of Manipur.* Directorate of Economics and Statistics. Government of Manipur.

Grierson, G.A. 1967 *Linguistic survey of India*, (Reprint). Delhi : Motilal Banarsidas.

Haimendorf, Furer, C. Von. 1948 Culture strata in the Deccan. *Man,* XLVIII:87-90.

1976 *Return to the naked Naga : an anthropologists view of Nagaland (1930-70)*. New Delhi : Vikas Publishing House Pvt. LTD.

Herskovits, Melville, J. 1974 *Cultural Anthropology,* (2nd Indian reprint). Delhi : Oxford & IBH Publishing Co.

Hodder, Ian. 1977 The distribution of material culture items in the Baringo District, western Kenya. *Man*, 12 : 239-267.

Hodgson, B.H. *Cf. Hudson, T.C.* Pp. 10 (Reprinted, 2003).

Hodson, T.C. 1982 *The Naga tribes of Manipur,* (Reprint). New Delhi : B.R. Publishing Corporation.

2003 *The Meitheis,* (Reprint). Delhi : Low Price Publications.

Hoebel. E. Adamson. 1958 *Man in the primitive world,* (2nd edition). New York : Mc. Graw Hill Book Company INC.

Hole, F and R. F. Heizer. 1977 *Prehistoric Archaeology: a brief introduction.* New York : Library of Congress Cataloging in Publication Data.

I.A.R. 1968-69, 1980-81, 1983-84, 1984-85 *Indian archaeology : a review.* Anuual Bulletin of Archaeological survey of India.

Irving, R. 1972 *Introduction to prehistory : a systematic approach.* London : McGrow Hill Book Co.

Jain, K. C. 1979 *Prehistory and Protohistory of India*. New Delhi : Agam Kala Prakashan.

Jochim, M. A. 1976 *Hunter gatherer subsistence and settlement – a predictive model*. London : Academic Press.

Johnstone, J. 1983 *Manipur and the Naga Hills*, (Reprint). Delhi : Cultural Publishing House.

Kabui, G. 1988 Glimpses of land and people of ancient Manipur. In, Naorem Sanajaoba (ed), *Manipur past and present, Vol.1*, Pp.3-21. Delhi: K.M. Mittal Publications.

1991 *History of Manipur: pre-colonial period. Vol. I.* New Delhi : National Publishing House.

2002 *Jadongang, a mystic Naga rebel,* (2nd edition). Imphal : By the author Keisamthong.

2004 *The history of the Zeliangrong Nagas : from Makhel to Rani Gaidinliu.* Delhi : Spectrum Publications.

Kamson, M. 1976 The customs and traditions of the Kabuis. *Quarterly Journal* (Oct. –Dec.), Vol. 1, No.4. Imphal : Manipur State Kala Akademi.

1977 The Kabui. *Quarterly Journal special issue on modernisation in tribal culture*, Vol. 11, No.1. Imphal : Manipur State Kala Akademi.

Kramer, Carol. 1979 *Ethnoarchaeology: implications of Ethnography for Archaeology*. New York : Columbia University Press,

Kroeber, A.L. 1976 *Anthropology,* (3rd Indian reprint). Delhi : Oxford & IBH Publishing Co.

Laiba, M.T. 1988 *The Geography of the Manipur*. Imphal : Thoudam ongbi Memcha Leima, Thangmeiband.

Lebar, F. M., Gerald C. H., John and K. M. 1964 *Ethnic groups of Mainland Southeast Asia*. New Heaven : Human Relations Area Files Press.

Lee, R.B. 1972 'Work effort, group structure and land use in contemporary hunter gatherers'. In, Ucko, P. ; R. G.W. Doubleby (eds), *Man, settlement and urbanization.* London: Duckworth.

1974 Male-female residence arrangements and political power in hunter gatherers. *Arche, Sex, Behave.* 3 : 167-73

Leshnik. 1964 Sociological interpretation in Archaeology, Ph.D. thesis, Chicago University. *Cf. Nagar, 1975.*

Lowie, R, H. 1956 *An introduction to Cultural Anthropology,* (Reprint). New York : Rinehart & Company, INC.

Lynton, Nandini, 1984 'The use of the ethnoarchaeology in interpreting south Asian prehistory'. In, Kenneth, A.R. K. ; L. Possehe, G.L. (eds), *Studies in the archaeology and palaeoanthropology of south Asia.* New Delhi : Oxford and IBH Publications Co.

Mackenzie, Alexander. 2004 *The North-East frontier of India,* (Reprint). New Delhi : Mittal Publications.

Majumdar , D.N. , T.N. Madan. 1987 *An introduction to Social Anthropology*. Delhi : National Publishing House, Darya Ganj.

Majumdar, D.N. 1976 'Shifting cultivation, is it a way of life ?: an analysis of Garo data'. In, Pakem, B., J.B. Bhattacherjee, B.B. Dutta, B.Datta Ray (eds), *Shifting cultivation in North East India,* Pp. 11-14. Shillong : North East Council for Social Science Research, Meghalaya.

Makuga, G. 1994 *Introduction to the Rongmei Nagas*. Manipur : Mr. Mrs. Makuga.

Manipur State Kala Akademi. 1974 Articles of Literary and Cultural Interest. *Quarterly Journal.* Imphal: Manipur State Kala Akademi.

Mathews, J. W. 1966 A Review of the Hoabinhian in Indo China, *Asian Perspectives 9.*

McCulloch, W. 1859 *Account of the valley of Munnipore.* Selections from the Records of the Government of India, Foreign Department, No. XXVII.

Medhi, D. K. 1993 *Man and environment in North East India, Vol.1.* New Delhi : Omsons Publications.

2002 *Man and environment in North East India, Vol. II.* New Delhi : Omsons Publications.

Michell, J. F. 1973 *The North East frontier of India,* (Reprint). Delhi : Vivek Publishing House.

Misra, V. N. 1974 Aarchaeological and ethnographic evidence for the hafting and use of microliths and related tools. *Puratattva*, (7) / 7 : 3-12.

Mohanty, P. 1985 The Mesolithic culture of Keonjhar District, Orissa : A preliminary report. *Bulletin of the Deccan College Research Institute*. 44:103-111.

Morgan, L. H. 1877 *Ancient society, or research in the lines of human progress from savagery through barbarisms to civilization*. London : MacMillan and Co.

Muller, F. Max. 1977 *Anthropological religion*. New Delhi : Asian Educational Service.

Murty, M.L.K. 1978a Symbiosis and traditional behaviour in the subsistence economics of the Kunchapuri Yerukulas of South India : a predictive model. *Puratattva*, Bulletin of the Indian Archaeological Society, (10) : 50-61.

Murty, M.L.K. 1978b Use of plant food by some hunter gatherer communities on the south east coast of India, its possible relevance to prehistory. *Unpub. Proceedings Indo-Pacific Prehistoric Association X^th ICAES* : Pune : Post plenary symposium on Recent Advances in Indo Pacific Prehistory.

Murty, M.L.K. 1981 Hunter-gatherer ecosystem and archaeological patterns of subsistence behaviour on the south-east coast of India : an ethnographic model. *World Archaeology*. London : Routledge and Kegan Paul, 13 (1) : 47-58.

Murty, M.L.K. and K. Thimma Reddy, 1975 The significance of lithic finds in the cave areas of Kurnool, India. *Asian Perspective*. XVIII : 214-226.

Murty, M.L.K and Gunther D. Sontheimer, 1980 Prehistoric background to pastoralism in the southern Deccan in the light of oral traditions and cults of some pastoral communities. *Anthropos*. International review of ethnology and linguistics, 75 :163-184.

Nag, D.S., 1958 *Tribal economy ; an economic study of the Baiga*. Delhi : Bharatiya Adimjati Sevak Sangh, Kingsway.

Nagar, Malti. 1966 The Ahar Culture : an archaeological and ethnographic study. *Unpub. Ph.D thesis*. Poona University, Poona.

1969 Clues to Aharian Prehistory in contemporary Mewar village life. Lucknow : *The Eastern Anthropologists*, XXII, I.

Nagar, Malti. 1973 Folk ornaments in Mewar. *Bulletin of the Deccan College Research Institute,* Poona, XXXI – XXXII (1) : 70-71.

1975 Role of Ethnographic evidence in the reconstruction of the archaeological data. *The Eastern Anthropologists,* 28 (1):13-22.

1978 'The use of wild plant foods by aboriginal communities in central India'. In, V.N. Misra and Peter Bellwood (eds), *Recent advances in Indo-Pacific Prehistory. pp*……… New Delhi : Oxford and IBH Publishing Co.

1983 Ethnoarchaeology of the Bhimbetka region. *Man and Environment,* VII: 61-69.

Nagar, Malti and V.N. Misra. 1989 Hunter gatherers in an agrarian setting : the nineteenth century situation in the Ganga Plains. *Man and Environment*, XIII : 65-77

1994 Survival of the hunting gathering tradition in the Ganga Plains and central India. In, Bridget Allchin (ed), *Living traditions : studies in the Ethnoarchaeology of South Asia,* Pp. 169-192. New Delhi : Oxford and IBH publishing Co. Pvt. Ltd.

Negi, B.S. 1996 *Human Geography : an ecological approach.* Delhi : Kedar Nath Ram Nath, Meerut.

Oakley, K. P. 1975 *Man the toolmaker,* (6th edition). London : Trustees of the British Museum, Natural History.

Odell, G. H., 1980 Toward a more behavioral approach to archaeological lithic concentrations. *American Antiquity*, 45 (3) : 404-431.

Oldham. 1883 *Report on the Geology of Manipur State and Naga Hills. Man,* Vol. XIX. *Geological Survey of India.*

Orme, B. 1974 Twentieth century prehistorians and the idea of ethnographic parallels. *Man* (N.S.) Vol. 9.

Oswalt, W.H. 1974 'Ethnoarchaeology'. In, C.B Donman & C.W. Clewlow (eds), *Ethnoarchaeology.* UCLA : Monograph IV, Inst. of Archaeol.

Pakem, B., J.B. Bhattachaerjee, B.B. Dutta, and B. Datta Ray. 1976 *Shifting cultivation in North East India.* Meghalaya : North East India Council for Social Science Research.

Pandit, T.N. and N.K. Das. 1993 *The pre-agricultural communities of India*. Calcutta : Archaeological Survey of India and Ministry of Human Resource and Development.

Paterson, N. 1971 'Open sites and the ethnographic approach to the archaeology of hunter gatherers'. In, D. Mulvaney, and J. Golson (eds), *Aboriginal man and environemnt in Australia,* Pp. 237-248. Canberra : Australian National University Press.

Patnaik, S.M. 1995 Material culture and archaeology. *Indian Anthropologists*, 25(2) : 59-64.

Pemberton, R.B. 1966 *Report on the eastern frontier of British India,* (2nd edition). Gauhati: Dept. of Historical Antiquarian Studies in Assam,

Raju, D.R. 1981 Early settlement patterns in Cuddapah District, Andhra pradesh: a Palaeolithic study. *Unpub. Ph.D. thesis, Deccan College, Research Institute*, Pune.

Raju, D.R. 1990 The settlement and subsistence pattern of the Neolithic cultures of the Lower Krishna valley. *Man and Environment*, XV (2).

Ramakrishnan, P.S., 1984 The science behind rotational bush fallow agriculture system (jhum). *Proc. Indian Science. (Plant Sci),* 93 (3) : 379-400.

Rami Reddy, V.. 1987 *Elements of Prehistory.* Delhi : Mittal Publications.

Rao, Nagaraj M. S. 1965 Survival of certain Neolithic elements among the Boyas of Tekhalkota. *Anthropos*. 60:480-486.

Remei, M. 1983 *Nagagi dharma amasung houna lonchat (Religion and the norms of the Nagas).* (in Manipuri). Imphal : Smt. Amubi Remei, Kakhulong,

Roy, Indrani Basu. 2003 *Anthropology the study of Man*. New Delhi: S. Chand and Company Ltd.

Roy, J.K. 1978 Alcoholic beverages in tribal India and their nutritional role. *Man in India,* 58 (4) : 298-326.

Roy, S. K. 1981 Aspects of Neolithic agriculture and shifting cultivation, Garo Hills, Meghalaya. *Asian Perspective*, XXIV (2): 193-221.

Ruivah, K. 1993 *Social Change among the Nagas (Tangkhul)*. New Delhi: Cosmo Publications.

Sali, S. A. 1990 *Stone Age India*. Aurangabad : Shankar Publishers.

Sanajaoba, N. 2003a *Manipur a British Anthology, State and country Vol. I.* New Delhi : Akansha Publishing House.

Sanajaoba, N. 2003b *Manipur a British Anthology, (Law, Customs, Hill-Men, Language and Religion) Vol. II.* New Delhi : Akansha Publishing House.

Sankalia, H. D. 1964 *Stone Age Tools, their techniques, names and probable functions*. Poona : Deccan college, PG & Research Institute.

Sankalia, H. D. 1970 *Some aspects of prehistoric technology in India.* New Delhi : Indian National Science Academy.

1974 *Prehistory and protohistory of India and Pakistan*. Poona : Deccan College Postgraduate & Research Institute.

Sanjembam, Vedaja. 1998 *Manipur Geography and regional development*. Delhi : Rajesh Publications.

Schrire, C. 1972 'Ethno-archaeological models and subsistence behaviour in Arnhem Land'. In, David, L. Clarke (ed), *Models in archaeology,* Pp. 653-671. London : Methuen.

Sharma, B.A.V., D. Ravindra Prasad and P. Satyanarayana. 1984 *Research methods in social sciences,* (Reprint). Jalandhar : Sterling Publishers Pvt Ltd.

Sharma, T.C. 1976 The prehistoric background of shifting cultivation. In, Pakem, B.; J.B. Bhattacherjee; B.B. Dutta, and B. Datta Ray (eds), *Shifting cultivation in North East India,* Pp. 1-5. Shillong : North East Council for Social Science Research, Meghalaya.

1981a A note on some prehistoric survivals in North East India. *The Bulletin of the department of Anthropology,* 7-8 :1-7. Assam.: Dibrugarh University.

Sharma, T.C. 1981b The Neolithic pattern of North-Eastern India. *Madhu : recent researches in Indian Archaeology and Art History,* Pp.41-52. Delhi : Agam Kala Prakshan.

Sharma, T.C. and D.N. Majumdar, 1980 *Eastern Himalayas : a study on Anthropology and tribalism.* New Delhi : Cosmo Publications.

Singh, C.B. 1984a Meitei ethnonym. *Journal Manipur University*, Pp.26-35.

Singh, C. M. 1984b The Meitei : Origin and affinity, *Journal of Manipur University*, Pp. 9-25.

Singh, K.B. 1976 *An introduction to tribal language and culture of Manipur (7 tribes)*. Imphal : Manipur State Kala Akademi.

Singh, K.S., B. K. Das Gupta, T. Bagchi, Pratima Chowdury. 1993 *Material traits survey additional data basketry of India*. Calcutta : Director, Anthropological Survey of India.

Singh, K. S. 1992 *Wildlife in Manipur*. Imphal : Public Book Store

Singh, L. I. 1987 *Introduction to Manipur*, (3rd edition). Imphal : S. Ibochaoba Singh.

Singh, M. K. 1980 *Religious development in Manipur in the 18th & 19th centuries*. Imphal : Manipur State Kala Akademi.

Singh, O.K. 1972 Antiquities of Manipur, *Manipur State Museum*. Bull. No. 1, Pp.1-3.

1980 'Archaeological researches in Manipur'. In, T.C. Sharma and D.N. Majumdar (eds), *Eastern Himalayas: a study on Anthropology and tribalism*, Pp. 147-162. New Delhi : Cosmo Publications.

1983a *Archaeology in Manipur: Napachik , a Stone Age site in the Manipur valley*. Imphal : State Archaeology, Government of Manipur.

1986 *Prehistoric Archaeology of Nongpok Keithelmanbi*. Imphal : Amusana Institute of Antiquarian studies, Manipur.

1988a *Archaeology of Manipur*. Imphal : State Archaeology, Arts and Culture Department, Government of Manipur.

1988b Aspects of archaeology in Manipur. In, Naorem Sanajaoba (ed), *Manipur Past and present*, 1: 59-71.

1991 *Neolithic stone tools of Manipur : a catalogue of neoliths in the People's Museum*, Kakching : Kakching Peoples's Museum.

1997 *Stone Age Archaeology of Manipur*. Imphal : Amusana Institute of Antiquarian studies, Okram Chuthek, Khongman.

Singh, O.K. and R.K. R. Singh. 1990 A preliminary report on an

Archaeological exploration at Singtom, Chandel District, Manipur. *Man and Environment*, XV (1) : 103-106.

Singh, O.K. and T.C. Sharma 1968 Studies on prehistoric archaeology of the Garo Hills, Jr. Assam Sc. Soc., XI :36-50.

Singh, O.K. and T.C. Sharma. 1969 On the discovery of Stone Age relics from Manipur, Jr. of Assam Science Soc. XII : 36-48.

Singh, R.K. J. 1992 *A short history of Manipur,* (2nd edition). Imphal : By the author at Yaiskul Hiruhanjaba Leikai.

Singh, R. P. 1982 *Geography of Manipur*, New Delhi : National Book Trust, India.

Singh, T. A. 1987 *Quaternary studies in the Manipur Valley. Unpub. Ph. D. thesis, Poona University, Poona.*

Singh, W. Y. 1935 *Report on the archaeological studies in Manipur*, Imphal : The State Library.

Sinha, R.K., 1975 *An Introduction to Geology*. Delhi : Vikas Publishing House Pvt. Ltd.

Sinha, S.C. 1996 *Medicinal plants of Manipur*. Imphal : Mass and Sinha, Manipur Cultural Integration Conference, Palace ground.

Solheim, W. G. 1975 Reflections on the new data of south east Asian prehistory : Austronesian origin and consequences. *Asian Perspective,* XVIII (2) :146-160.

Sollas, W.J. 1911 *Ancient hunters : and their modern representatives.* London : MacMillan.

Stanislawski, M.B. 1974 The relationships of ethnoarchaeology, traditional, and systems archaeology. In, C.B. Donnan & C.W. Clewlow (eds), *Ethnoarchaeology*. UCLA., Monograph IV, Inst. of Archaeol.

Stiles, D. 1977 Ethnoarchaeology : a discussion of methods and applications. *Man,* 11-12 (1-4): 87-103.

Subba, T.B. and G.C. Ghosh. 2004 *The Anthropology of North East India,* (Reprint). Delhi : Orient Longman Private Limited.

Szabo, Katherine, R. Hazel; A. Anderson and P. Bellwood. 2003 Prehistoric subsistence strategies on the Patanes Islands, Northern Phillipines. *Bulletin of the Indo Pacific Prehistory Association*, 23:163-171.

Tan, H.V. 1976 The Hoabinhian in the Context of Veitnam, In, *Veitnamese Studies* No. 46, N.K. Vien (Ed). Hanoi.

Thaimei, M. 1976 'The Kabuis (or the Rongmeis)'. In, Singh, K.B., (ed) *An introduction to tribal language and culture of Manipur (7 tribes),* Pp. 31-61. Imphal : Manipur State Kala Akademi.

1995 'The Rongmeis'. In, Naorem Sanajaoba (ed), *Manipur Past and Present : the ordeals and heritage of civilization*, Pp. 378-408. New Delhi : Mittal Publications.

Thapar, B.K. 1965 Neolithic Problem in India, In, *Indian Prehistory* 1964, V.N. Misra and M.S. Mate (Ed). Deccan College, Poona.

Thomas, D.H. 1972 'A computer simulation model of Great Basin Shoshonean subsistence and settlement patterns'. In, D.L. Clarke (ed), *Models in Archaeology*. London, Methuen.

Thomas, P.K. 1974 : Zoological evidence from prehistoric India, with special reference to domestication. *Bulletin of the Deccan College Research Institute*. XXXIV: 1-4.

Topo Sheet, 1970 Survey of India.

Tylor, E.B. 1913 *Primitive Culture*. 2 Vols. London.

Tylor, E.B. 1865 Researches into the early History of Mankind and the Development of Civilization. London. *C.f. Engels, F., 1952.*

Umeov, A.I. 1970 'The basic forms and rules of inference by analogy' *In.*Ta Venee. P.V. (ed). *Problem in the logic of Scientific knowledge.* Dordecht, Holland, D. Reidel Publishing Co.

Verma, A.K. 1988 *Neolithic Culture of Eastern India.* Ramanand Vidya Bhawan, Delhi.

Watson, P.J; A. Steven; LeBlanc and C.L. Redman 1971 *Exploration in Archaeology: An explicity scientific scientific approach.* New York : Columbia University Press.

Wobst, H. M, 1974 : Boundary conditions for Paleolithic social systems : a simulation approach. *American Antiquity*, 39 (2) : 145-177.

Worman, E.C. 1949 The Neolithic problem in the prehistory of India. Jr. of Washington Academy of Science 39 (6).

Wylie, M.A. 1980 'Analogical inference in archaeology', paper presented at the Society for Americal Archaeology conference, Philadelphia.

Yellen, J.E. 1974 The Kung settlement pattern : an archaeological perspective. Thesis, Harvard University. *C.f. Stiles, D., 1977.*

1977 *Archaeological approaches to the present : models for reconstructing the past*. London :Academic press.

1978 Settlement patterns of Kung: An Archaeological Perspective. In, Lee, R.B. and I. DeVore (eds), *Kalahari hunter gatherers studies of the : Kung Sian and their neighbours,* Pp. 47-73. Cambridge: Harvard University Press.

Zehol, Lucy. 1998 *Ethnicity in Manipur: experience, issues and perspective*. New Delhi: Regency Publications.

(ZNU). 1985 Hamei : *Eikhoigi jatigi ming (Hamei the nomenclature of our nation), (in Manipuri)*. Manipur : Zeliangrong Naga Union.

Index

A

Agricultural cycle, 154-155
Agriculture, 151-152
Antiquity of the hunting, 96

B

Barak River system, 26
Beliefs, 10
British military and the political officers, 36

C

catchman area, 25
Chindwin River system, 27
Clans, 58-60, 61
Collection of wild bees and honey comb, 90
Consumption and distribution patterns of food, 234

D

Domesticate animals, 234
Domestication of plants and animals, 138

E

Economic activities, 8
 of the Kabuis, 9
Economy, 89
Ethnoarchaeological approach, 7
– studies, 2
Ethnoarchaeology, 1, 3, 4, 5
Ethnoarchaeology, 233
Ethnographic Analogy, 237

F

Female Costumes, 69
– Dance Costumes, 70
Findings, 239
Folk culture, 6
Food of the Kabuis, 119

G

Geographical Setting and the People, 12-86
 about the villages under Study
  Chingkhulong, 39
  Khonglong, 39
  Konthoujam, 39
  Marangching, 39
  Phungong, 38
 house type, 42-52
 Kabuis, 52
  age grading system, 77
  clan structure, 58
  dress, 62
  engagement, 56-58

family, 55
festivals, 72-77
grading of social status, 77
inheritance, 60-62
Kabui language, 81
marriage, 55-58
migration, 52-55
origin, 52-55
ornaments, 62
property, 60-62
religious beliefs, 77
village polity, 78

Manipur
climate, 28-30
flora and fauna, 30-32
geological formation, 17-19
hydrography, 25-28
lakes, 28
location, 12
natural vegetation, 16-17
people, 32
physiography, 14-16
rock formation, 19
soil, 22-25

rock types and age of formation, 21
settlement pattern, 41-42

H

Human food exploitation, 88
Hunting and gathering, 88

I

Introduction, 1-11
aim and object of the study, 8-9
methodology, 9
theoretical orientation, 1-8

K

Kabui villages, 8, 40
Kabuis, 10, 89, 96, 236, 240, 241, 241, 243, 245
Khangkhui cave, 194
Khonglong, 40
Kuki-Chin
people, 36
tribes, 37

L

Liangmei, 52
Lifeways of the Kabuis, 9
Loktak Lake, 28

M

Male Costumes, 64
– Dance Costumes, 68
Manipur, 8, 12, 21, 25, 32, 194, 196, 236
Manipur or Imphal river system, 25-26
Material Culture and Subsistence Pattern, 86-194
agriculture / wet cultivation, 151-154
aquatic animals and fishes, 169
distribution of meat of the games, 119
division of labour, 154
domesticated animals, 169
domesticated fowls, 169
domestication of animals, 139
fishing techniques, 123
fishing, 119
food collection, 89
food gathering, 90
food habit, 155-160
food preparation, 170-171
food production, 137

gathering, 86-89
horticulture, 140
household implements, 178-191
- Bu (Wooden barrel), 180
- Dui-lai (Earthen water pot), 180
- Goi-chei jou-bung, 179
- Guliang (Sac), 190
- Gu-panthon, Gu-mei, 178
- Hanthai, 179
- Humsaf jou bong, 179
- Jou-lai (Earthen wine pot), 180
- Kaluang, 189
- Kampho, 185
- Khok (Storing basket, 190
- Ku-wak (Adze), 190
- Kwak dung, 185
- Langpa/Langom (wooden bed), 190
- Langpai (Threshing bow), 190
- La-tai-kwak, 185
- Maigang, Mailu, 180
- Nangmoi (Spindle whorl), 190
- Nappurak, 189
- Panthon, Mei, 178
- Rangtang-ka, 189
- Ta dop (Gourd mug), 180
- Thing-nap-kwak, 185
- Thing-nap-kwak-phai, 185
- Thing-piban (Wooden pillow), 191
- Thing-tam-kwak-phai, 185
- Zou-mu (Gourd wine pot), 180

hunting, 96-98
- tamed animals, 118
- trap, 100
- weapon, 98-100

insects, 168
material culture, 86, 87
pastoralism, 138
patterns of subsistence economy, 89
preparation of
- field and sowing, 142-147
- *khai*, 175
- liquor, 171-174

preservation of food, 175-178
production of food, 86-89
shifting cultivation, 142
tools and implements, 140-152
- Bang (Dao), 148
- Bangkhoi (Sickle), 148
- Dri (Axe), 149
- Indhi (Umbrella), 150
- Jhap (Winnowing Fan), 150
- Ka and Kaluang (Bamboo baskets), 151
- Laogek (Harrow), 151
- Malek (Threshing Implement), 150
- Phu (Hoe), 149
- Phu (Spade), 149
- Shep (Digging stick), 151
- Thing/Tha (Threshing mat), 151

transportation, 154
traps for animals, 100-101

traps for birds, 101-118
weeding and harvesting, 147
wild animals, 165, 166
wild birds, 167
wild perennial plants, 161
wild summer plants, 160
wild winter plants, 161
Material way of life of the Kabuis, 236
Mats of bamboo strips, 96
Meitei Pangans (Manipuri Muslims), 37
Meiteis, 14, 32, 33, 34, 35, 37, 38, 42, 194
hill tribes, 35
Kuki Group, 36
Naga Group, 35
Origin, 33-35

N

Naga tribes of Manipur, 36-37

P

Palaeolithic stone tool industry of Nongpok Keithelmanbi, 214
Prehistoric Evidences, 194-231
artifacts and tools, 196
blades, 203
bone tool industry, 208-211
burins, 206
chisel-edged microlith, 204
chopping tool, 222
chopping tools, 206
cores, 208
dorsal surface, 206
economy, 211
edge-ground knife, 222
flakes, 203, 206, 207, 215
fluted scars, 203
handaxe, 206
Hoabinhian Culture, 217
– industry, 221
Khangkhui Cave Site, 200-202, 211
Machi, 217
microliths, 205
Napachik at Wangoo, 195
Neolithic culture, 224-230
Nongpok Keithelmanbi, 212, 218
locality-1, 218-220
Palaeolithic Culture, 197
Pebble tools, 219
Phunan Site, 230-232
Prehistoric Cultures of Manipur, 194-196
Scrapers, 222
Singtom, 216
Songbu cave, 195, 197
Stone Tool Industry, 202-208
stone tools of the Songbu cave, 197-200
Tharon cave site, 220-224
Preservation of food items, 243

R

Rituals, 10
Rotten wood, 96

S

State Museum, Government of Manipur, 195
Stone Age relics, 195
stone artifact type, 217
Stone Tool Types, 216
Subsistence Economy, 232-237

T

Technique of making the clothes, 63
Techniques of fishing, 123-131
Fishing by
bare hand, 124
hook and line, 125

making barriers, 131
net, 128-129
poison, 129
spear, 125
trap, 126-128
Thoubal river, 196
Tools and implements used by the Kabuis, 245
Tribes of Manipur, 37

W

wooden utensil, 240

Z

Zemei, 52, 63
Zou tribe, 197, 216

Plate 1 : A Traditional Kabui House (P. 48)

Plate 2 : Tarangkai - A well decorated traditional house (p.49)

Plate 3 : *Langom* - a wooden bed near a fire place (p. 50)

Plate 4 : *Panthon-Mei* (Mortar and Pestle) (p. 50)

Plate 5 : A hanging rack of three tires over a fire place (p. 51)

Plate 6 : A small granary beside a house (p. 51)

Plate 7 : A Kabui lady wearing Pheingao pheipong (Shawl) in her loom (p. 65)

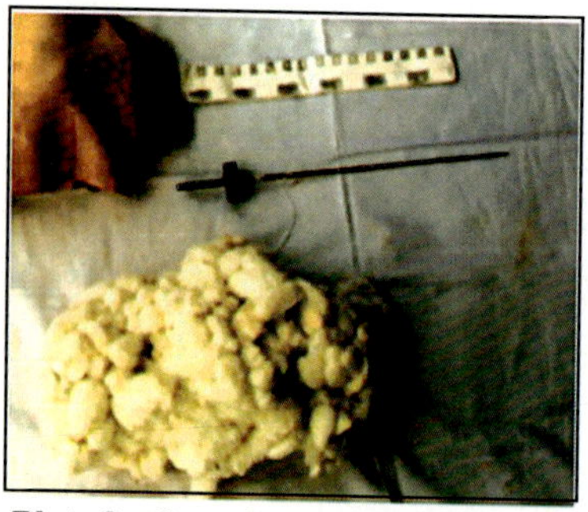

Plate 8 : Cotton in raw, collected from the jhum field (A) and a spining whorl (B) (65)

Plate 9 : Research observing the weaving technique at Phungong (p.66)

Plate 10 : Researcher (Middle) with the villagers at Konthoujam (p.66)

Plate 11 : An old couple wearing bead chains for aesthetic and magical values (p.67)

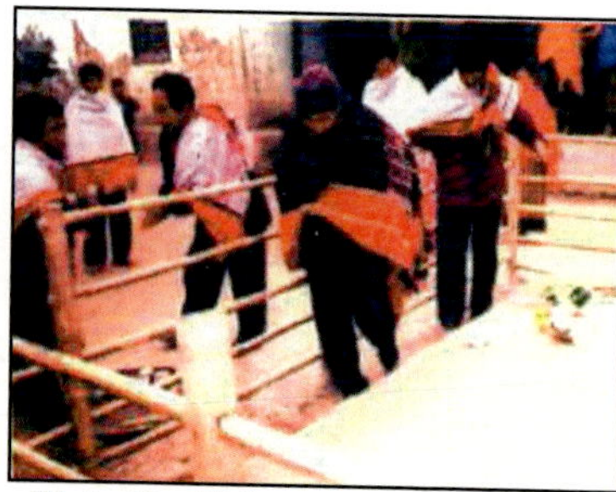

Plate 12 : Elders wearing *Pheingao pheipong* (white shawl) and *Chingkhongphei pheipong* (black shawl) on a memorial occasion in Gan-Ngai festival (P.67)

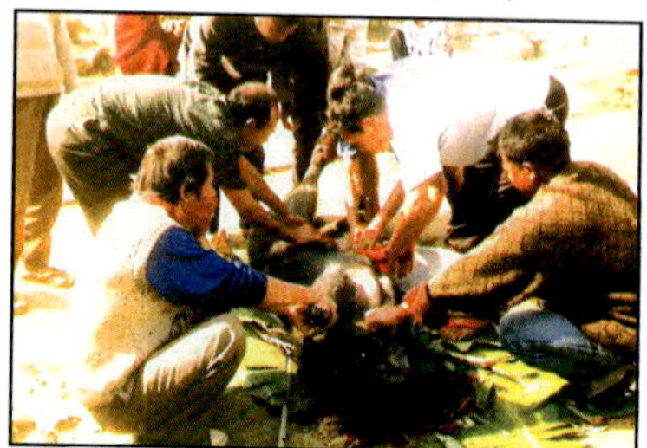

Plate 18 : Processing of pig for *Gakpai-jaomei* (p.82)

Plate 19 : *Gakpai-jaomei*- observation of spleen as an omen (p.82)

Plate 20 : Bamboo tubes for carrying rice beer (p.83)

Plate 13. Pheipong (A & B. *Pheingao*, C. *Mareipan*, D. *Masinpheipong*) (Male shawls)

Plate 14 . A male Kabui in dance costume

Plate 15. *Pheisoi* (A. *Langhu*, B.*Pheingao*, C. *Langjin*, D. *Phaisoi* of different colours (Female loin clothes)

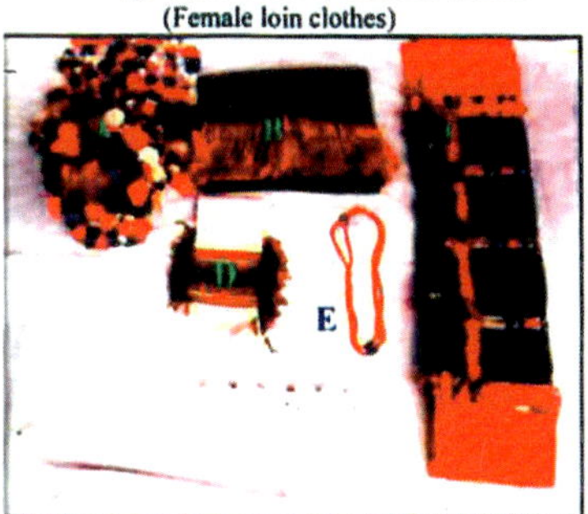

Plate 16. Dancing dresses and ornaments
A. *Duangh* (Hd.dress) B.*Phang phei*,
C. *Langhu- pheisoi* , D. *Pheilak* (waist belt),
E. *Tadan-tu* (bead chain)

Plate 17. A Kabui lady in dance costume

Plate 21 : *Tamcha-ponmei* (p.93)

Plate 22 : Bamboo – a village deity (p. 84)

Plate 23 : Taokhon - a memorial stone (p.85)

Plate 24 : Boys, collecting vegetables from the jhum field, on the way to home (p. 91)t

Plate 25 : Girls, collecting vegetables from the jhum field, on the way to home (p.92)

Plate 26 : A young girl collecting firewood from the surrounding hill (p.93)

Plate 27 : An old lady taking rest after collecting plantain leaves from the hill (p. 94)

Plate 28 : Bui- A. A bamboo having pointed tip (reng bui) used as a spear B. Iron tipped spear heads (p. 95)

Plate 29 : *A model of Keikang-bei* (Rack fall trap) (p. 120)

Plate 30 : A model of Thing-dang-pha (Beam trap) (p. 120)

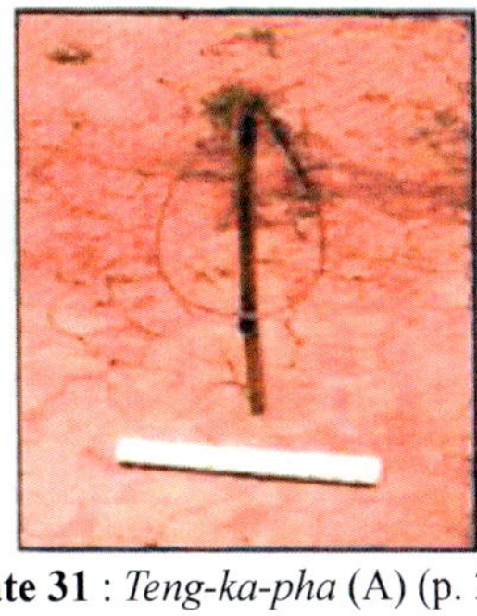

Plate 31 : *Teng-ka-pha* (A) (p. 21)

Plate 32 : *Teng-ka-pha* (p. 121)

Plate 33 : *Tao-pha* (all purpose trap) (p. 122)

Plate 34 : Iron tip of a fishing spear that resembles a double barbed Harpoon (p. 133)

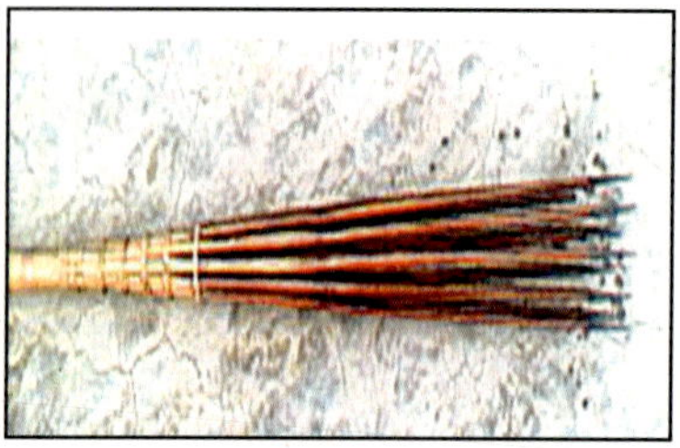

Plate 35 : A multiple headed fishing spear (p. 134)

Plate 36 : Single body valveless trap (p. 134)

Plate 37 : Double body valveless trap (p. 134)

Plate 38 : Plunge basket (p. 135)

Plate 39 : Hemishperical trap (p. 135)

Plate 40 : Cage trap (p. 136)

Plate 41 : Cast net (A) Net sinkers (B) (p. 136)

Plate 42 : Dip net (137)

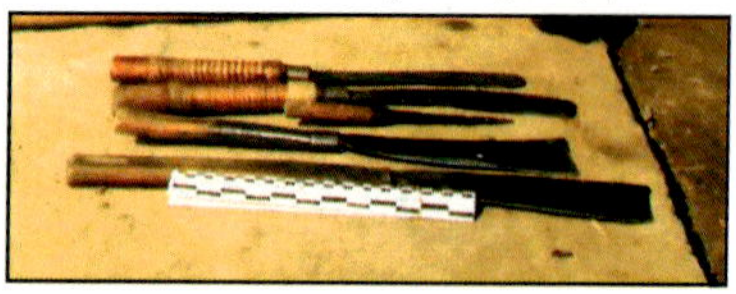

Plate 43 : Bang (Dao, iron blades of different shapes) (p. 157)

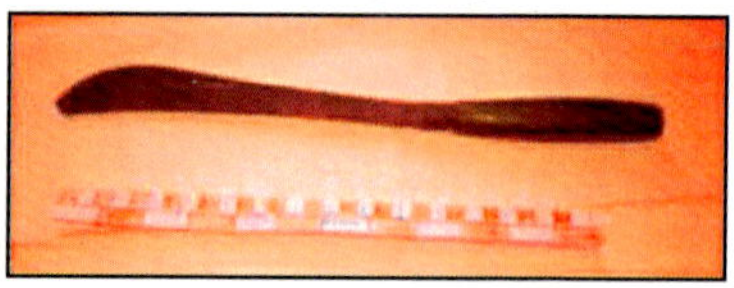

Plate 44 : Bangkhoi Sickle, a plain iron blade

Plate : 45 Phu- Spade, of different sizes (p. 157)

Plate 46 : Dri- axe (p. 158)

Plate 47 : Phu-Hoe, different sizes of hoes (*A. Lougai, B. Loupun phu, C. Nuchou/phu*) (p. 158)

Plate 48 : Buffalo yoke and plough (p. 158)

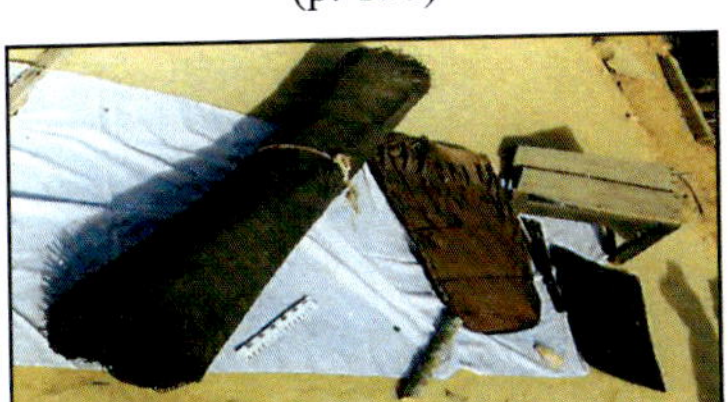

Plate : 49 *Jhap*-Winowing fan; B.Malek - Threshing implement; C. Indhi –UmbrellaD. Thing/tha -threshing mat (p. 159)

Plate 50 : Indhi-an umbrella used by the plain Kabuis and the researcher (159)

Plate 51 : A and B. Village elders drinking rice beer using A. Goicheibung (mithun horn) and B. Humsaf jou-bong (bamboo cup) C. Gu-panthon -wooden mortar (p. 181)

Plate 52 : Bu-wooden barrel with three legs (p. 181)

Plate 53 : Ta-dop (small gourd mug) (p. 182)

Plate 54 : Jou-mu (large gourd wine vessel) (p. 182)

Plate 55 : Earthen wine pot protected with cane strip (p. 183)

Plate 56 : Earthen wine pot of smooth surface (p. 183)

Plate 57 : Dui-lai- Earthen water pot (p. 184)

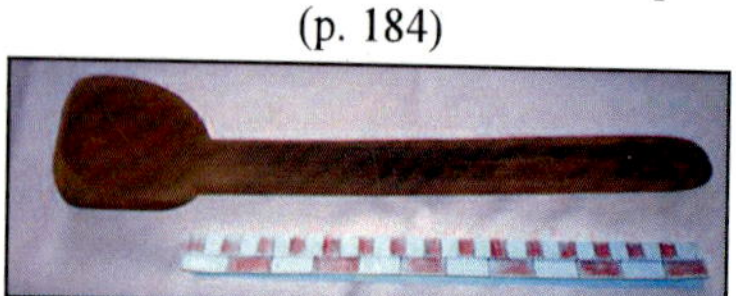

Plate 59 : La-tai-kwak -Bamboo stirrer (p. 186)

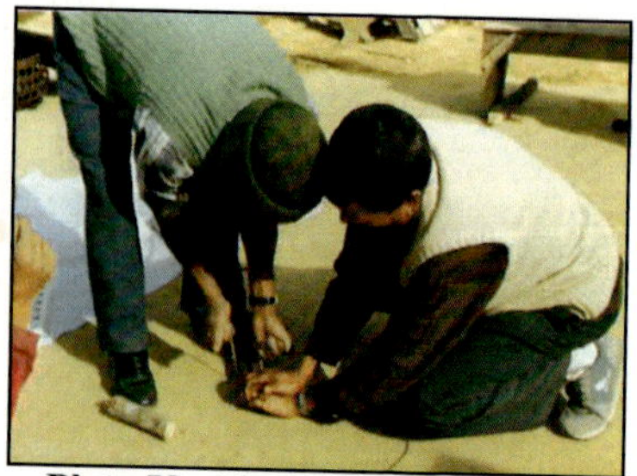

Plate 58 : Fire making with a log-Meigang (A) and a string-Meilu (B) (p. 186)

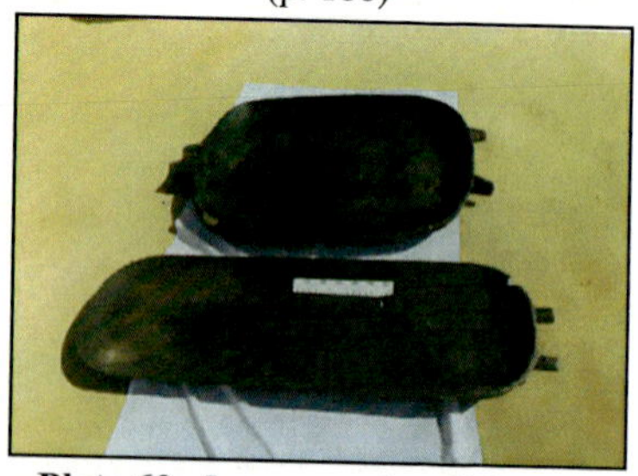

Plate 60 : Large wooden dishes for keeping dressed meat (p. 187)

Plate 61 : Thing nap-kwak - Wooden dish (p.187)

Plate 62 : Thing tam-kwak phai- Bowl with stand (L) (p. 188)

Plate : 63 Thing nap-kwak phai- Dish with stand (R) (p. 188)